To Patrick —
whom I know
champions The
Ethical Workplace!
Nan DeMars

# Praise for *You've Got to Be Kidding!*

"With Ponzi schemes cropping up everywhere, social media exploding around us, and confidentiality breaches on the front page news, *You've Got to Be Kidding!* is a must read for everyone in a business setting—from mail clerk to CEO. From my perspective as an employment practices lawyer, this book is a how-to for workplace ethics. Nan DeMars spells out *your* accountability at every work level and recharges your inner compass. Read it and use it as a reference source."

**—Stacey A. DeKalb,**
Attorney-at-Law,
Lommen, Abdo, Cole, King & Stageberg, PA

"Nan's new book is a timely, well-thought-out, experience-based message on shoring up ethical performance in the workplace. She is an impressive, values-based practitioner—making a positive difference to many audiences."

**—Dr. Robert MacGregor,**
Author of *Leadership: A Team Sport
Surrounded by Saints and CEOs*;
Founder of Center for Corporate Responsibility,
University of St. Thomas

"*You've Got to Be Kidding!* is a thought-provoking guide to ethics in the workplace, which is clear, interesting, and often humorous. Every supervisor, employer, manager, politician, military officer, and employee will learn valuable lessons from Nan, who has been in the trenches and speaks from experience."

**—General Dennis Schulstad,**
Retired Air Force Brigadier

"*You've Got to Be Kidding!* nails what the age of accountability means to those on the front lines of business, academia, and government alike. This book is a virtual 'one-stop shop' for ideas and answers to real-world ethical challenges seen in every workplace. This book is highly recommended for anyone in the business world."

**—Christopher Bauer, PhD, HSP, CFS;**
Author of *Better Ethics NOW: How to
Avoid the Ethics Disaster You Never
Saw Coming*

"BAM—Nan DeMars has done it again! In user-friendly, example-studded language, *You've Got to Be Kidding!* brings a black-and-white clarity to the issues that so often confront today's employee. Nan has made the seemingly complex simple to understand and to apply."

**—Dr. Marlene Caroselli,**
Corporate Trainer;
Author of *Quality Games for Trainers*

"Nan DeMars's judgment remains the first and last word on workplace ethics. Her experience and common sense approach, reflected in her excellent new book, *You've Got to Be Kidding!*, will serve as the ultimate guideline for appropriate workplace relationships."

—**Warren Spannaus,**
Former Attorney General,
State of Minnesota

"Nan DeMars pulls off a perfect trifecta. She's serious, hugely informative, and entertaining."

—**Dr. Robert F. Premer,**
Clinical Professor of Orthopedics
University of Minnesota;
Emeritus Chief of Orthopedics
Minneapolis VA Medical Center

"Nan DeMars does more than suggest you 'do the right thing' when faced with moral and ethical dilemmas in today's workplace. She tells you exactly how to maintain your personal and professional dignity and integrity above all else. Nan's wit and compelling examples make this an engaging and eye-opening must-read book for employees at all levels of an organization."

—**Erin O'Hara Meyer, PHR,**
Author of *Administrative Excellence:
Revolutionizing Our Value in the Workplace*

"Before I read any of Nan DeMars's books or heard her speak, 'ethics' to me was a deadly dull subject from the musty pages of an ancient book. I was totally wrong! Nan brings ethics to life with humor and real-life stories that illustrate how much she understands our challenges in the workplace. Her genuine empathy and 'Ethical Priority Compass' guide us to the correct path, and *You've Got to Be Kidding!* is the perfect template to maneuver in a digital world where issues and demands for decisions appear at lightning speed. Everyone's phone should have an app for Nan!"

—**Alberta Esposito,**
Assistant to Chairman, President, and CEO,
The McGraw-Hill Companies

"Nan DeMars owns the topic of workplace ethics. This book will assist all career-driven professionals (and their bosses) in the practicality of communication and mutual respect."

—**Susan K. Shamali CPS/CAP,**
2010 IAAP® International President;
Office Services Coordinator,
PricewaterhouseCooper LLP

"Nan DeMars has written another engrossing 'page-turner' on workplace ethics. This is a book everyone should have on their desks to remind them about the importance of accountability and following their Ethical Priority Compass."

—**Mary Ramsay-Drow CPS/CAP,**
2011 IAAP® International President;
Executive Assistant, Harley-Davidson, Inc.

"This book (like her previous books) is actual, factual, to the point, and easy to read and use. Especially in a time of recession and aggression, it is a wonderful tool to learn how to handle sticky situations, what is acceptable and what is not. Thank you, Nan!"

—**Ilja Kraag,**
SCPMG Legal Department;
Executive Assistant, Kaiser Permanente

"Nan DeMars knows ethics inside out. In a world where integrity seems to be hard to find, Nan's knowledge of the subject is complete and her insights are very helpful."

—**Gerri Kozlowski CPS,**
Executive Assistant;
Past IAAP® International President, M&T Bank

"Read this book and, you will know that, when it comes to ethics in the workplace, Nan DeMars 'gets' the pressures today's management and their staffs are under and understands the workplace from the trenches because she's been there. Do yourself a favor—when Nan DeMars speaks, listen!"

—**Barbara Adelman,**
Virtual Assistant

"As we say in the South, Nan 'practices what she preaches.' If there is ever a question about workplace ethics, just ask Nan—keep this book at your fingertips! She *is* the authority!"

—**Ina Simpson,**
HRD Professional;
Past IAAP® International President

"Nan provides ethical solutions to unethical situations and coaches the reader to meet these challenges with integrity, perseverance, and accountability. She offers real-time scenarios where men and women have succeeded in their endeavors to perform at a high level when faced with difficult decisions. Nan's delightful sense of humor and respect for office professionals will engage you until the end."

—**Nancy Torell,**
Executive Assistant to President/CEO Kemps

"Nan's insight and common sense approach to ethical behavior both in the workplace and sharing space on this complex planet is, in one word . . . brilliant. With wit and wisdom, you will learn that being honest truly is a virtue, and you *will* fall in love with Nan."

—**Terri Hill,**
Executive Administrative Assistant, Opportunity Partners

"As a human resource professional, time is of the essence in resolving employee issues in a satisfactory, all-inclusive manner. Keep *You've Got to Be Kidding!* at your fingertips—it will provide you with a positive outcome for all involved in any workplace ethical dilemma."

—**Rochelle Hummel,**
Human Resource Generalist,
Spring Lake Village

"Nan DeMars is the foremost expert on ethics in the workplace. With humor, this book takes our complex ethical issues and shines on them the light of integrity and personal dignity. You'll enjoy this read!"

—**Pat Sandkamp,**
Executive Administrator,
Northstar Balloons LLC

"After opening my door to FBI agents who questioned me about the conduct of an attorney I worked for early in my career, I can especially relate to Nan's chapter on loyalty."

—**Karen Eide,**
Professional Executive Administrative Assistant

"We're excited about this book at Monsanto! In the spring of 2010, our Administrative Professional Network (APN) invited Nan DeMars to present two office ethics seminars to its approximately 300 administrative professionals. We bridged the seminars over the lunch hour with a talk by our own business conduct director. Even he learned something from Nan! For those who have encountered unethical situations and felt alone (and who hasn't?), *You've Got to Be Kidding!* will show you how widespread these types of situations are and provide concrete information about what to do. Nan's new book (along with her training) should be required for all."

—**Connie Verberkmoes, Sarah Faraone, and Tina Gonzenbach,**
Monsanto

"Nan DeMars has written another groundbreaking book on workplace ethics. This book is a primer for all employees in the workplace who find themselves, from time to time, in the crossfire of ethical complexities. Here are the practical guidelines to deal with those dilemmas in order that you, your boss, and your company all share a collective win. This book should stay front and center on everyone's desk!"

—**LaWayne Reuter Yaeger,**
Executive Administrative Assistant
to the Chairman, President, and CEO
Sempris, LLC

"In my 48 years as an executive administrator to CEOs, I have seen much of what Nan writes about. Today is a different world, and Nan DeMars has brought business ethics to the forefront and given each of us guidelines to live by. Nan's real-life stories are written with humor, which makes her work easy and fun to read. Every company should provide every employee with this book to set the tone of the company's expectations. Enjoy and learn!"

—**Peggy Jo Danielson-Fortner,**
Executive Administrator to CEOs at
General Mills, Ziegler, Toro, Valspar,
NCS, and PLATO

"Nan DeMars's books always make you stop and listen to that little voice in your head when something doesn't seem ethically right. This book is a must–read for the newbie as well as the well-seasoned assistant."

—**Gale Shuster,**
Executive Assistant,
Xcel Energy, Inc.

"With passion and dedication, Nan gives you the tools to work with as she walks you through some of the ethical dilemmas she has encountered in her work and provides you with guidelines. *You've Got to Be Kidding!* is a must for every human resource department, administrative professional, leader, and educator. A company with good ethical standards will have a good reputation."

—**Geri Ronningen,**
Executive Assistant to Chairman/CEO/CFO,
Despatch Industries

"Thanks to this new book (and the teachings) of Nan DeMars, management and ethics are no longer just a polite oxymoron! Nan has empowered employees with the tools and courage to do the right thing, even if it means challenging those in positions of authority. Thank you, Nan!"

—**Jennifer Fuller,**
Executive Administrative Assistant,
CarVal Investors

"Workplace ethics seems to be a no-brainer, until you come face to face with reality. Then, all the complexities that surround these issues rear their ugly faces. This book gives you the tools of communication to peel back the layers and face the issues. This is thought-provoking and practical—a must-read for all professionals."

—**Lynda B. Boulay, CPS/CAP,**
Director, IAAP® Trust Foundation

# YOU'VE GOT to BE KIDDING!

# YOU'VE GOT to BE KIDDING!

## How to Keep Your Job without Losing Your Integrity

## NAN DeMARS

WILEY

John Wiley & Sons, Inc.

Published by John Wiley & Sons, Inc., Hoboken, New Jersey.
Published simultaneously in Canada.

For general information on our other products and services or for technical support, please contact our Customer Care Department within the United States at (800) 762-2974, outside the United States at (317) 572-3993 or fax (317) 572-4002.

Wiley also publishes its books in a variety of electronic formats. Some content that appears in print may not be available in electronic books. For more information about Wiley products, visit our Web site at www.wiley.com.

ISBN: 978-0-470-94751-7 (cloth)
ISBN: 978-1-118-08650-6 (ebk)
ISBN: 978-1-118-08652-0 (ebk)
ISBN: 978-1-118-08660-5 (ebk)

Printed in the United States of America

10  9  8  7  6  5  4  3  2  1

*This book is dedicated to—*

1. *The three greatest men in my life: Hans Wessel, my father; Lou DeMars, my husband; and Judd Ringer, my first boss. These men of honor, far ahead of their times, proved to me it's always good business to take the ethical high road.*
2. *All of you who so candidly shared with me your stories and insights. I'm so proud of your quest to do the right thing without losing your jobs.*
3. *And especially the administrative professionals throughout the world who are too often caught in the ethical crossfire of business activities. You are all my everyday heroes.*

# Contents

# Preface

I was recently in Gillette, Wyoming, getting ready to present a city-wide Office Ethics Workshop, and I was delighted to see a group of employees from a local mining company enter the room. Several rugged-looking coal miners dropped themselves into the front row, arms crossed, and looked me over with a what-the-heck-am-I-doing-here attitude!

Nevertheless, they soon warmed up. They were great contributors, especially to the lively discussions at the tables about "real-world" case studies. One miner's comments were particularly poignant. He cornered me during a coffee break to profusely thank me for the session. He went on to say that he and his buddies hadn't wanted to come to the workshop and wondered why their boss had insisted they attend. Then, tears welled up in his eyes, and he said, "Nan, at about 11:00 this morning, you hit on the exact ethical dilemma I have been struggling with for months. And now I know how to proceed!"

I was surprised and, of course, wanted to hear more. But he was gone before I could ask him what his dilemma was, and, later on, we were surrounded by attendees that made it difficult for him to share. Though the moment had passed, the pained look in his eyes stayed with me.

This coal miner personifies what I believe to be our collective reality today: *everyone* faces ethical dilemmas from time to time, even when their "office" is in the bowels of the Wyoming mountains.

My first book, *You Want Me To Do WHAT?: When, Where, and How to Draw the Line at Work* (Simon & Schuster, 1998), helped administrative professionals—the artists formerly known as "secretaries"—resolve their most common ethical dilemmas. As someone who's been there/done that myself, I've been a champion of the admin profession throughout my office ethics training programs. In my mind, the person in this particular role is in one of the best positions to improve office ethics. Because they're usually in the middle of the action, they have lots of leverage to influence coworkers' behavior by virtue of simply being a good role model. I am extremely proud to hear that the book has become something of a must-have "bible" for all admins.

I find myself writing this book today because admins—and everyone else in the workforce, miners included—tell me they *still* get stuck by ethical dilemmas in the workplace, and there are plenty of new ones out there to drive us crazy. I am the number one advocate for the *Ethical Office*—no matter what kind of "office" you work in. I am happy to see that admins are being treated more often as the professionals they are. However, I am worried that we don't yet fully understand that being a professional also means living up to a stricter code of ethics and being 100 percent accountable for our actions—no exceptions.

I've written this book to help with that. There's no preaching or finger-wagging here because I know you're smart enough to draw your own conclusions from the stories. I also know that ethical dilemmas are causing more stress because the ranks of employees left standing after recent rounds of layoffs are stretched pretty thin. This stress hits productivity—and profits—hard. Based on my seminars, the so-called Great Recession seems to have brought a lot of ethically suspect situations to a boil all at once, thereby forcing many people—admins and nonadmins alike—to choose between their ethics and job security.

This book invites you to help me expand the national dialogue about what it will take for us to build a culture of ethical offices. Everyone who works with others makes choices about how to treat their coworkers, so every one of us can contribute. If we want more ethical offices and all the benefits that come from that environment, we need to up the ante and tackle the tough "what if" questions before a crisis of conscience overwhelms and paralyzes us.

As it has with my ethics training, this book has morphed into guidance for *all* employees in the workplace. I witness more and more people who find themselves in the ethical crossfire of business activities. It's simply become a fact of professional life! Together, we can learn to navigate the thorny and often treacherous minefield of ethical choices employees face today.

This is a how-to handbook for the practical resolution of common workplace ethical dilemmas. I hope you find it useful, even indispensable. I am especially hopeful for those of you worried about keeping your job during these difficult times, in perhaps the toughest job market in decades. I know that employees everywhere are feeling the pressure to accomplish more with fewer resources, so the temptation to cut corners is ever present.

We are making significant progress toward our goal of more ethical offices. The time during which we will be tested is when it's most essential to stand up for what we know is true: doing the right thing is best for business success (and your own personal success) in the long run. To those asking, "Is it possible to keep my ethics *and* my job?," I say, "Yes, it is—and, yes, you can!"

*Nan*

# Introduction
# Why Do We Care about Ethics in the Workplace?

## Are We Really That Vulnerable? More than Ever Today!

*"Nan, why do I need ethics training anyhow? I'm ethical, my boss is ethical—in fact, the whole darn company is ethical!"*

I love to hear this question because it means managers aspire to run an ethical ship, and most employees want to get on board!

But I am a realist. Human relationships—and the ethics that guide our conduct—are dynamic, unscripted, and imperfect. As certain as you are that you, your boss, and your company live in a state of grace, I'm equally certain that you and your company will be surprised time and again by moral dilemmas. This is the nature of the workplace, where personal ambition, organizational goals, egos, and work styles compete. To the extent that this competition is offset by cooperation, you will have more or less of an ethical office. But, because people are people, ethical dilemmas will always exist. This book can help you prepare for their inevitable—and hopefully infrequent—occurrence.

Let's review the basics. An ethical dilemma occurs when we must choose between two negatives, for example, disobey our boss or defy our conscience. The costs can be high: Dilemmas cause stress that hurts our personal health and productivity, while the company's reputation and profits eventually suffer as well. Dilemmas can cost us our jobs and put us behind bars. And since everyone has a boss (even top executives have to answer to boards of directors, shareholders, and their financial institutions), no one is beyond a dilemma. Our never-sleep business environment often means that ethical dilemmas come at us too quickly to take time for mature reflection. We're usually forced to make a decision and take immediate action, before the ax falls or the dam bursts.

What did it look like when you first encountered an ethical dilemma at work? Was it when you were asked to "fudge" an answer to someone on the phone? When you were asked to falsify attendance or inventory or expense account records? Was it when you were tempted to show favoritism to a vendor because of a gift? Were you on the wrong side of a lawsuit because of a breach of client confidentiality or computer security? Maybe you had your reputation shredded by gossip and innuendo, or you were the last one standing in a take-no-prisoners financial scheme?

These are a few of the more egregious dilemmas that will hopefully never cross your work threshold. However, there are somewhat more minor daily situations that frequently challenge your ethical and moral standards. Ethical dilemmas come in all shapes, sizes, and dollar amounts—and can occur when you least expect them.

## Admins Have Always Been in the Middle of the Action

Administrative professionals do not work in isolation—far from it, in fact. They see coworkers, bosses, vendors, and customers being their best and worst selves. Because they could be deemed the "nerve center" of the office, they're usually among the first responders to a mess. Anyone who manages to keep their ethics without losing their job is a *hero* in my book!

As a pioneer in the workplace ethics field, I've had a front-row seat to a parade of ethical dilemmas, especially those administrative professionals encounter. I myself was an executive assistant to a CEO for years, and then had the privilege and good fortune to lead the International Association of Administrative Professionals. As international president and a six-year member of the board of directors, I was privy to the "big-picture" challenges we faced behind closed doors. Some of the stories I heard would shock and anger you. You would probably ask—as I often did—"What *planet* are these people on?"

The legal protections against discrimination and harassment were not always present, and a lot of tears were shed for the wrong reasons. In 1981, I helped our association write and adopt the first code of ethics for the administrative profession. It was a defining milestone that signaled to the world that we have the same responsibility—and deserve the same respect—as other professionals.

I launched my executive assistant search firm during this time. I also began to present my ethics workshops and keynote presentations to companies, organizations, associations and educational institutions that had become aware of their office ethics problems and wished to change their culture by incorporating my principles of the Ethical Office. This is when I *really* got an earful. Indeed, some of the ethical (or unethical) situations seminar participants related would set your hair on fire. Gradually, I saw the patterns of dysfunction that made corporate cultures toxic and unethical.

I poured everything I'd learned into my first book, *You Want Me To Do WHAT?: When, Where, and How to Draw the Line at Work* (Simon & Schuster, 1998). It was a true labor of love that, I hope, helped a lot of people. I also authored several international surveys of admins to get an accurate measurement of what was going on in the trenches at companies of all types and sizes. The results grabbed a lot of headlines because they reflected both qualitative and quantitative dimensions.

Then, almost overnight, it seemed that employees at *all* levels of responsibility were finding themselves on the witness stands! Enron . . . Martha Stewart . . . WorldCom . . . Arthur Andersen . . . Bernie Madoff and dozens of other "Ponzi schemes" became emblematic of scandals in the headlines. Suddenly, workplace ethics became a part of the national discussion as we all wondered, "How could these people do what they did?"

Fast-forward to today. Unscrupulous behavior has become a mainstay of the blogosphere and the 24-hour news cycle, and falls from grace regularly occur in the political, environmental, medical, educational, and commercial work world. Codes of ethics and conduct can be found from large companies on through the mom-and-pops. Job descriptions have been written for the newest type of organizational leader, the ethics director. "Hot lines" to report ethical lapses are common; so are "point persons" designated to handle ethical dilemmas and "do's and don'ts" in expanded employee handbooks. The number of colleges and universities with ethics curriculums has grown from less than 10 to more than 300 in less than a decade. And ethics training has become the most popular training on the professional development docket.

## Everyone Now "Gets It!"

Unlike my previous title, this book lands in a "we get it" climate. Not only are *employees* recognizing their accountability and resulting vulnerability in the workplace today, but *employers* are recognizing the same as well. By using real-world examples—some ripped from current headlines—this book will increase awareness of ethics in the workplace in the twenty-first century—from both the employee's and employer's perspective. This is an employee- *and* employer-friendly book.

*You've Got To Be Kidding!* is filled with comments and stories from my *OfficePro* column readers, seminar attendees, and talk show call-ins, all of which reflect the many ethical dilemmas with which employees and employers alike struggle. Some participants have identified themselves while others are given a false first name because they wished to remain anonymous. But *all* of these stories are taken from real-life experiences. My husband, Lou, says I am now "unshockable" because I've heard it all before.

However, I'm not so sure. I am still surprised by the things people do at work. Stuff happens; people are still people, and they sometimes behave badly. French novelist Alphonse Karr put it this way: "The more things change, the more they remain the same."

## I'm Optimistic

Though this book has a few snapshots from the past, it focuses mostly on the future. I refuse to resign myself to the fact that people will always disappoint and misbehaving companies will always deny. I have witnessed firsthand what can happen when improvements take hold, and I assert that we are much closer to the universal Ethical Office than ever before. Never mind that we still have a ways to go; you care, and your bosses care, and that's more than a good start. Together, we make zillions of small, everyday decisions to do the right thing, and this truly makes a difference.

This book is for everyone trying to do the right thing *and* keep their job. It is packed with ideas, suggestions, tools, and strategies to help you "see" the ethical problems in your workplace and "remodel" to fix them. What might appear at first glance to be a lose-lose scenario (e.g., lie and keep your job or be honest and lose your job) doesn't have to be. This book offers many suggestions to handle your current ethical dilemmas—and possibly head off future problems.

Yes, these stories reflect the tough dilemmas employees face. But, more important, they reveal the ways in which office professionals—regardless of title—are *solving* these problems. Their stories will make you proud and ratchet up the "ethics IQ" of your coworkers, your bosses, the people you supervise, and your employers. As we become collectively better at recognizing and resolving our ethical dilemmas at work, we will all enjoy a higher, more sustainable quality of life, do a better job of serving our customers, and improve our bottom lines. Doing the right thing is good for business after all.

Gertrude Stein once said: "The difference—to *be* a difference—must *make* a difference." You—just by focusing on ethics in the workplace today—are *making* that difference!

*We are being the change we want to see!*

—Mahatma Gandhi

# YOU'VE GOT TO BE KIDDING!

# Part I

# Take Care of Yourself

# 1

# When Morals Become Ethics

## *Your Beliefs Become Your Behaviors*

---

*Whatever we want our children to be, we should become ourselves.*
—Carl Jung

A gentleman stood up in one of my citywide seminars in Knoxville, Tennessee, that many University of Tennessee students were attending. He announced that he was "only speaking to the young people in the audience" and went on to tell the story below. I'm so glad he did:

> I had just graduated from college and had my first job with an oil company in Oklahoma City 25 years ago. Jobs were scarce at the time, and I especially needed mine because my wife was pregnant. My boss called me into his office one day and gave me two envelopes—one with a round-trip ticket to Phoenix, the other with $10,000 in cash. He told me to fly to Phoenix and give the envelope to the chief of a Native American reservation in the area. I don't know

where I got the nerve at the time, but I remember asking him "why?" He replied, "We are trying to buy the oil rights of his reservation."

To this day, I can tell you the suit I was wearing, the color of my shirt and tie, and how my knees were wobbling. I mustered up my courage and replied, "Then, this is a bribe?" My boss immediately responded, "No, no, no—this is just the way we do business!"

Now, I had a choice, and it turned out to be the choice that framed my future business career. In a slightly shaky but firm voice, I replied: "Then, I can't do that."

I can't remember my boss's exact words, but they were something to the effect of "my way or the highway." And I never did figure out if, in that moment, I was fired or I quit! Regardless, I was on the street.

After a good amount of time and trauma, I eventually found another job in the banking industry. I am now executive vice president of (a major bank) in Knoxville.

I am telling this story to you young people out there for two reasons: First, I don't care how old you are, you can stand up for what you believe is right. And, second, every ethical decision I had to make in my career from that point on was easier to make!

The applause seemed to go on and on.

This man probably didn't get up in the morning on the day that he refused to deliver the bribe and declare, "Today, I will stand my ground and behave in an ethical way." His decisions came automatically from within—from his moral compass, the internal guidance system that pointed toward what was right and away from what was wrong. In short, his *moral beliefs* directed his *ethical choices*. He learned early on in his professional life that "doing the right thing" means making the difficult choice even when there is a steep price to pay, or even when no one at all—except you—would ever know the difference.

## A Few Definitions

Before we proceed, I want to share my definitions for *values*, *morals*, and *ethics*. These terms are commonly used interchangeably since they each provide behavioral rules. However, you have to appreciate their distinctions to understand why good people sometimes behave badly. So let's split a few hairs:

*Values* by themselves are not a matter of good versus bad, moral versus immoral, or ethical versus unethical. Our values are personal; we choose and assign to them varying degrees of importance. Not all are equal, and they change as we grow and encounter various life experiences. Some of our values might be qualities like comfort, stress, accountability, friendship, security, honesty, stability, achievement, status, autonomy, loyalty, competition, cooperation; it's a long list. But whatever values we choose, those that are most important to us are essentially what define us.

*Morals* are the principles of a person's character that are deemed "right" or "good" according to a community's standards. We learn morals when we are very young, and they do not change. *Ethics* describes the social system—like your office—in which those morals are applied. Ethics usually refers to a set of rules or expectations that are accepted by a group of people, whereas a person's morals stay private. A useful way to think about how morals and ethics relate is this: We *accept* our morals and *choose* our ethics based on our values.

These distinctions allow us to talk confidently about social, medical, office, company, and professional ethics, but not about moral or immoral people. We cannot know another person's moral code; however, we can observe a person's ethical behavior. When we refer to another person as moral or immoral, we impose our moral standards on them and presume that we know their internal character, their innate "goodness" or "badness." We're better off simply saying that someone is ethical or unethical, based on whether we observe their behavior to be aligned to our group's accepted code of conduct.

## What Do You Think?

I attended a holiday party a few weeks after Bernie Madoff's Ponzi scandal erupted in New York City. A gentleman came up to me and posed this question: "Nan, I sit on the board of trustees of a prestigious college on the East Coast. A few months ago, the college received a huge monetary gift from Madoff. The money is currently in the bank but has not been allocated to any particular branch of the college yet. Can we keep this money?"

I started to give my standard disclaimer, as I often do: "I'm not an attorney, nor am I a licensed CPA . . ." when he interrupted me with, "I know you're not, but you're an ethicist. I would like your opinion on what we should do!"

I looked him right in the eye and replied, "It's not *your* money!"

Well, to say he went "ballistic" would be an understatement. He peppered his justifications at me at rapid pace: "We were given and accepted the money in good faith" and "We are totally innocent in the Madoff scheme." His defensive diatribe went on so long it brought to mind Shakespeare's line: "Methinks you doth protest too much!" Why was he even asking me the question in the first place if he had no doubt about what he should do?

When he finally ran out of steam, I caught two attorneys who are friends of mine by the sleeve, brought them over, and asked the gentleman to ask them the same question. He did, and both of them immediately responded: "It's not *your* money, so you have to give it back!"

We discussed at length how this was a unique ethical dilemma because the money had not yet even been allocated to a particular branch of the college (it was just sitting in the bank). My attorney friends both said if the funds had been already spent, you *could* argue it was too late to do anything. However, there was a clear choice in this case. This was also a great example whereby the gentleman was justifying keeping the money because "We're not doing anything illegal." But was it the *right* thing to do?

Fast-forward a few months. I was chatting with a golfing friend, Andy Weiner, about this very subject, when he shared the following story with me. Andy was serving as a board member of Faith's Lodge, a Minnesota-based charity that supports families facing the loss or severe illness of a child. At their annual fund-raising event, Andy said the chair was standing at the podium ready to close out the evening when "a nice-looking gentleman in formal business attire took the stage and told the story of losing his son—and then handed him a $25,000 check!" Andy added, "We were all elated. What a wonderful way to wind up our fund-raising year!"

Four days later, the man who presented the check, Tom Petters, was arrested for heading a "mini-Madoff" Ponzi scheme. (Petters has since been sentenced to 50 years in prison.)

I asked Andy, "What did you do?" He replied, "We immediately had an emergency board meeting via e-mail and we *unanimously* voted to return the check." Andy looked me right in the eye and said, "Nan—it wasn't *our* money!"

# Are There Morals We All Agree Upon?

Yes. There is a short list of *universal moral principles* that appears to be accepted by all religions, cultures, and societies:

- Empathy
- The ability to distinguish right from wrong
- Responsibility
- Reciprocity
- Commitment to something greater than oneself
- Self-respect, but with humility, self-discipline, and acceptance of personal responsibility
- Respect and caring for others (the Golden Rule)
- Caring for other living things and the environment

While each culture may label and express these universal moral principles in slightly different ways, you can look for them anywhere and you'll find that common moral sense is always the same.

Ethics, then, is a *system of moral values*. We all start with universal moral principles and, as we mature, choose our most important values based on our upbringing and social networks. If our morals and values are in alignment, we can relate to others in an ethical way. We can also look at ourselves directly in the mirror while shaving or tackling bed hair in the morning. Even Mickey Mouse used to say, "You have to be *yourself!*"

While it's difficult—nearly impossible—to change another person's morals, their values may be negotiable, and this is where hope for the Ethical Office lies. If we can align our coworkers to a commonly accepted code of ethical behavior—that is, our professional ethics—our ethical dilemmas will disappear, and productivity will go through the roof!

# Growing Up Ethical

Where do our morals—these "generally accepted standards of goodness and badness in conduct or character"—actually come from? It is widely thought that we do not choose our morals, but rather learn them and accept them from our culture—some combination of our parents, teachers, religious leaders, media, coaches, friends, and experiences—at a very young age, hence our societal imperative that children receive sufficient care and nurturing. In the words of James Baldwin, "Children have never been very good at listening to elders—but they have never failed to imitate them."

I once sat with radio talk show host Danny Bonaduce in his New York City studio for a live interview. You may recall Danny, at a young age, as the little red-haired, freckle-faced actor who played the banjo on *The Partridge Family* TV show. Danny took our workplace ethics conversation seriously, but he also teased me (and his listeners) with questions such as: "Nan, I don't make much money here, so what if I take the dictionary home and keep it for my kids? Is that ethical? What if I just take the Scotch tape home every now and then? Is that ethical? Everyone does it—what's the big deal?" Ms. Ethics (me) kept responding to his questions, "No, Danny, that's not ethical." Finally, at one point, with a twinkle in his eye, he replied with frustration, "You remind me of my TV mom—Shirley Jones! She never let me get by with anything, either!"

I told Danny *he* reminded *me* of one of my favorite cartoons featuring a little boy who was suspended from school for stealing pencils. His father was driving him home and scolding him all the way: "Johnny, how can you possibly be suspended from school for stealing pencils?" In the last cartoon frame, the papa says, "What do you do with all the pencils I bring home from the *office?*" It certainly makes one think.

However we come by them, our morals provide the context, or framework, for our actions. These are our most fundamental beliefs—our core values. These are the principles and values we have internalized. We make moral decisions without a lot of thought because they are based on the principles in which we believe most deeply. Morals are a part of who we are—our internal guidance system.

In order to live happily and at peace with ourselves, we have to live in ways that are congruent with our morals. For us to work happily and productively, we need to share common ethical standards with our coworkers. Therefore, we encounter a classic ethical dilemma when the ethics in the office are at odds with our personal values. And the larger the gap, the greater your level of stress. That's what makes the discussion of what the Ethical Office is, and how to build one, so essential to the quality of your professional life. You have the power to *choose* whether to behave in ways that are congruent with your values and morals, and you have the power to *act* to influence the group's ethics.

Acting on what you believe is "right" creates a positive and productive workplace, whereas acting in opposition to what you know is "right" causes discontent, low esteem, angst, frustration, pettiness, and—surprise, surprise—low productivity. I have observed this time and time again in my consulting work and have found that an ethical workplace outperforms an unethical (or ethically conflicted or confused) workplace every time.

## But Aren't Laws Sufficient?

Unfortunately, no. Laws are the minimum, essential requirements that maintain social order. They apply to everyone and are attractive because they are actually written down. However, conforming to a standard that is merely the minimum for behavior is hardly an achievement.

Laws are poor substitutes for ethical awareness and conduct at work for two reasons: First, you cannot possibly codify all aspects of the interpersonal relationships that comprise an office environment. If someone in the workplace is going to treat someone else unfairly, he will find a way to do it. Second, it is possible to satisfy the letter of the law even while still committing an act that most reasonable people would consider unethical or immoral. It may be technically legal to accept a gift from a supplier, but does that make it the right thing to do?

Still, it's tempting to use a simple, minimal legal standard for our conduct. When called to account for our questionable behavior, how many of *us* would hide behind the flimsy statement, "I did nothing illegal," or "What I did was perfectly legal," as if legality equals "rightness."

Let's sum it up in reverse order.

*Legal standards* are the minimal standards that provide the outer boundaries of conduct ("If you go beyond this point, you risk going to jail"). They tell you what you *cannot* do, but provide no positive guidance about what you *should* do. Workplaces that are guided solely by the law tend to be negative, petty, and mean-spirited. We, of course, must comply with the law, but it's not enough.

*Ethical standards* are the next step up. Ethical conduct is the set of behavior standards established for, chosen, and accepted by a group of people working together in the same place, group, or profession. There may be differences among corporate, professional, office, and personal ethics, depending on your situation.

*Values* are the bridge between morals and ethics. They are personal, variable, and adaptable. They carry no "rightness" or "wrongness" in and of themselves, but they must be aligned to morals and ethics to avoid dilemmas and the accompanying stress.

*Moral conduct* implies the highest standards of conduct guided by universal principles. If the law is the minimal standard, and ethical standards a reasonable expectation, then a moral code is the highest personal standard.

In short, the law tells you what you *should not* do, ethics tell you what you *should* do, and morals tell you what you should *aspire* to do.

This way of thinking explains why and how there can be several acceptable answers to ethical dilemmas. While I certainly don't want to suggest that you lower your standards, I must tell you the truth. Sometimes the best you can do in the practical world is to choose the answer closest to your personal values. They define who you are, and the closer you are to your "true" self, the happier and more satisfied you will be at work. Each of us has to make choices about keeping things confidential, respecting coworkers, telling the truth, and so on—choices that routinely test who we are and what we stand for.

## We Grow Ethically as We Mature (Thank Heaven)

People will continue to grow ethically as long as they continue to be challenged. One of my favorite stories about maturing is the father who devised a method of disciplining his young son. Whenever the boy was naughty, he had to drive a nail in the fence. Whenever he was good, the boy was allowed to remove a nail. Simple rules, right? One day, the boy noticed that the fence was all full of holes and looked bad. He remarked about this to his father and said, "I can take the nails *out*, but I can't remove the holes" (an important observation). His dad was wise to point out that, although we may balance our mistakes with good deeds, sometimes the mistakes still leave their mark.

This potential for predictable moral growth is the *single best hope* for building a more ethical office environment. Questioning and discussing the ethical dilemmas that take place in the office prompts everyone who participates to move a little further toward their next stage of development.

So there *is* hope! The ethical dilemmas you are thrashing out this year with your supervisors, peers, and coworkers are actually helping people grow, which hopefully means you will not have to deal with the same dilemmas next year. There's still no guarantee that your boss will "see the light" and stop submitting bogus expense reports on her own; after all, she has her own set of values. But as you learn to identify and handle these dilemmas better, your boss's ethics might even improve a bit (albeit often at a glacial pace)!

Fortunately, we have choices about how to handle our ethical dilemmas, which means we have some power over what happens to us professionally. Good thing, too, because dilemmas, by definition, defy simple, black-and-white decisions. We'll see this recurring theme time and again in this book because the decision you make depends on the given situation's unique circumstances.

I received the following letter that presents a classic dilemma, which pits moral standards against job obligations:

---

Dear Nan:

I am a legal assistant to a high-profile attorney who often takes on controversial cases. I love my job because it's never boring and challenges me daily. My boss's new client is an abortion clinic in our city; he is defending the clinic in a malpractice lawsuit. I am a staunch pro-life supporter and campaign often for candidates of my persuasion and, for that reason, I do not want to support my boss in this case. I know that if I have to do so, my personal feelings will prevent me from doing a good job. Do I have the right to refuse? And, if so ... how do I do it?
—Elenita in San Antonio, TX

---

I know my seminar attendees struggle with this situation because the room is always split on this particular issue. The conundrum is: You are not being asked to do anything illegal, immoral, or unethical; you are simply being asked to do your job! But you are struggling with the question: Can I keep my personal morals out of the job—and do I have a right to express them? Again, you have a choice.

Keep in mind that you have been hired to do your job, and one of your responsibilities is to support your boss in his or her job. You haven't been hired to pick and choose which part of your boss's responsibilities you wish to support. What if your boss were defending a child abuser? *That* case would kick us all in the stomach. Legal assistants who are familiar with these dilemmas remind us that, when you join a law firm, you accept two principles: (1) everyone has the right to a vigorous defense, and (2) everyone is innocent until proven guilty.

This woman's options were as follows: She could do her job while trying to separate her emotions about her personal morals from her performance. She could also talk to her boss about the situation, explain her objection, and express her concern about being able to perform at top level. If she works for a large law firm, perhaps they can find another assistant to work on this case and/or hire a temp to do so (both of which are, unfortunately, costly solutions). If it is a small law firm, neither of these solutions may be an option. This assistant may be fortunate to have an understanding boss who will make an adjustment for her, or this may quickly become a nonperformance black mark in her next review. She may even be fired on the spot. All of these outcomes are legal, and she would have no recourse. But, again, everyone has the right to say "no" to anything—and the price you may pay for not being able to separate your personal beliefs from your job responsibilities may be too high for you. Then again, it might be a price you are willing to pay. Only you can decide.

Phew. Whoever said these jobs were easy?

## We All Have Regrets

Jean was a Midwestern secretary who worked for the fund-raising arm of a nonprofit operation. Her specialty was planned gifts, and the executive she worked for was an attorney. Her organization encourages donors to seek their own attorney's counsel for document preparation during the estate planning process. One particular donor, who procrastinated in having her will made out, was, according to Jean, "sort of coerced into signing a will we made out for her." Jean's boss asked her to prepare a will for the elderly woman to sign and put their organization in it for $50,000, which she did, and "we became beneficiaries of this gift." At her boss's request, Jean destroyed all evidence "that we drew up the will." She was also instructed to have "no memory of this situation." Jean claimed to have a good relationship with her boss and that she "always did what he asked." Despite the fact that she knew at the time that what she was doing was wrong, she went ahead and followed her boss's instructions. The elderly woman died, and Jean's organization received its gift accordingly. However, Jean will forever have regrets that she did not object to her boss's request. She also realizes now that, if the family ever contested the will, "I could be taken into court for questioning." Jean considers this to have been a substantial ethical, moral, and legal lapse in her judgment.

Mark was chief operating officer of an engineering firm. He told me that he once "sat in the CEO's office while the CEO ranted, raved, and scolded (complete with expletives) one of my subordinates!" He added, "I knew this was verbal abuse of the worst kind, and yet I did nothing about it." Mark confessed to me, "Today, I would have stood up, told the CEO I would handle this myself, and made a fast exit with my employee in tow." He added that while he knows this would have made the CEO furious, he would have sat down with him later and explained how this kind of behavior falls into the hostile environment slot of harassment guidelines and the like. To add to Mark's regret for not defending his employee at the time, he told me he also lost him to a competitor shortly thereafter. And, as he said, "I can't blame the guy for leaving."

A woman named Julie told me she was an executive at a privately owned industrial firm. Her boss, the CEO, was a staunch supporter of a particular presidential candidate and party, and Julie happened to be supporting the opposition. The CEO often held fund-raisers at his home, which, according to Julie, he "expected his executives to attend and, if they could not attend, to at least write a personal check to the candidate." In addition, a few weeks before the national election, he "brought in posters of his candidate for each of us to put up in our private offices and also handed out bumper stickers." Julie said while all of this made her furious, she wanted to "remain in good stead with my boss ... so, I plugged my nose and put up the poster but could not go so far as the bumper sticker."

To this day, Julie regrets not standing up for her rights as a citizen. She claims (with 20/20 hindsight—we all have it) that she should have informed the CEO of the fact that it's illegal for an employer to foist his/her ideology, religion, and/or political beliefs on employees. His behavior qualified as employee intimidation, and he was creating a hostile work environment. To make it worse, she said, "I know he would have listened to me because he respected me and we had a great rapport." Julie also believes that, had she stood up to him, she might have saved the company from the resulting exodus of employees. Like several others, Julie left the company shortly thereafter.

Both Mark and Julie told me they did nothing in these circumstances because they needed their jobs. Mark said he was always "one paycheck away from serious cash flow trouble," and Julie was a single mom who constantly worried about her kids' welfare. Mark and Julie represent the kind of everyday heroes from whom we can all learn something. They both are individuals who obviously think about "doing the right thing," feel strongly about their principles, and actually have the intestinal fortitude to walk the talk—at least among their peers, most of the time. Yet even they were not beyond intimidation. There are many of us who have experienced similar situations when we felt we had to do something we knew was wrong.

Andrea, the secretary in Lauren Weisberger's popular book-turned-movie, *The Devil Wears Prada*, faced a classic dilemma as well. She was working for the-boss-from-hell in the New York fashion industry and was staying only because the boss promised to give her a recommendation that would be her entrée into any fashion publication she chose thereafter—if she could hang onto her job a little while longer. However, even if she survives, she has to decide if "the job that a million other women would kill for is worth the price of my soul." In the end, she decides it is not worth it, but it's a choice she must grow into on her own. There are countless professionals out there who can relate all too well to Andrea's story.

## Should We Lower Our Standards to Make Our Lives Easier?

As we grow more mature ethically, we often find ourselves under pressure to relax our own standards when we're told by way of justification, "Everyone does it." However, it's always perilous to lower your own standards, as it may put you on the first step of a slippery slope. Perhaps no one has ever more clearly expressed this danger than German philosopher Goethe, who once spoke these powerful words: "We *become* that which we tolerate!"

### It's Up to You

While the decision to do the right thing may be difficult, it's really not complicated. Either you do or you don't. But if you compromise your integrity by opting to take the unethical route for yourself, you can expect to feel badly about the decision later on. Remember the boy we met earlier in the chapter who put the nails in the fence and pulled them out later? The holes were still there. The deed could not be undone.

We have all had that pit-in-our-stomach feeling when we caved to something we knew we should not have. But recognizing this is half the battle. The other half is acknowledging we will do better next time and appreciating the fact that our moral growth is an ongoing process.

In the chapters that follow, we'll explore the values most relevant to employees in the workplace and the ethics that support them. I predict that you will feel more and more confident and empowered to be the agent of ethical change in your office. I can't wait!

> *One's philosophy is not best expressed in words; it is expressed in the choices one makes ... and the choices we make are ultimately our responsibility.*
> —Eleanor Roosevelt, U.S. First Lady (1933–1945)

# 2

# The Age of Accountability

## The "My Boss Told Me to Do It" Defense Is No Defense!

*That's when I realized we were all on our own.*
—Eleanor Squillari, Bernard Madoff's secretary

Eleanor Squillari remembers December 12, 2008. Her boss had been arrested for securities fraud the day before, and FBI agents were swarming throughout her office building. She recalls, "The phones were ringing off the hook, the fax machines were spitting out reams of paper from clients demanding redemptions, and a group of at least 25 angry investors down in the lobby were screaming for someone to come and speak with them."

Eleanor found Peter Madoff, Bernie's brother and the company's chief compliance officer, and asked him, "What am I supposed to be telling all these people?" His response, according to Eleanor: "He just threw up his hands and walked away."

That's when it hit her: Eleanor—and everyone else in the company, for that matter—was completely and utterly on her own.

The FBI agents confirmed this point to Squillari when she later told them she had agreed to coauthor the June 2009 Bernie Madoff story in *Vanity Fair*. "You need to take care of yourself," one of them said, "because nobody else will." Amen to that!

## Welcome to the Age of Accountability!

Here's another true story from the front lines: As I was sitting in the office of a CEO for a large manufacturing company, he explained why he was hiring me to present some ethics training sessions for his employees. His company has strict travel guidelines for its salespeople—"caps," he explained, for airfare, accommodations, rental cars, meals, and other expenses. One of his "top producers" was spending far beyond the caps, and his admin knew it. Apparently, the assistant was uncomfortable processing her boss's expense reports, but never said or did anything. Eventually, the salesman was fired.

Afterward, the CEO, along with the vice president of sales and the human resource director, had a meeting to address the question of whether they should also fire the assistant. They had determined that the assistant was fully aware that her boss was breaking the rules but chose to remain silent. The admin had been caught in a loyalty squeeze—loyalty to her boss versus loyalty to her company—and she had unfortunately made the wrong choice!

I congratulated the CEO for having had a discussion that would probably not have even taken place a few years ago. The salesperson would have been fired, but the admin would have simply been reassigned to a new boss with no further discussion. But not today. Nowadays, both employees and management realize that everyone is personally accountable for their actions in the workplace.

For those of you wondering, I happen to know the "rest of the story" at the manufacturing company. The admin in question was not fired. Instead, she received a second chance, a new boss, and a long lecture about her concept of loyalty. Her managers told her that while they appreciated the difficulty of the position in which she had been with her previous boss, any future boss who committed an unethical act did not deserve her loyalty. The bottom line was that loyalty to the company trumped loyalty to the boss. Just because her boss "asked me to do this" didn't mean she was off the accountability hook!

I commended this CEO and his management team for accepting their responsibility in failing to provide guidance in this respect to their employees. If they had had the accountability conversation with their employees before any problems occurred, they could have nipped the situation in the bud. But they didn't, and the admin was conflicted and did not know what to do or even whom to talk to. However, the CEO eventually got extra credit for rectifying the problem: because he was hiring an ethics trainer (me), he found a surefire way to avoid future problems.

## New Ethics Expectations and Rules for Employees

The most dominant trend in the evolution of office ethics is the rise of *personal accountability*. Employees today are acutely aware that they must avoid being associated with wrongdoings because they are likely to be held personally accountable for their actions or inactions.

My latest *OfficePro* magazine survey results of over 900 respondents make it crystal clear how fully admins understand *their* place in the accountability food chain today. The days of being able to use the defense "My boss told me to do it" are long gone. Employees nowadays may find themselves at any time on a witness stand with no one to take responsibility for their actions but themselves.

## Thank You, Enron—You Woke Us Up

I was giving a seminar in Houston at a hotel three blocks from the Enron trial. I walked out of my hotel room to find a copy of the *Houston Post* lying at my feet. The front page displayed a photo of an Enron admin behind the witness stand, hand in the air, being sworn in. Joannie Williamson, former assistant to Enron chiefs Kenneth Lay and Jeffrey Skilling, was testifying in the trial. Though she was never charged with any crime, she was still right there in the middle of the fray. I held up the paper from the podium and began the seminar with these words, "If you are wondering why you are attending this ethics workshop today—this could be *you!*"

Administrative professionals are often the employees most likely to find themselves in the ethical crossfire at the office. Because their accountability is now front and center, they are entitled to knock on (or kick open) the door to ethical conversations. And they are doing just that.

They are identifying ethical issues and generating solutions; as a result, they are making their organizations stronger in the process. I believe that these particular staff members are more sensitive than ever to their organization's ethical conduct due to the fact that they resolve so many of the daily operational dilemmas. An admin's unwritten job description now even seems to include "corporate conscience keeper."

## What Would You Do? How Would You Decide?

**Imagine you are an Enron employee facing these dilemmas:**

1. Your boss tells you to shred documents you know have been or are about to be subpoenaed. Do you comply or refuse?
2. Your boss is lying to conceal the company's serious problems. Do you challenge her?
3. You have heard and seen enough to know the company is in serious trouble. Do you warn your friends to take action, such as selling their company stock, to protect themselves?

One seminar attendee stood up and responded to question 3 with a twinkle in her eye: "Nan, I'd go home and tell my husband to sell all our Enron stock!" Of course, we know that such an action would likely trigger a charge of insider trading by the Securities and Exchange Commission and that both this woman and her husband would be in deep you-know-what.

Enron's ethical lapses jumped to the front page because the issues involved a huge enterprise. Many people were financially ruined, and the headlines were accompanied by a juicy political scandal. But, then again, haven't many of us witnessed—or even experienced—our own, smaller versions of Enron? Companies go bankrupt every day, and behind many of them are principals who tried to save the company and employees who were asked to help.

Though the scale may be smaller, the ethical dilemmas that involve personal accountability and loyalty to company and boss versus loyalty to friends and coworkers, along with all the accompanying confidentiality issues, are the same. And an organization doesn't have to be headed for bankruptcy for these dilemmas to surface. The normal ups and downs of the business cycle cause stock prices to fluctuate and layoffs to occur.

I have found most ethical dilemmas to be "it depends" choices that are highly situational and conditional. There are no obvious answers—that's why they are called dilemmas—and too many are a choice between two poor alternatives.

To help with these kinds of situations, I offer my signature Ethical Priority Compass as a simple, effective guide to orient yourself to any ethical dilemma, and thereby equip you to make the right ethical decisions even under extreme pressure. If you follow these three points—in this order—you will never be lost.

**Nan DeMars's Ethical Priority Compass provides a hierarchical approach to resolving ethical dilemmas:**

*First, take care of yourself.* You must protect your professional reputation and your financial security—and do so in a way that is aligned with your personal morals and values.

*Second, take care of your company and its customers.* Without them, you have no livelihood. So they deserve your best efforts and your loyalty.

*Third, take care of your supervisors.*

Let's examine each of these more closely.

## Take Care of Yourself

I cannot overstate the importance of protecting yourself, especially before it becomes too late to do anything meaningful. Regardless of what your boss has instructed you to do, you are totally accountable for your own actions in today's business world. No matter what happens, you have to defend yourself against legal action as well as physical, financial, and emotional harm.

Whatever the situation—your supervisor is harassing you, you see a coworker stealing, your manager asks you to lie for her, or you unexpectedly discover an explosive file of compromising e-mails—*document* the incident for your protection. *Do not* confuse character with compromise. If you feel that it's absolutely necessary to do something you consider questionable, safeguard yourself with documentation that makes your ethical position clear, even if it is nothing more than a "memo to self." And don't forget: at the end of the day, you're the only one who has to look at yourself in the mirror. Be careful not to compromise your personal morals and values, even when those around you behave in a manner to which you object. Your choices and decisions define who *you* are.

Taking care of yourself also means taking care of the reputation of your industry and your profession by adhering to agreed-upon standards. Most industries have their own versions of a code of ethics, all of which are readily accessible online through your search engine. For example, the legal, medical, accounting, real estate, and other professions have lengthy codes of conduct to use as a baseline for any of their ethical decisions. Do you know what the industry standards are for the business or field in which you work?

If you are an admin, you are bound both by the standards of your industry as well as the standards of your profession. You can find your professional standards on the International Association of Administrative Professionals (IAAP) Web site: www.iaap-hq.org. Adhering to your industry and professional codes of conduct can keep you centered. Hopefully, the standards of your industry and the standards of your profession are rarely in conflict.

## Take Care of Your Company and Its Customers

Immediately after your own interests come the interests of your organization. You must do your best to protect your company from any harm whatsoever and to continually act in its best interest. Sometimes, this requires that you act as the company's conscience to protect it from itself!

At the very least, you must protect your company from participating in illegal behavior. Better yet, you can try to keep its members from committing immoral and unethical actions, although different people will have contrary opinions about what "the right thing to do" is. Will jobs or profits be protected? Does environmental protection trump economic development? Which would you rather see, rigid compliance to a zealous regulator or obsessive adherence to a purist's idea of consumer rights? No one said that any of these were easy decisions, which is why the very conversations about ethics in the Ethical Office are so helpful. You may not always arrive at the perfect answer, but you'll have a much better chance of reaching consensus.

Your company deserves your loyalty on an ethical front purely because it provides you with a livelihood by giving you a paycheck. Practically, your company can demand your loyalty because it is more powerful than you, your managers, your coworkers, your union, your customers, and your suppliers. The company itself will remain long after you and whatever problem you're facing have gone away. In a dispute, your company will be your best defender or your worst adversary.

You must speak up about anything that affects your company or your ability to do your job for your company and attempt to resolve the dilemma. Report your concerns according to protocol; if that isn't effective, go to your company's human resource officers, the legal department or executives beyond your supervisor. It isn't always fashionable to take care of your company, but it *is* the *right* thing to do—that is, until you have proof your company no longer deserves your support.

And, don't forget your company's *client*. Protecting your company's customer is part of protecting the company. The reasoning is that if the company does something that hurts the client, the company will ultimately be harmed as well.

Who will ever forget the toppling of the two giant industries that will forever live in infamy: Enron, the failed energy corporation, and Arthur Andersen, their accounting firm found guilty of criminal charges relating to the firm's handling of its auditing. It became apparent during the Enron trials that, although some Arthur Andersen employees who worked on those books sensed something was amiss, they chose not to say anything. Then, when the you-know-what hit the fan, *both* Andersen (the company) *and* Enron (the client) were held equally accountable—and both organizations ended up going down for it.

## Take Care of Your Supervisor

Behind you and your company are the interests of your supervisor. Though this is a professional relationship that merits a lot of your loyalty, it should not be blind or unconditional loyalty. You share a history, and your manager probably holds considerable power over you regarding compensation, the benefits of mentoring, networking, advancement, resources, scheduling, work assignments, and the quality of your work life. However, your supervisor is also a person with warts and worries; he or she is neither angel nor devil.

Imagine that you're facing an ethical dilemma. If your supervisor is not the problem, then, by all means, seek his or her counsel. If your supervisor *is* the problem, do not immediately leap to the conclusion that he or she is the enemy. After listening to literally thousands of stories about trouble with supervisors, my counsel is that it is always *well* worth the extra effort to try to mend and preserve this relationship.

Let me emphasize your boss deserves your loyalty, but only as long as it is earned. Again, your loyalty is neither blind nor unconditional. You must rid yourself of the tendency to "help him until it hurts you" by asking yourself the tough questions: Are you actually doing "the right thing," or are you just looking the other way because it's easier? Are you enabling his or her bad behavior? Who will stand by *you?* And the really tough one: for what could you potentially be held accountable? These personal auditing questions don't mean you're being disloyal to anyone. You're simply being smart.

"I have found Nan's Ethical Priority Compass to be spot-on," says Mary Ramsay-Drow, CPS/CAP, 2011 IAAP international president and executive assistant at Harley-Davidson, Inc., in Milwaukee, Wisconsin. "Keep it handy—it will serve you well."

Equipped with your Compass, let's address the three Enron questions from earlier in the chapter.

## Your Boss Asks You to Shred (Subpoenaed) Documents

As legendary football coach Vince Lombardi would say, your best defense is a good offense. Replay your boss's request: "In other words, Caroline, even though there is a court order not to do so, you wish me to continue shredding these documents?" This statement both establishes the fact that you are aware you are being asked to commit an illegal act and gives her the opportunity to withdraw the request. If your boss presses on with the request, simply refuse to comply with this simple explanation for your refusal: "Because I may have to be held accountable." No one can argue that claim.

## Your Boss Is Lying

If you think your boss is disseminating misleading information, give him the opportunity to defend his actions. Ask questions; after all, you may not have all the information. If you determine you have incorrect or incomplete information, then no damage is done. If, however, you realize that you *do* fully understand the situation—and that your boss is in fact lying—document your conversation and communicate with the appropriate person above your boss so the company has a chance to protect itself.

## You Believe Your Company Is in Serious Trouble

Do you sell your stock if you suspect your company is crashing? Trust your Ethical Priority Compass here: because your decision to sell your stock will probably not affect your boss or the company (unless you are very vocal about it), this is about guarding your own financial security. If you know you must protect yourself, your questions are how to best do so. First, get the best-quality information you can by asking questions of your boss and whomever else you deem appropriate to approach.

Then, consult your attorney and perhaps your accountant. Your actions will depend on why the company is failing, what is public information versus "insider" information, and how much you can reasonably be held responsible for. Again, document your efforts to do the right thing. If you're ever asked to testify, your best defense will be your notes from these conversations.

## Your Boss Owns the Company

Consider the following letter I received from Yolanda in Duluth, Minnesota:

> Dear Nan:
>
> I have always worked for publicly held companies and agree with the order of your Ethical Priority Compass. However, now I work for a privately held company owned by my boss, the CEO. Shouldn't I put my boss before the company now (i.e., take care of myself, then my boss, then the company)?

This is a great question, and Yolanda should be happy to hear that her Compass still works—and in the proper order. Whether you work for a privately or publicly held company, you obviously should take care of yourself first. But your company is still next in order because if you take care of your company, you take care of your boss (the owner). This is important because if your boss starts to do something illegal and you are supporting her, it will bring the company (and you) down if discovered. If you take care of your company, then you are taking care of your boss. Keep your Compass pointed in the right direction—and in the right order!

# Consequences of Not Following Your Ethical Priority Compass

Your Compass and its sequence of *self, company, manager* will keep you grounded when you are facing all ethical dilemmas. Mix up any of these priorities, and you run the risk of losing your job, your reputation, and your self-respect.

Most professionals will constantly strive to do everything they possibly can to reconcile their ethics with their boss's requests. Sometimes, however, ethical dilemmas can morph into slippery slopes of denial and rationalization. For example, you believe you are doing your job and supporting your boss on a project. Then, in the middle of the night (when we usually get our sudden revelations), you realize that your boss is participating in an unethical (maybe even illegal) practice—and what's even worse is that you are an accomplice!

It's time to work your Compass. First, you realize you now have to take care of yourself because you're involved. Next, you have to protect your company because it will be affected. Finally, your boss no longer deserves your loyalty or protection, so you want to get out while you still can!

## A Few Horror Stories

I heard this one from the executive assistant to an officer of a large insurance firm. The assistant and her boss were invited into a meeting with the CEO, during which her boss was fired. He was told he had until noon to clear out his office, and the admin was asked to assist him in the packing.

All morning long, the admin helped her now-former boss with a lot of shredding. She was uncomfortable with some of the material she was shredding; however, she "felt sorry for him and did as I was told."

At noon, when her former boss was ushered out of the building, she was as well, thereby learning an incredibly tough lesson. She put her (former) boss's interests before those of the company—a substantial mistake. In retrospect, of course, she should have questioned the shredding and/or walked out and voiced her concern to the CEO. However, we'll never know if that would have been enough to save her job.

Another sad story came from a woman named Mary Ellen, whose state legislator boss gave her permission to use his state telephone credit card to call her ailing mother in another state. Mary Ellen was grateful for this kind gesture and proceeded to use the credit card for the next nine months until her mother died. Coincidentally, there was an investigation shortly thereafter of all state legislators' use of their telephone credit cards based on recent complaints of misuse that had occurred. Heads started to roll as the state's attorney general discovered that many legislators had used the cards illegally for lobbyists and various personal reasons. Mary Ellen, who was caught in the web of investigations because it was determined that there were about $500-plus worth of charges on her boss's phone card traced to her mom's phone number, was consequently fired!

This might not seem fair at first blush because Mary Ellen's boss had given her permission to use his card. The problem was that he had no right to let her personally use her state's taxpayer funds. Even though her boss was not thinking ethically, *she* should have been. It was another hard lesson of failing to recognize one's own accountability.

## Taking the Fall

The night before a citywide seminar in Columbus, Ohio, the business teacher at the Ohio Reformatory for Women contacted me. Her class had read my book and was studying the topic of workplace ethics, so she invited me to come out to the prison and speak to her students. Of course, I was happy to do so.

It was a great evening. All of her students were receptive to the topic and we had a lively discussion. I will never forget when I started talking about the topic of accountability in the workplace today. A woman in the back of the room waved her hand, stood up, and interrupted me with her statement: "Nan, you don't have to talk to *us* about accountability . . . we're in the *can!*"

She brought the house down—and I saluted her.

Afterward, I had dinner with the instructor, who told me there were more than a few women in the room who were convicted of "white-collar" crimes and their defenses were that their bosses said, "Don't worry—I'll protect you" (or words to that effect). Of course, at the end of the day, they were convicted along with their bosses—and one even *instead of* her boss.

## Embracing Accountability Is a Two-Way Street Today

We're figuring it out! Both supervisors *and* their employees are acknowledging each other's accountability for their respective actions today. Savvy managers are increasingly demanding relationships with their employees that routinely improve the ethical dimensions of a decision or practice. Such a partnership allows both parties involved to feel confident enough to bring discussions to the table without fear of being judged. After all, if you and your partner agree on absolutely everything all the time, then you probably need a new partner!

## The "Puffed with Importance" Conversation

My best example of this new attitude is clearly reflected in the last conversation I had with late U.S. Senator Paul Wellstone. Wellstone, who died tragically in a plane crash in 2002 while campaigning for reelection to the U.S. Senate from Minnesota, once told me, "Nan, I have a meeting with each new employee on the first day of their job, in both my St. Paul and Washington, D.C., offices. I tell them: 'If I get all puffed up with the importance of being a U.S. senator and you believe I am sliding off my ethical and moral compass, I want you to come in, sit down, and shore me up!'" Indeed, another executive told me she often has the same "puffed with importance" conversation with her assistants because she wants her employees to act as the "constant monitors" that keep her on the right track!

No employee today can afford to become an active (or passive) coconspirator in unethical, illegal, or immoral activity. Your position does not matter; whatever your job title, you are accountable for your own actions because those actions may some day land you in a court-room.

Texas Instruments has been an award-winning, international leader in the movement for corporate ethics programs for the past 60-plus years. They frequently print on the back of their employees' business cards these three simple guidelines they call the *"TI Ethics Quick Test"*:

- If you know it's wrong ... don't do it.
- If you're not sure ... ask questions.
- Keep asking until you get an answer.

*If you don't stand for something, you will fall for anything.*
—Deborah Perrotta, former Enron
executive assistant

# Nan DeMars's Ethics Dilemma Audit

The following are the questions you need to ask yourself when faced with a potential ethical dilemma in the workplace.

Warning: Ethical dilemmas ahead!

1. Is this an ethical or a communication problem?
2. What, exactly, are the choices in this ethical dilemma?
3. How serious is it? Can you live with either potential result? Can you live with it not being resolved at all?
4. Will the dilemma affect your—or another person's—job?
5. Do you believe that the "rightness" of a decision is "relative"?
6. Do you decide which action to take based on which course of action harms the least number of people?
7. Do you believe an unethical act is justified if it causes another unethical act to cease?
8. How would you feel if your resolution to this dilemma appeared on the evening TV news?
9. Can you explain your actions to your kids, spouse, or parent?
10. Who will this decision impact? What are both the potential damage and benefits to those affected? What are their needs, wants, values, expectations?
11. What are the alternatives to solving this dilemma?

# 3

# The Twin Faces of Loyalty

## The "New Loyalty" at Work Is a Two-Way Street

---

*Loyalty to whomever you work for is extremely important. The problem is—it is not the most important thing. When it comes to not admitting mistakes, or covering up, or not rectifying things just to save face ... that's a problem.*
—Coleen Rowley, 24-year veteran FBI Agent,
Testifying before the 9/11 Commission

received the following letter recently from one of my readers:

Dear Nan:

My assistant challenged me to get your opinion through your column—so here goes.

> I think a boss deserves unconditional loyalty, and my assistant disagrees with me. As a manager, I value loyalty above all else. In fact, loyalty is my simple definition of professionalism. None of our jobs are so tough that 100 other people could not do them. The only really special thing we bring to the table is our loyalty to each other because that is what inspires our team to be great performers.
>
> Some call this chemistry; I call it loyalty. When one of us isn't a saint and does something wrong or stupid, I believe loyalty trumps everything and you should do whatever it takes to protect each other.
>
> —The Boss, Elburn, IL
> P.S. I promise no one will get fired because of this disagreement.

You can imagine the flood of mail I received in response to *this* missive! Loyalty is the up-close-and-personal aspect of the "new accountability" we explored in the previous chapter. As we assume an increasing amount of legal and other liabilities, we have to keep our beliefs about loyalty up to date as well.

Like the manager who sent me the above note, I happen to be a fan of loyalty. Anyone who has been married, partnered, started a business, maintained a lifelong friendship, or gone through a difficult time knows that loyalty can be the air in our life raft when the big ship starts to founder. It's not necessarily a flashy virtue, but it can keep things afloat. I always loved actress Elizabeth Taylor's definition when referring to loyalty in one's personal life: "You know who your real friends are—when you're involved in a scandal!"

Because we value loyalty, we instinctively want to be loyal to those with whom we work. That "I'll watch your back" kind of allegiance is certainly desired and appreciated in a boss/employee relationship. But under what circumstances is that kind of loyalty deserved?

## The Dark Side of Loyalty

Unfortunately, for all its virtue, loyalty has a dark side as well. When a company overemphasizes this kind of blind devotion, we have what FBI whistle-blower Coleen Rowley terms *groupthink*. The result is a dangerous lack of skepticism and debate, denial of factual reality, and suspension of personal responsibility.

Corporate cultures that tolerate nothing less than unconditional obedience take a short cut to a dead end. This is a familiar excuse at these companies for poor outcomes: "Right or wrong, if my boss tells me to do it, I do it." In this environment, anyone raising questions is seen as "disloyal," even when they have crucial and perhaps lifesaving concerns. This was the case in both the *Challenger* and *Columbia* space shuttle tragedies wherein a "little guy" at NASA challenged the group-think up the chain of command—and was systematically rebuffed and vilified in response.

Loyalty gone awry is betrayal at its worst. The previous chapter touched on the Madoff-like scandal in my city in the form of charismatic CEO Tom Petters, who allegedly spent years building a multimillion-dollar Ponzi scheme to finance his luxury lifestyle. This all came to a crashing end when—as it had with Bernie Madoff and other operators of such mind-boggling, unprecedented pyramid schemes that surface periodically—Petters was arrested and his empire shut down by the government. A few days later, his stunned executive assistant, DeAnne Anderson (who had no involvement or knowledge of this scheme) told me: "Nan, I feel like I've been married to a man for five years and suddenly found out he's been cheating on me the entire time—and now wants a divorce!" I will never forget her devastated reaction.

A friend of mine, Pam Peterson, CPS, of Minneapolis, appeared with me on a panel on *NBC Dateline* when my first book was launched, and shared a similar experience. Pam had worked for a real estate developer who was convicted and served a prison sentence for fraud. Completely innocent of any charges, Pam testified that, as a part of her job, she signed tax documents that she had no reason to believe were false. A part of her boss's defense in court was his statement that "Ms. Peterson signed those documents without my consent." Our astute *Dateline* host, Keith Morrison, responded: "He betrayed you!" And Pam replied: "Yes ... to save *himself*, he betrayed *me!*" Fortunately for Pam, the courts did not agree with her boss.

## New Expectations

It used to be the case that if your boss was in trouble, you were pretty much automatically in trouble as well. Loyalty was blind, and it was expected that all employees—especially assistants of any kind—would take the blame, fall on their swords, catch the darts and bullets for their bosses, and always—always—be gracious about their scapegoat role. These expectations have gone the way of the job-for-life expectations, and to that I say, good riddance! Who wants to share a prison sentence with their boss, anyway?

A paycheck doesn't buy blind loyalty anymore. We are all professionals with our eyes open and our own set of responsibilities. As such, we remain personally accountable for our actions until we leave our jobs. The one-time defense that "My boss told me to do it" no longer holds water today—because no one else will be in that courtroom to defend you or take the blame for your actions.

Almost every single response to the boss's letter (above) was that their loyalty was "conditional." In essence, most people are willing to give loyalty to a boss who deserves it, "as long as I don't have to do something illegal. Or immoral. Or unethical. Or against my personal beliefs about right or wrong. Or something that will hurt my company."

I think it's fair to say that the blind and unconditional loyalty of yesterday has morphed into a more nuanced view of allegiance to our companies and managers. And if you look behind the headlines, you'll find a whole slew of new loyalty dilemmas.

## The Martha Stewart Trial

Many people followed the insider trading trial of domesticity diva Martha Stewart—a scandal that served as a wake-up call for all administrative staff. These professionals were particularly riveted to the travails of their peer, Doug Faneuil, who was suddenly thrust into the middle of a no-win ethical dilemma that the poor guy was forced to play out on the world stage. Faneuil worked at Merrill Lynch as executive assistant to Stewart's broker, Peter Bacanovic. Originally, he backed both Stewart and Bocanovic's stories. He later recanted and admitted to prosecutors that he had indeed lied for his boss.

Almost overnight, Faneuil became the government's star witness in trials against his boss and one of his boss's biggest clients, both of whom were charged with lying to securities investigators about why Stewart dumped her ImClone stock.

There were likely many employees who felt a collective chill when they heard Faneuil claim during testimony that he was pressured into lying about what his boss said and did—and felt equally sympathetic (not to mention anxious) when he admitted his role in covering up those lies because "I felt I would be fired if I didn't lie." Perhaps instinctively, Faneuil believed his defense could be a simple statement: "My boss told me to do it!" After all, it worked for Fawn Hall, Colonel Oliver North's assistant, when, during the Iran-Contra hearings in the 1980s, Hall explained why she shredded documents and smuggled them out of North's office just ahead of the law. Hall, however, was lucky. She narrowly missed being prosecuted when, at the last minute, she received immunity (a luxury that probably would not be afforded her today). By the way, did you know that, from the moment Hall and North left their Washington, D.C., offices together after shredding papers and smuggling them out in Hall's underwear, Colonel North *never* took a single phone call from Hall again? If *that* outcome doesn't nail into the coffin the old-fashioned "blind loyalty to your boss" adage, nothing will!

Doug Faneuil's situation hit a nerve with administrative professionals and assistants everywhere. The unfortunate truth is that bosses can frequently place pretty intense pressure on employees, even though it may be subtle at times. And unluckily for Faneuil, this pressure was related to an illegal act.

Former International Association of Administrative Professionals (IAAP) president Adella LaRue, CPS, sums it up best:

> Let's not forget that an executive assistant in Faneuil's position must surely be aware of the applicable rules and regulations of the industry—and blind loyalty should not even be on his radar screen. If he was unaware of all of this, then he should not be deemed a professional executive assistant in the first place.

Incidentally, Doug Faneuil was not the only admin to testify during this high-profile trial. Both the secretary to Sam Waksal, the now-jailed ImClone Systems Inc. founder, and Stewart's personal secretary were key witnesses as well.

## The "Old Loyalty" Is No Longer Relevant

In the bygone world where all assistants were called secretaries, loyalty to the boss was always blind and one-way only—meaning that assistants complied unconditionally and without thinking or questioning their manager's requests. It was even standard operating procedure for some bosses to blame a mistake on the secretary. In fact, a boss who stood up for his secretary was so uncommon that reciprocal loyalty often was suspected as evidence of hanky-panky!

The consequences of blind loyalty present us with familiar drama. Faneuil joined the ranks of not only Fawn Hall, but U.S. President Nixon's secretary Rosemary Woods as well. Some 40 years ago, Woods testified under oath that she erased those famous 18 tape-recorded minutes so critical to the Watergate hearings "accidentally" by a "slip of the foot." Whether it was indeed an accident will never be known. However, what *was* obvious was the unconditional loyalty she exhibited to her boss, the president. Like so many other anonymous assistants who subscribed to the loyal-no-matter-what philosophy, these high-profile employees suffered severe personal losses.

I am happy to report that the unconditional loyalty embraced by yesterday's assistant seems to have gone the way of the manual typewriter. The "just-do-it-and-shut-up-about-it" expectation is still out there, but it's less common. This is due to the fact that assistants nowadays realize they are at higher risk for suffering personal and professional consequences of their actions, inactions, complicity, or silence.

Ask Joannie Williamson, former assistant to Enron chiefs Kenneth Lay and Jeffrey Skilling, about her loyalty's limits. The defense launched its case by introducing Williams, who testified that she believed a key prosecution witness (another former boss) had lied on the stand. Innocent of any Enron mischief herself, her position still put her—completely by herself—alone in the legal crosshairs.

## "Good" versus "Bad" Loyalty

Everyone who works above, below, or among coworkers in an office lives in a constellation of complex relationships that can breed loyalty dilemmas. So how *do* we discern the "good" loyalty from its evil twin? How can we tell if our company is trumpeting loyalty in an attempt to build camaraderie or to shellac over wrongdoings and discourage dissent? What are the characteristics of loyalty when it's done correctly, as well as when it's gone terribly wrong?

Dictionary.com states the definition of *loyalty* as:

> The state or quality of being loyal; faithfulness to commitments or obligations.

An office cannot function without a certain level of loyalty. Employees are not a bunch of mercenaries sharing a vending machine and printer toner. Our commitments, obligations, and relationships deserve our steadfastness and our loyalty.

A glaring example of loyalty done right versus loyalty done wrong was management's handling of the aftermath of the 9/11 terrorist attack. Sue Shellenbarger of the *Wall Street Journal* explained this in the following way:

> Handling the aftermath of the terrorist attacks posed an acid test for employers that often fundamentally changed the employer-employee relationship. The mass emotions aroused by the tragedy were so primal—fear, grief, anger and the drive to protect loved ones—that any managerial missteps took on larger-than-life importance.
>
> The employers who rose to the occasion with understanding, empathy, and concern for their employees' fears and welfare—as reflected in e-mails, an outpouring of encouragement and educational materials, and even charitable contributions—were rewarded by their employees' deepened and lasting commitment. These employers were starkly compared to those who ordered employees to return to "business as usual," even on the day of the tragedy itself, which resulted in a shattering of employee commitment from thereon.

Jane Pierce of Coeur d'Alene, Idaho, writes:

> Loyalty to one's employer is vital to business's success. ... Ideally, we would all like to work for someone who sees eye-to-eye with us all of the time, but that's pretty unrealistic ... loyalty can be expressed and displayed by one's ability to remain as professional and supportive to your employer as you can be.

No office can survive within a system of finger-pointing and self-interest—no matter how profitable it is. Being willing to provide a bit of grace under pressure and overlook each other's human failings from time to time create a realistic and supportive atmosphere, instead of one based on fear and fault-finding.

Former president of the Fredricksburg Chapter of IAAP Rose Carle explains it in the following way:

> Blind loyalty is not a virtue in an administrative assistant. I had an executive a few years ago who routinely double billed

his travel expenses, whose previous assistant had "looked the other way." What she did not realize is that had he been found out, she would have been just as legally liable as he was since she actually prepared the billing and had full knowledge of what he was doing. We're talking jail time here.

## Team Loyalty Comes in Good and Bad Flavors, Too

The notion of loyalty, having each other's backs, forgiving minor failings, and working with the collective good in mind are magic ingredients for any type of team—and a unit of employees is no different. Some of us have had the experience of working in a group in which everyone truly has the best interests of each other and the company at heart. This is a great experience, and an essential feature of the Ethical Office. This type of group does not permit pettiness, gossip, and undercutting, and a sense of goodwill and lightheartedness prevails. People are not afraid to make or admit their mistakes because they know they'll be treated with dignity. In fact, a team like this is able to transcend individual mistakes and foibles—and isn't that the point of a team, after all? The sum becomes greater than its parts, and together, we can accomplish amazing things.

The antithesis of this—the antiloyal gang—is fueled by self-interest, pettiness, even backstabbing. Those who embody this approach are overly concerned about self-preservation and, in this environment, Me-First-ism is king: the only loyalty to be found is to me, myself, and I. We see a lot of "monitoring" in this kind of office; instead of a commitment to doing good work and being as supportive as we can to those around us, there's a group of underminers and judges.

I have been hearing a lot about new types of loyalty dilemmas lately. For example, what do you do when "the team" is in jeopardy and you respond by trying to protect the wrong person or promote the wrong cause for the wrong reason? The danger of misplaced loyalty to a charismatic boss remains a risk as well. While it's certainly exciting and gratifying to work for a highly visible, charming, wealthy, and popular politician, entertainer, salesperson, what have you, it can lead to a loss of objectivity, blind allegiance bordering on obsession, and trouble with other relationships—because no one else can compare to the boss whom you worship! Fortunately, most of us learn that there is a real person behind the mask and begin to relate to that personality in a way that promotes trust and honesty.

In situations in which you and your office mates struggle to meet a goal or solve a problem, you may feel pressure from multiple sources to bend the rules and cut corners. You are committed to the outcome because this is your battle, too; you are emotionally involved with your teammates, who also happen to be your friends. You genuinely want to be helpful. You have a natural desire to remain bonded to your group and to be accepted as a "good team player." It can be especially difficult under these circumstances to be the one who puts the brakes on an unethical plan. Who wants to be the wet blanket or the one who squelches the team's opportunity to meet the goal or solve the problem? It can be complicated to make the right decision when you feel you are hurting others' incentive pay or chances for promotion or success.

## Resolving Team Loyalty Dilemmas

Is it really in your best interests—or that of any of your team members—to cut corners when negotiating the copier contract? Shopping the printing bids? Evaluating the performance of the temporary staff? Reorganizing the data-entry system? If you think about it and raise the tough questions about the right thing to do, you'll usually find that most people will support you and respect you for being a moral leader. Being able to persuade your office mates to look at the bigger picture and the longer view will allow you to build an ethical office environment that much more quickly.

This is true even when your only teammate is your boss; in fact, the pressures to yield to the path of least resistance are greater here. After all, your boss controls your career in many respects, so you have to be more diplomatic and tactful when you argue to take the moral high road. But this should not deter you. You are doing your boss a favor when you "remind" her to stop trying to make short-term solutions work for long-term results.

So if your teammates get derailed and start cutting ethical corners to meet a deadline, you *can* be their moral decision leader. Challenging someone else's plans or activities on ethical grounds is always potentially explosive. You are, in a sense, questioning his or her "goodness" as a person. So, keep your Ethical Priority Compass in place and functioning to guide you through these ethical judgment calls.

The following are some practical suggestions that may help you broach the delicate subject of doing the right thing when it comes to loyalty. Remember, *your* loyalty to your *personal values* and account-ability, as well as to the long-term interests of the company and to your boss and/or teammate, are what motivates you to speak up.

*Challenge your boss.* Here's one approach: "Susan, can we talk about this report? I think it's in our best interests to consider the long-term consequences of inputting this questionable data. I'd like to explore a couple of other ways to do it." Then be prepared to offer your suggestions.

*Challenge your teammates.* "Hey, gang—this just doesn't seem like the way to meet our goal here. I feel uncomfortable about how we evaluated this situation. What do you say we try it a different way?" Again, be ready to suggest another, more ethical way to do this.

Be careful in both situations not to come across with your ethical "guns blazing." Keep your comments and suggestions positive so as to avoid putting anyone immediately on the defensive. You are not accusing anyone of any wrongdoing. Arguing the "high road" is actually easier than trying to defend cutting corners. You might consider saying something like, "This is too important a project to take a chance on having it blow up in our faces. What do you think about this idea? ..."

Other dilemmas will emerge that will force you to choose between various competing loyalties: friends versus friends, boss versus coworkers, company versus coworkers, team versus friends, Vendor A versus Vendor B, and so on. Trust your Ethical Priority Compass to guide you. As long as you keep your priorities in mind, you can take care of yourself first, your company second, and your boss (or teammates) third.

## "Torn" Loyalties with Bosses

Let me tell you about three assistants who barely survived their no-win loyalty dilemmas, all involving their bosses.

Sondra called me one day with a real doozy of an ethical loyalty dilemma and asked if I had ever heard a similar one, and I certainly had not. This was a first for even me. Sondra worked for an executive search firm whose partners had just split and started their own competitive search firms. Both wanted Sondra to work for them half-time, essentially "sharing" her via joint custody. This meant that she would work $2^1/_2$ days a week as an office manager for one gentleman, and the other $2^1/_2$ days as the office manager for the other one. Search firms are highly competitive and the reverence for confidentiality is always crucial because clients and candidates often interchange. Consequently, both her bosses told her that she would be fired on the spot if it ever were determined that she shared *anything* about the other's business.

I told Sondra that the good news was that both her bosses paid her a huge compliment by believing she could handle this professional scenario. But she wasn't so sure and claimed she was a "basket case, worrying constantly about never getting any of their clients/candidates mixed up." Although this surely was not her bosses' intent, it looked to me at first blush like a complete recipe for disaster. If Sondra (accidentally or otherwise) leaked *any* confidential information, she was in a vulnerable position to be blamed. I told her that her only chance of survival was to (1) "compartmentalize" the two jobs in her head every moment that she was working; (2) concentrate on keeping *everything* confidential on both jobs; and (3) constantly focus on her Ethical Priority Compass. She almost had to decide not to even *talk* during her workdays. Most important, due to these unusual, pressure-cooker circumstances, I also advised Sondra to continually and realistically evaluate her progress and monitor her own personal stress levels. This just might be a case whereby she may have to throw in the towel for her own self-preservation.

I don't know how she did it, but being the professional she is, Sondra was able to complete both roles for several months. However, when she was eventually laid off from both jobs (solely due to the economic downturn), she had to admit she was tremendously relieved and had not realized the toll it had taken on her health until it was over. Hindsight is always 20/20, and when I asked her if she would do it all over again, her response was: "No way!" Sometimes totally unrealistic expectations are placed on us by virtue of our jobs—and we recognize them too late.

Joel, however, had a problem that was "sending me home every night with a splitting headache." He had worked for his boss, the company president, for 10-plus years and he was someone with whom Joel had a "great working relationship." Two weeks prior to meeting me, Joel's boss had been fired. It was an overnight "coup" that had been solely based on company politics. Joel arrived at the office the following morning to find his new boss—the recently elected president—sitting at his boss's desk. He had just flown in the night before.

Joel then began assisting both men—his current boss and former boss (who had a one-month contract to remain to aid the transition). For that reason, he was suffering all the obvious torn loyalties to his "old" boss (regretting his imminent departure), but also wanted to assist his "new" boss because he represented his future security. To make matters worse, the two gentlemen "were archenemies and barely spoke to each other."

Talk about being caught in a loyalty squeeze! Joel's "old" boss needed and depended on his assistance to wrap up his affairs, but he wasn't handling the situation in a professional manner. Consequently, Joel had two major problems: (1) his "old" boss was asking him to gather information, additional files, books, and material that made Joel question whether he should comply; and (2) he had to listen to his old manager ask inappropriate questions about the "new" boss ("What's he planning? What's he saying about me? What's he like to work for?"). To add to his trauma, Joel's new boss viewed any help he provided to his old boss somewhat suspiciously because he was understandably uncertain about his loyalties at this point. Joel went home each night wondering how he was even going to survive the ensuing two weeks.

I met Joel in the middle of his month of hell, as a guest speaker at his association's annual conference. I, of course, explained my Ethical Priority Compass in my program. Joel was first at the podium following my presentation to thank me (or so I mistakenly thought). Instead, he told me, "I now know how to handle the mess I'm in," and proceeded to explain his predicament. We had a conversation about how he had to follow his Compass and take care of himself first, since he wanted to keep his job; his company second, since it provided his livelihood; and his bosses third—"new" boss first and "old" boss second.

Joel called me a month later to let me know that this approach had worked beautifully. After he and I spoke, he stayed centered and said to himself whenever a dilemma arose: "I work for XYZ Company, and I'm going to do what I think is best for the company, period." Consequently, he sought permission and approval of his "new" boss for everything he gathered for his "old" boss. He also informed me that he ended up telling his former boss he was running his requests by his "new" boss accordingly; and the requests ceased. In addition, to halt his old boss's barrage of questions, he ended up explaining his Ethical Priority Compass to him. To his credit, he got the picture. Consequently, Joel said he got through that difficult month without any more Tylenol.

Then there was Monie, a woman who had been an assistant to her boss—the company owner—for over 30 years. She loved her job until her boss began to plan his retirement and brought in his son and daughter as heirs apparent. Overnight, Monie's well-organized professional life was upended. She not only was assigned to "bring them both up to speed on what's going on around here," but she also had to deal with two Gen-Xers—colleagues whose professional approach differed from both her own and her former manager's. It didn't take long before Monie's efforts to navigate this transfer of power plunked her in the middle of the "new" and "old" regimes *and* the consequent conflicting ways of doing business.

Monie admitted to me that the *only* way she got through that difficult transition time without losing both her sanity and her job was by remaining focused on doing the best she could for the company first, and her "boss-for-the-moment" second.

## Loyalty Can Be Seductive

I was recently presenting a seminar at an insurance company when Lindsay, an accountant for the agency, shared her story with me during a coffee break. Lindsay told me that she thoroughly enjoyed working for her boss and the accompanying salary. She became aware, however, that her boss was calling in late, leaving early, and taking extended lunch hours—and soon realized that these absences were all alcohol related. She also knew her boss was dealing with some serious personal problems at the time, including divorce and a grandson's terminal illness. Consequently, Lindsay felt great sympathy for her boss and began making excuses for his erratic behavior and unproductive performance. As the situation evolved, Lindsay found herself drawn deeper and deeper into her boss's deceptions, covering more frequently for his absences until one day she blatantly lied to the company president about the progress of a project her boss was working on.

Lindsay said she never planned to be a coconspirator in cheating the company in any way but that she was gradually compromised over several months' time. She said she stopped eating right, got little sleep, and, in her words, was "en route to a mental breakdown." One day, while combing her hair, she "didn't like what I saw in the mirror." So she walked into work that very morning and quit her job. Though her shocked boss tried to talk her out of it, she walked out the door that day and never looked back.

Lindsay began to cry when she got to this point in her story. She explained that she had just realized, in sharing her story with me, that her circumstances were similar to those of an abused spouse. She had slowly been drawn into an unhealthy situation, stayed much too long, and enabled her boss's behavior because she needed the salary and security. In addition, she liked the company and her boss. She also added that she hadn't realized how much she had compromised herself until she quit her job.

Later in the day, Lindsay shared with me that her boss was ultimately fired from his position. We sat down and talked about how she got derailed and how she could have handled the situation differently. She agreed that she should have confidentially reported her concerns about her boss's alcohol problem to the correct personnel at her company. This would have given the company the opportunity to provide her boss with possible assistance and, ultimately, might even have saved his job.

It always burns my biscuits (as my husband often says) when someone has to quit an excellent job because someone *else* is behaving poorly. I was gratified to know that Lindsay had learned from the experience, but was sorry the lesson came at such a high cost.

## Loyalty Is Almost Always Personal

Susan shared a similar story with me; unfortunately, hers had a tragic ending. Several years ago, Susan had worked in the credit department of a well-known department store and had observed her boss open the cash register and take one of the large bills on several occasions. What was even worse was that he commonly blamed one of his employees for the theft and, consequently, fired the individual. Susan stayed below the radar and never said anything because she did not want to "jeopardize my own job." Finally, the "big boss" called her into his office and inquired if she had ever witnessed any such behavior on the part of her boss, and she reluctantly revealed her observances. Her boss was fired, his wife divorced him, and he moved to another state. Susan learned a few months later that he had been hospitalized with depression and ultimately took his own life.

Tears welled up in Susan's eyes as she told me, "Nan, had I known what would happen to him, I never would have said anything." I knew exactly how she felt. Susan knew logically that she was not responsible for her boss's suicide; she also knew his thievery would have probably been discovered eventually, even without her testimony. Emotionally, however, she struggled for a long time with "the guilt of being a part of his demise." And it only added to her self-inflicted guilt that she also wondered if she had reported his stealing earlier, he might have been able to receive the counseling he desperately needed.

Situations like this remind us once again that ethical dilemmas are *rarely* simple black-and-white decisions. The late Tip O'Neill, Speaker of the U.S. House of Representatives, often said, "All politics are local and personal." I believe one's ethics are the same: local and (deeply) personal as well.

It's also vital to appreciate the difference between loyalty to *whom* versus loyalty to *what*. The "what" we choose to be loyal to ought to be the greater good, also called the moral standard. The winning strategy is *always* the moral standard; our challenge will be to find our way to it.

"Good" loyalty—a feature of the Ethical Office—is essential to our professional happiness. Because we are human beings, we will inevitably stumble and fall. We will make awkward gaffes in meetings, and we all need someone to supply a gracious chuckle now and then. Support among colleagues brings out the best in our team and in each other. The benefits of being in a functioning, productive, supportive, creative, and mutually energized team every day are priceless.

An assistant named Carol Gonazales from Lake Oswego, Oregon, puts it this way:

> I feel that loyalty, in the early stages of developing a work-ing relationship, could be helped along with good chem-istry. I think chemistry is taken to the next level—which is loyalty—once everyone is secure in the fact that the right thing is done when presented with ethical choices, for our department, clients, and our company. None of us would put the other in a position where this would be jeopardized.... Loyalty in a working team is a secure feeling that the right thing will be done, no matter the situation.

Problems begin to mount when personal integrity takes a backseat to loyalty. And big problems can snowball into catastrophes—until someone with enough integrity is willing to be accountable, admit the error, and begin rebuilding trust, one commitment at a time. In the "loyalty first" scenario, whistle-blowers stay silent out of loyalty to their companies. Those situations are what allow tragedies like the *Challenger* and *Columbia* space shuttle catastrophes to continue to occur.

Patti Ferguson from Wichita, Kansas, reports:

> Loyalty is a timely topic for me personally as I have just gone through a trial in federal court in which my former boss was convicted for several white-collar crimes. Because of my loyalty—and what I thought was a vital characteristic for a successful boss/assistant team—he was able to get away with these crimes. Doing so was probably easier for him because of his assistant's (my) loyalty. It is very clear to me now that once my boss realized he had a "loyal" assistant working for him, he took full advantage of my loyalty and used it in a most unethical way. During past interviews, I always described myself as a loyal assistant; however, I no longer consider that a plus for a good administrative professional and will not use "loyal" to describe what I bring to the table as an administrative professional.

Clearly, a lesson learned in the most difficult of ways.

Wendy Griffin Anderson, an executive administrative assistant for a firm in Memphis, Tennessee, writes:

> My motto used to be, I'll do whatever it takes to protect my boss and cover for him when he blows it, no questions asked. I was taken advantage of, treated unprofessionally, humiliated, abused, and ultimately rejected. I had given everything—taken blame for things that were not my fault, sometimes even lied—to protect and support this person, only to have them turn on me. I've come to understand that loyalty comes down to respect—and out of mutual respect grows loyalty. It is false loyalty to cover another person's mistakes and shield them from taking responsibility and learning from their mistakes. ... Corporate life isn't about keeping individual people in certain positions. It's about delivering on the corporate mission—that assistant is the TRUE professional.

# The New Loyalty Means Being Committed to Doing the Right Thing

Employees today describe loyalty as a dedication and commitment to doing the right thing for your personal and professional standards, your company's mission, and your bosses. For example, Kay Enlow, CPS/CAP, past international president of IAAP, states: "I believe our understanding of loyalty has shifted dramatically. I now think of loyalty as a commitment, not blind allegiance. I must remain committed to my personal values and beliefs—what I feel is right or wrong." Well said! Superintendent of the Ames Water Plant in Ames, Iowa, Philip Propes, concurs by defining the old-fashioned loyalty as compliance:

> There are 100 other folks who could "do the job," so it's the commitment I'm concerned about. I would much rather have commitment than compliance. I may have good workers who are compliant, but I'll have excellent workers if they're committed to doing the right thing.

Enlow (Hallmark, Kansas City) also adds:

> When I personally think of "loyalty," I think more internally ... it's more of a dedication or commitment to my employer. I believe dedication and commitment come from a true "buy-in" to your company's beliefs and values and their goals and objectives. And when you feel aligned to that direction, dedication and commitment just come naturally. Another key indication of this new loyalty is not being afraid to share thoughts and opinions when asked.

In other words, loyalty as commitment includes a commitment to debate and discussion. Other additions to a "big-picture" definition of the new loyalty include qualities such as trust, honesty, integrity, pride, elevated skill levels, high moral standards, and unwillingness to take advantage of the system.

Trust is a substantial element to loyalty as well. As Elizabeth Black says in her April 2008 *OfficePro* article, "Confidence trust is the belief that you can count on the other person to do the right thing or act in positive, ethical ways. Competence trust is the belief in the person's capability to do the job at hand." When both of these exist, loyalty is a natural result.

## Managers' Alert: Start Talking!

The loyalty conversation is one that needs to occur, and preferably sooner rather than later. This discussion needs to take place on various levels and across groups—between bosses and employees, among management, and even at the board level. I encourage you all to start talking about loyalty's new limits and expectations in your organizations and to do so in such a way that will result in enhancing your mutual trust and respect. It is a conversation that must transpire well before a loyalty crisis occurs.

Savvy management supports employees and wants them to recognize and feel the limits of loyalty, as well as the increased accountability that is a reality today. They want employees to take full responsibility and control of their jobs, and to be proactive and alert to ethical infractions. And they are demanding a *partnership* with employees that creates an atmosphere of challenge and debate, whereby raising ethical questions about a decision or practice is simply a part of managing well. In a way, the definition of *loyalty* has evolved to include the practice of questioning, debating, and advocating for the highest good of the company. I believe that loyalty and integrity issues can usually be solved with frank discussion or outside intervention such as ethics training.

Managers and employees nowadays agree that they must view loyalty as a reciprocal commitment to help each other "do the right thing." Both are aware of, and even hypersensitive to, their separate accountabilities, and both realize that no one gets to play the blame game anymore. Each can hold the other to higher expectations, and neither ought to expect the other to sacrifice himself. Loyalty now is something to be *negotiated*, not presumed.

There's only one way for management and employees to inoculate themselves against a loyalty crisis, and that is to start talking. Managers ought to ask employees about the limits to their loyalty, while employees should seek a reality check from their bosses regarding expectations. Both of you need to start talking about these limitations and expectations *now*—before you need to talk to a lawyer about your defense. Use the talking points at the end of this chapter to launch your loyalty conversation.

# No More Eyes Wide Shut

We need loyalty more than ever to keep ourselves grounded in today's fast-paced, rough-and-tumble world. We certainly need the sense of teamwork and camaraderie that come with loyalty if we are going to be productive and positive focused. Though loyalty has morphed from unconditional to conditional, it still is vital.

However, let's all be smart about this. Loyalty today must be earned equally by all parties involved. It is the by-product of establishing mutual respect and trust. The new definition of *loyalty* is provisional, and it does not extend to compromising your personal ethics or the well-being of the company. Cynthia Lynch (a column reader) writes:

> Integrity, doing what is right, correct and honest—*that* defines the limits of loyalty. If a simple, honest mistake is made within those boundaries and can be correctly and diplomatically righted with no fingers pointed—why not do so? But, could you respect someone, however loyal, if they lacked integrity? "Do whatever it takes to protect each other" is a very suggestive phrase, and a slippery road to travel.

No employee today can afford to become a coconspirator in unethical, illegal, or immoral activity. Most employees want to take the high ground and do the right thing, and managers are no different. Your professional connection can help keep each other out of trouble. And isn't that one of the goals of every good business relationship?

## Talking Points to Help Understand the New Loyalty: For Managers and Employees

**Kick start the discussion by asking your boss these questions:**
- What should I do if I am uncomfortable with something you request?
- Do you always want me to make you look good? At what cost?
- Do you want to know of any gossip I overhear that might be potentially damaging to you or the company?

- Does my loyalty to *you* trump my loyalty to *your* boss? Or to the company?
- Do you think a job applicant is ethically bound to reveal she's pregnant?
- What if you oversleep one morning, call and ask me to tell your boss you are visiting a client, and I refuse? Is this okay?
- How do *you* think Doug Faneuil should have handled the pickle he was in?
- Should I process a report I *know* contains misleading information?
- What should I do when my personal integrity conflicts with a request of yours?

Remember: just launching the conversation should open the door for all kinds of healthy ethical discussions.

*The price of blind loyalty is incompetence. Unconditional loyalty means issues don't get aired and downside risks remain unassessed.*
—Ron Suskind, author of *The Price of Loyalty*

# 4

# True Myths? It Depends!

## *Let's See Things as They Really Are—Not as We Want Them to Be!*

*The great enemy of the truth is very often not the lie—deliberate, contrived and dishonest—but the myth—persistent, persuasive and unrealistic.*

—President John F. Kennedy

Take a look at the letter I recently received from Vangie in Lincoln, Nebraska:

Dear Nan:

I'm beginning to think I'm in the middle of an episode of the popular TV series, *Mad Men!* I process my boss's expense reports each month. He is client manager (and main producer of our midsize advertising agency. My boss has begun visiting a city I'm familiar with and, appropriately, takes clients to lunch several times during his weeklong visits. Recently, however, he has been listing his lunches (with receipts) at a well-known "gentlemen's club." I don't think this would pass the smell test in our compliance department and, yet, is it my job to bring the subject up with him? Should I just look the other way (he's the one going to the strip club—not me), or should I take some action about it?

Bad news, Vangie—it *is* your job!

Before we focus on practical strategies that you can use to improve the ethical climate in your office, I would like to rid you of some common misconceptions about ethics. We will be better at spotting potential ethical dilemmas—and coming up with good resolutions to those dilemmas—if we set aside some of our naïveté about organizationwide ethics.

Most of us tend to be optimistic—perhaps even a bit idealistic—when it comes to ethics. We tend to give the other guy or gal the benefit of the doubt, and take things at face value. As professionals, we instinctively try to help others do their jobs, trusting that they share our "all for one, one for all" attitude.

Well, it's time for a reality check, folks, and the bad news is: not everyone is as nice as you are. The good news, however, is that you, your boss, and your coworkers *can* learn to make better ethical decisions *if* you question and discuss specific dilemmas that matter to you. If you're going to effectively challenge the status quo in your office, however, you're going to have to get used to asking the tough questions. And the toughest ones might just be the ones you ask yourself.

Let's first challenge a few of the most common myths I keep hearing from otherwise reasonable office professionals—what I've labeled as the "Top Ten Office Ethics Myths."

## Myth 1: "It Isn't *My* Job to Police My Boss and/or Coworkers"

*Reality:* Yes, it is! If you care about your job, your company, and your professional reputation, you should be highly concerned with maintaining the ethical standards of your workplace. Monsanto Global Ethics Director Scott B. Baucum puts it this way:

> I like to see myself as a good, honest person; but, I am often imperfect and in a hurry. I need ... someone near me with a prudent perspective and courage enough to say, "uh, you might want to rethink that one, Boss!" The *last* thing I need is someone who questions nothing, accepts everything, and thinks he/she is being a "good employee." I need a partner with a strong sense of integrity and courage enough to use it.

Progressive leaders like Baucum appreciate the tactful reminders and reinforcements they receive from their staff to keep everyone on the right track.

The earlier case involving Vangie and her boss is a good example of the fact that when her boss is in trouble, *she* is in trouble! Vangie apparently is well aware of her company's rules about appropriate expenses. Her instincts are spot-on; she knows there's a problem festering.

Therefore, my advice would be for Vangie to have a frank talk with her boss about the greater transparency expected these days and the likelihood that his shenanigans will eventually be uncovered. She should point out she is accountable as well because she handles his expense account reports, and she might someday be asked if she was aware he was frequenting this club on company time and at company expense.

Vangie should stress that she is acting in her boss's interests by discussing the situation with him. While she can also suggest "what if" scenarios that involve the IRS and unflattering publicity, it should be sufficient to point out that he is violating company policy and she is, in essence, a coconspirator.

If Vangie is uncomfortable talking with her boss about this situation (as many employees would be), she can meet instead with an appropriate individual in her company, for example, a human resource director, compliance director, corporate attorney, or even her boss's boss. She should tell the person she would like to speak confidentially with him or her and, also, that she is going to document the conversation.

Vangie's Ethical Priority Compass is a helpful guide here. She must protect herself (due to her involvement in processing his reports); she must protect her company (by preventing an embarrassing and perhaps costly incident); and she must protect her boss from himself (her boss may be reprimanded or even lose his job).

## Myth 2: "Women Are More Ethical than Men; They Are More Moral and More Principled"

*Reality:* Not necessarily true! The most recent research is that there is a universal sequence of the stages of moral development for *both* genders. I have found in my own research, however, that the *process* of how men and women reach their moral and ethical decisions often differs.

My sister-in-law, Dolores, is a pastoral care chaplain who has raised four boys and two girls. She says her sons and daughters both wanted to win equally in sandbox games, but her daughters were quicker to complain, "That's not fair!" And that's when the squabbling began.

At the risk of being mislabeled a sexist, I do believe many females' approach to handling ethical dilemmas differs from our male counterparts. Maybe Dolores is right; as women, we generally seem to place a premium value on the *process* by which we win. Perhaps we need to *feel* we won fair and square. But I think it is a stretch to say that men are therefore more willing to fight unfairly. Males have a cultural history defined by sportsmanship and "playing by the rules," so they care about winning fairly, too, just in a slightly different way than we do. Now that more of us are growing up with organized athletics (thank you, Title IX!), we are—like the men—also looking at ethics through the lens of "good sportsmanship."

Men and women certainly *communicate* about ethics differently. I was a guest on an East Coast radio show exploring this topic when a caller said to me:

Ms. DeMars, when I was growing up, my father was just as ethical as my mother, and each taught me right from wrong in their own way. My dad always told me what *not* to do, with the reason "It's wrong!" My mom told me the same. However, my mom always went one step further. She would sit down with me and explain "why" it was wrong because of the consequences.

This caller experienced firsthand the difference in styles of male and female approaches.

## Myth 3: "What Others Do Is None of My Concern"

*Reality:* What others do *is*—and should be—of your *great* concern. You work for an organization that pays you a salary, and you work in a profession with standards. You cannot afford to make the hollow statements: "It's none of my business" or "It's not my job."

I presented a workshop to a group of employees at Kraus-Anderson Construction in Minneapolis. There were over 100 guys (plus a few gals), all in various positions of responsibility for this well-respected Midwestern construction company. In fact, I deemed the company a "handshake firm" (i.e., their word is their bond) because they have a legacy of honorable dealings that dates back several generations.

I offered this potential scenario to the group: Let's say you were out for dinner one evening and saw an employee of your firm at the bar acting "way out of line." You don't know the guy, but he is wearing a sweatshirt with a company logo, and there's a company car parked outside. What do you do? I gave them three options: (1) join him so you can keep an eye on him; (2) try to get him out of there; or (3) do nothing because it's none of your business.

The room erupted; then, a most interesting thing occurred. By happenstance, I called on several 20-something guys in the front row with their hands up who opted for number 3—to do nothing! Since their responses surprised me, I then began purposely calling on the silver-haired attendees in the room. *They* all chose option 2—to get the guy out of there. Each of them went on to say, "This is not only our company's reputation that is at stake; our *profession's* reputation is at stake as well!"

I ended this segment by asking the company president, Bruce Engelsma, for his input. He stood and resoundingly agreed with the silver-haired gang. I was proud of this company and its management for having instilled that professional pride in its employees. I have to cut the younger guys some slack, however; they probably had not been working for the company long enough to internalize the sense of loyalty and pride.

The bottom line: what your colleagues do *is* your concern; their actions reflect on you and your company. No workplace professional can be successful with an isolationist, blinders-on, "I'll just do my job" attitude.

## Myth 4: "I'm the Only One Who Sees What's Going On, and I'm the Only One Who Cares"

*Reality:* This is doubtful. It may seem that way at times because we're often all wrapped up in our own world. But the reality is that we're never alone. You may have some silent observers at the moment, but people do notice and care. They are often simply waiting for someone else to be first, to be a leader.

Wanda Simeona, former executive assistant to Arizona State Treasurer David Petersen, provides an inspiring role model. Petersen was the target of an investigation for allegedly improperly pocketing speaking fees, billing the state for personal travel expenses, hiring political allies, and improperly using state computers. His troubles came to light only after Simeona quit and made numerous allegations against him in a blistering four-page resignation letter. Once she stepped forward, Petersen's chief of staff and chief deputy provided information and documents to investigators. So do the right thing; you never know who is ready to follow you.

## Myth 5: "I Can Trust My Boss to Always Be Fair (or Unfair)"

*Reality:* Wrong. Bosses are human—sometimes wise and sometimes clueless. Generalizing about how your boss always thinks or acts can limit your view and leave no possibility for positive change. His or her managerial skills may or may not be an ideal match to your own personality and skills. Or perhaps your supervisor has some personal problems that affect his or her judgment at times (e. g., an ill relative, a divorce pending).

# Myth 6: "I Have to Do What I'm Told to Keep My Job"

*Reality:* This is probably the most self-defeating myth of all, not to mention the fact that it's also a cop-out. Yes, your boss has more power than you do, but that doesn't mean you have *no* power at all. You can assert yourself by expressing your best ideas and alternative approaches wherever possible. Look for a reasonable middle ground on which you can both agree.

Let's imagine that your boss has essentially told you that it's "my way or the highway," and her way is the unethical route. While coercion will probably not be that blunt, you'll likely get the picture. Again, this is reality. Unless you have a signed employment contract with your company—which most people do not—you can be fired "at will." The best approach here is to assert yourself and push back as much as you dare when she pushes you. Offer constructive solutions when you encounter an ethical dilemma. Talk it through with your boss or others to start that long-overdue dialogue about office ethics.

# Myth 7: "I Really Made a Bad Mistake; I'm a Bad Person"

*Reality:* Whether you made the error inside or outside your office walls, you are simply a good person who just made a bad choice. Lapses in ethical judgment are not terminal; you can use them to learn from the experience, and see what you'd do differently should a similar situation arise.

# Myth 8: "A Person Cannot Be Talked into Acting with Greater Moral Courage"

*Reality:* I know for a fact that this is false because of what I've seen during my interactive ethics training. Employees have "aha" moments all the time and experience ongoing development of individual moral judgment (thank heavens). And nothing stimulates this growth more than examination of the ethical dilemmas that are likely to affect your company.

People often ask me, "Why don't you, as an ethicist, tell your seminar attendees what to do and what not to do?" I always respond by reminding them that not even a psychiatrist tells you what to do. All anyone can do is help a person understand the ramifications of his or her actions. In the end, it's up to every person on his or her own to make personal choices about right and wrong.

Ethics training is most effective when it asks questions that help people think through their dilemmas. Lecturing, sermonizing, telling, or reading about moral dilemmas have little impact—and would likely put my attendees to sleep. Likewise, casting shame and assigning blame on someone at the point his hand is in the cookie jar, so to speak, yields very ineffective results. It's not until people actually address and discuss relevant moral and ethical dilemmas that they care about—with people they care about (their coworkers)—that change occurs.

## Myth 9: "You Are Born with Your Morality; You Believe What You Believe, and, By Golly, You Will Cling to It throughout Your Life"

*Reality:* Wrong again. People grow up. They mature because of their experiences and opportunities to reflect and examine their decisions.

At one seminar I led, a woman stood up and told us about the company officer for whom she once worked who had "one wife and three mistresses." (This busy guy had obviously slid off his moral compass.) She said she managed to "keep them all straight" (and make sure that no one ever learned about the others) and, in the process, she never had a better job, better salary, better bonuses, or better raises than she did in that position. Then, I asked her (because I *had* to know) was it all worth that extra effort, and would she do it again today? She didn't hesitate for a second when she answered, "Not in my lifetime!!" Thankfully, we can learn and make better choices next time.

And finally, the biggest myth of all . . .

# Myth 10: "People Instinctively Do the Right Thing When Confronted with an Ethical Dilemma"

*Reality:* Oh boy, if only that were the case. But ethical dilemmas are by definition *dilemmas* because they involve people, and people are complicated. I *do* believe that most people instinctively respond with "Well, it depends" somewhere in the first few minutes of a discussion about an ethical dilemma. It is reminiscent of the oft-repeated words of Tevye, the anguished papa in the musical *Fiddler on the Roof*, as he continually struggled with moral dilemmas, defined them, and repeatedly ended up saying, "On the *other* hand..."

I speculate that if we were placed in a room all by ourselves, and *no one would ever know the consequences of our actions*, here's what we would do when confronted with an ethical dilemma: 10 percent of us would instinctively do the right thing, and another 10 percent of us would automatically do the wrong thing. The other 80 percent of us will struggle with the dilemma, conclude "it depends on the circumstances," and act unpredictably.

**Here is a sampling of a few "it depends" questions you may encounter at work:**

- Are there any circumstances that would cause you to "look the other way" if a friend at the company were taking advantage of disability benefits?

- Your coworker comes in late, leaves early, and takes long lunch hours. Would it make a difference knowing that she is a single parent with a difficult child care situation?

- You witness a married supervisor out to dinner in a cozy situation with an employee who reports directly to him—and who is not his wife. A problem?

- What would you do if your boss constantly ignored company policy and used the company car for personal vacations?

- Do you always automatically blow the whistle on inflated expense reports when you learn of them?

- If you were aware of a job applicant's prior chemical dependency problem that might cripple his chance to be hired, would you speak up?

- If you believed your boss was "cooking the books" to make herself look better or cover up for a problem, would you say something to her? Would you speak to anyone else? Would you say anything if it was likely you would lose your job as a result?
- If you became aware that a coworker was bending the rules in some way, would you tell your own or his supervisor? Would you handle the situation any differently if you knew that you probably would cause this individual to lose his job?
- A coworker tells you she has been sexually intimate with her supervisor. She confides that she was coerced into the liaison at first, but now she says, "It's not too bad. We have a good time, he's giving me more money and better assignments, and when it ends, I'll have a great lawsuit." Would you do anything about this train-wreck-waiting-to-happen?

Virtually all ethical decisions you make at work fall into this "it depends" category. You must decide these situations on the basis of what is right for you, your company, and your boss—*in that order*. It's entirely normal for you (and everyone else) to be tempted to bend the ethical rules because of various needs and pressures. It's also normal for people to choose to act in their short-term self-interests. If the ethical standards need to flex, stretch, or twist a bit to cover not-so-ethical behavior, then they say so be it. In other words, "What's right is right, and what's *wrong* is right, as long as it's convenient and suits my needs."

I am continually amazed at people's capacity to bridge the gap of inconsistency between what they say they believe is ethical and their unethical actions. If and when their deeds happen to be aligned with their core values, it is only a happy coincidence.

You can see the problem this causes. If people make all their "it depends" decisions based only on their short-term self interests, and do not see the satisfaction of their personal needs as linked to the welfare of the team, the office environment will quickly become unmanageable and unbearable. This selfish decision making is expected in small children at play, but not acceptable among professional colleagues in a modern office!

The rationalizations that make it possible for a person to live with what I call the "dynamic discord" of actions he or she knows to be unethical carry a cost. They will pay a hefty personal price in terms of stress and unhappiness—and the organization will suffer as well when this stressed and unhappy individual reports for work with a bad attitude, low energy, poor motivation, poor concentration, and overall subpar capacity (or desire) to perform.

It therefore makes good sense to *minimize the likelihood* that an employee will have to live with an unresolved ethical dilemma. This book is packed with suggestions about how you can minimize your "it depends" questions, resolve your ethical dilemmas, and, in the process, build a more ethical office that supports and reinforces your natural desire to "do the right thing."

**The following three questions are the ones I pose most often to my seminar attendees along with information on how they usually respond:**

1. You've just received an offer for your dream job and are planning to go into the new company, meet with the human resource director, and formally accept the following day. However, you learn that afternoon that you are now pregnant! Do you also reveal this fact when you accept the job—which you still fully intend to do? We all know that it's none of their business; you're not obligated in any way to reveal this information, nor is it legal for them to ask you the question. However, my seminar attendees are still split down the middle on this one: 50 percent say they would reveal this new situation, and 50 percent say they would not. Well, "it depends." ...

2. You are a production manager and your boss, the VP of production, is married with a large family. However, he also has a mistress and is careless about letting you (and others) know about this fact. He often says to you, "If you need to reach me today, here's my 'friend's' number; but make something up if my wife calls." How would you handle this? I am happy to report that 90 percent of my attendees say they would *not* lie to the boss's wife, and would tell him so. However, their responses to dodge this conundrum differ greatly—so I guess it depends....

And ... the real lulu:

3. You are Doug Faneuil, executive assistant to Martha Stewart's investment broker, Peter Bocanovic, at Merrill Lynch. You are suddenly thrust into a no-win ethical dilemma concerning your boss and one of your boss's biggest clients—the one and only domesticity diva Martha Stewart! Even though you know they

are lying, do you support both Bocanovic's and Stewart's stories denying involvement in passing on any "insider" stock tips? Well, it depends. . . .

What would *you* do in these situations? It's difficult to predict, isn't it? I suppose it would depend. . . .

*Golf is like life in a lot of ways. The most important competition is the one against yourself. And all the biggest wounds are self-inflicted.*

—President William Jefferson Clinton

# 5

## Mea Culpa—I Screwed Up!

### *How to Recover from a Major Goof-Up!*

*I screwed up!*
> —President Barack Obama, three weeks into his
> presidency, taking the blame hours after former
> Senate Majority Leader Tom Daschle withdrew
> his name for a cabinet post due to tax problems

Dear Nan:

Help! I've really screwed up at work. Fortunately, my boss is willing to give me a second chance, although I feel her watching me constantly. My coworkers, however, two of whom I supervise, appear less supportive, and I'm afraid I've lost their respect. My self-confidence as a professional has plummeted. Logically, I know I am probably not the only one this has ever happened to, but it

sure doesn't feel that way. It's very stressful to even go in to work.
I probably need to look for another job, but who's going to hire
a loser like me? How can I get past this?

—Janice in Branson, MO

**W**ill anyone who has never made a mistake on the job please
stand up? Some of us have made minor errors; some of us have
made major boo-boos; and some of us have even made utter fools of
ourselves. But every single one of us has erred at some point. As Donna
Ferguson, assistant with Manchester Tank & Equipment Company, in
Quincy, Illinois, accurately states, "I believe that someone who doesn't
make a mistake once in a while isn't doing anything productive in the
first place." Great point.

*Mea culpa* is a Latin phrase that translates into English as "my
fault" or "my own fault," the modern equivalent of which would be
"my bad." This chapter will help you recover from a major screw-up
in your professional life (you're still on your own with any personal
issues). There isn't one of us who hasn't "been there."

Take heart—most professional mistakes are not career killers (although they can certainly feel like it at the time). However, *not* learning
from them can be fatal to your profession.

One thing you can be happy about is the fact that you aren't
playing them out on the international stage. We can learn something
from the celebrities who had the most to lose when they screwed up
big time. What did Presidents Richard Nixon and Bill Clinton and
domestic diva Martha Stewart do that made their mistakes look even
worse? They lied and denied—and their denials were their downfalls.
Had they all simply admitted their mistakes in the first place, Nixon
would have remained president, Clinton would have headed off an
embarrassing impeachment trial, and Stewart probably would have
just been fined and scolded—but never sent to prison!

Why is it that the denials and cover-ups are everyone's Waterloo?
It's because we are left wondering what else they are hiding. Long after
high-profile incidents have departed from the headlines, we will forever
suspect there is a lot more fire behind all that smoke.

*The One Minute Apology* author Ken Blanchard (the guy who shows
us how to do anything in a minute) says corporations should realize
that "the longer you wait to apologize for a wrongdoing, the quicker
weakness is seen as wickedness." Blanchard explains that this is what

causes people to ask, "If they're not going to admit that they screwed up, I wonder what else they're going to lie about?"

Employees' mistakes are a very big deal to them. We all know the unwritten part of your job description often goes like this: "Help your managers avoid disasters. Help everyone with damage control. Keep things looking calm and collected and running smoothly, even when you are paddling frantically just below the surface. You are on the company's first-responder team, so fix any screw-ups that occur." Not surprisingly, this means that employees take their own mistakes very seriously—precisely *because* they are so uncommon.

So how *do* you go into reputation rehab after a serious mea culpa? You can follow the five-step program outlined below.

## Step 1: Assess the Problem

Since this is much more difficult to do if you panic, focus on what is real and don't let your imagination run away with you. Take a deep, cleansing breath. Overreacting ("The sky is falling!") is just as bad as underreacting ("Eh, I'll be fine—this should just fix itself"). Since you're likely to exacerbate the damage by overreacting, you must analyze the situation logically: What additional problems could occur as a result of this mistake? How might others be affected? What are the long- and short-term ramifications? Could you potentially lose customers over this? What is the value of that lost business?

Operating in a state of sheer panic may cause others to do things that are counterproductive, dangerous, or stupid. So please spare your coworkers unnecessary drama—take a breath and regain your perspective.

## Step 2: Acknowledge Your Mistake

Have a frank talk with yourself and acknowledge that this is *your*—and nobody else's—problem. As soon as you own it, you have a fighting chance of fixing it, and that has to become your priority. Now is not the time for denial, the blame game, lame excuses, or creative cover-ups; if you delay facing the situation for what it is, you'll only make things worse.

You must first determine if and when to acknowledge your mistake to your boss. But whatever you decide, *you* must be the one to tell your boss first. Do it immediately, and bring your ideas for a solution with you. If you've got no ideas (since panic sometimes causes our brains to freeze), admit that as well. If your boss hears about the problem or your mistake from someone else, you are left to defend yourself and correct her version of the story—not to mention having to explain why *you* weren't the one to let your boss know. At this point in the discussion your credibility is suspect; so who is your boss more likely to believe?

Look at all the high-profile individuals who have experienced "lapses in judgment," "ethical blunders," and other denials and cover-ups (John Edwards comes to mind). They only made their problems worse by attempting to dodge the truth, and when the facts finally came out (as they always do), it made their actions look 10 times worse. So take ownership of your mistake. You screwed up! In the words of the Dale Carnegie Sales Course, "When you lay an egg . . . stand back and acknowledge it!" If you don't recognize your mistake, you may be forever locked in the ranks of the credibility challenged.

Julia Baker, a division secretary/steno for U. S. Army Engineer Research & Development Center in Vicksburg, Mississippi, writes:

> I've done something that was devastating to my professional ego. I finally had a talk with myself. I knew my coworkers had blundered on occasion, but I really couldn't remember specifics about their errors, so it was probably my ego making me think they were focusing on *my* blunder. I reminded myself it's not *always* about me—that I am a very good secretary and I will continue to be a very good secretary.

Sharon Forston, senior admin assistant at GKN Aerospace Chemtronics Inc. in El Cajon, California, recommends, "Disclose the facts to your manager and be prepared to include a solution so the same error is not made in the future. My experience has been that when you demonstrate a sincere personal desire to be a part of the solution, your manager will respect your confidence to continue making appropriate decisions."

Do not try to dodge accountability. People are watching you, so remain a model of professionalism by taking responsibility for your actions. Use this experience as an opportunity to set the standard for open communication and mutually supportive teamwork. You might have to ask your coworkers for their help—and you may be surprised at how willing they are to give it.

"I've found it's very difficult for someone to be angry with you after you've taken full 'credit' for a mistake you've made," notes Rosemary Deitzer, CPS/CAP, Association & Meeting Services, West Chester, Ohio. And Carolina J. Wilson from the University of Northern Iowa in Cedar Falls adds, "If they [your teammates] make a mistake, they will now know they must bring it to your attention immediately so it can be corrected—just like you did. It will take a while, but honesty and consistency in your own performance will restore any of the respect they've lost for you."

## Step 3: Forgive Yourself, and Then Apologize to Whomever You Need To

Your confidence has taken a hit after you make an error, so it's only natural to beat yourself up. However, if you've honestly acknowledged reality, you can focus instead on taking action toward a resolution instead of stewing in a soup of anxiety and fear (and barraging yourself with questions like, "Who knows? Who will find out? What will they think of me? What's going to happen?").

"Learn to look at yourself in the mirror and like what you see again," advises Maryann E. Winfield, human resource administrative specialist at Dell Inc. in Austin, Texas. "From that point on, you should have no trouble aligning your actions with your values." This is an internal dialogue you have to have with yourself before you can proceed in a constructive way. Why? Because you have a few potentially difficult conversations ahead of you, and you will be less effective if you don't mentally prepare yourself for them.

Apologize sincerely but briefly to the people you've affected, and assure them that this situation will not be repeated. This will probably include your boss; consider whether you cost the company money or credibility. It might also involve coworkers and outsiders whose lives you made more difficult. You must take ownership with confidence and humility and acknowledge your mistake to whomever it affected. If you do so without blaming others—or using any terms or phrases that cause people to doubt your sincerity—you become part of the solution, not the problem.

"Quit kicking yourself and get back to work. We all screw up to varying degrees," says Carol McBride, assistant VP/office manager for Haylor, Freyer & Coon Inc., in North Syracuse, New York. "Think about how you would treat someone who had made the same mistake you did. Often, we are so much harder on ourselves than we would be on others," points out Jill Mahoney, admin assistant with the Principal Financial Group in Des Moines, Iowa. And Sally Costello of the Shaw Group Inc. in Ross, Ohio, advises: "If you continue to show outwardly that you are beating yourself up, others will beat you up as well. Some people feel good about themselves if they can pick on a 'loser'—so don't let them. Do not give your power away."

Secretarial specialist Keri Younker from the Munroe Meyer Institute in Omaha, Nebraska, suggests that you "call a meeting with those affected, openly discuss what has happened, apologize publicly to everyone at the meeting for making the mistake, and then state that you will do whatever you can to fix the problem. Then, you have to move on. The people you supervise will respect you more if they see that you can admit your mistake."

## Step 4: Do What You Need to Do So This Doesn't Happen Again

Start by looking inward to see what you have learned from this screw-up. Rethink your behavior and your systems. Answer the question, "How on earth did this happen?" And be truthful about it. Ask yourself some tough questions: Are you a good enough listener? Are you sufficiently thorough/careful/organized/focused? Were you distracted by outside influences? Were you in a rush? Or—the real biggie—were you just plain careless?

Tracy Heslop, CPS/CAP, executive assistant at Husky Energy, Inc. in Calgary, Alberta, Canada, writes:

> Mistakes are meant to be learned from. Make sure you identify what it is that caused you to make the mistake in the first place. Perhaps your workload is too heavy, you have been putting in too much overtime, or the expectations being placed on you exceed the position you are occupying. Or maybe you were just having a bad day.

In addition to applying what you've learned in order to ensure that you don't repeat your screw-up, you have to take action. Acknowledging and apologizing for your mistake will be much more effective if you get back to work, do whatever you can to fix the problem or—at the very least—take steps to make certain it will not happen again. Use your actions to let people know that you've learned from this mistake so you will not repeat it.

It may also take some special effort to rebuild trust with your boss. I recall one particular manager who told me his assistant made a huge financial error that ended up costing the company a considerable sum. When asked if he fired her, he replied: "Why would I do that? I know she won't make the same mistake again. I don't know that about someone else I may hire."

"It speaks volumes that your boss is willing to give you a second chance. To me, that says there is a history of solid work performance," says Rebecca Carlisle of the University of Florida in Gainesville. Yes, your boss is probably going to be watching you a bit closer for a while; after all, that's her job. But a little extra communication back and forth may be just what you need to rapidly increase your confidence and credibility. A true professional knows when to call on his backup team, and this is the perfect time to request a little extra support and ask for the supervisory encouragement you need. When you're a member of a team that's working on many things at once, there is never enough time to double-check everything— right?

Karen Samuelson, purchasing admin assistant at John I. Haas Inc. in Yakima, Washington, emphasizes the fact that a single heartfelt acknowledgment, apology, and promise to help fix the problem should be enough for the boss (and coworkers). After that, "Your boss should stand up for you to your coworkers, assert that you are a valued employee, and say that you would appreciate their support and assistance." The people around you will see that while you may have made this mistake, they may well make the next one—so only a fool will fail to help you move forward.

"I completely understand how the person who makes an error feels," writes Carolyn O'Connor, CPS, executive assistant to the City of Holland in Michigan. "Any mistake seems catastrophic; when I make a huge one, I feel the earth should swallow me whole and think that I should be banished from existence. However, I have learned that the key to professional growth is to learn from my mistakes. When we look back, we can always see a trail of bread crumbs leading to that mistake. Take steps to pay attention to those little things."

# Step 5: Finally, Maintain a Positive Attitude

Do not dwell on your contrition, and don't wear your mea culpa on your sleeve like some badge of nobility or heroics. People are attracted to upbeat, future-looking people who make good things happen. "Don't plague yourself with 'what if's,'" says Jeanette Sanders at Honda of America in Marysville, Ohio. "Move on while maintaining the same professional integrity that you have always had." Laura Black of SBC Global reminds us that, "Obsessing on what happened will only drive you crazy and accomplish nothing other than showing your peers and supervisor that you truly are not the right person for the position." After all, as Susan L. Auyer, Bechtel National subcontract administrator in Richland, Washington, reminds us: "We're all in the same boat. And as we preach here at Bechtel, if you handle it well, your mistake will not be the focus; your solution is what will be remembered."

No one really cares how you feel about making the mistake, nor is anyone interested in your chattering about it. They're busy, too, so try not to get stuck in the whiny place (they don't understand me, it's not really my fault, my cell phone died, everyone is against me, the job was too hard, I was busy doing something else, blah, blah, blah). Skip the drama (I'm so stupid! I can't ever do anything right! etc.). Your best bet is to pick yourself up and fix the problem, starting with an honest appraisal of what happened. This is not about self-blame; it's about understanding and using that knowledge to work smarter the next time. If you've learned something from the screw-up—and if you stay positive and focus on moving forward—then your ability to overcome this event will only add to your value as an employee.

I once had an office manager tell me about the time she had too much wine at the office holiday party (when such activities were allowed), kissed the "wrong guy" under the mistletoe, fled the premises, and didn't return to work for a week! When she did, she said it was "really too late to recoup my reputation" and, unfortunately, she left the company soon thereafter. If she had followed the above advice and addressed her blunder head-on, instead of hiding out in shame, I wager she would still be employed at the job she loved.

On a personal note: I once fell off the podium right after I had been introduced (all gangly six feet of me—not a pretty sight). Fortunately, only my pride was hurt. The audience had been applauding, but stopped abruptly with a gasp as their seminar leader disappeared from sight. I slowly crawled back up onto the platform, dusted myself off, reached for the podium, and said to my hushed audience, "As Seinfeld would say . . . *that* went well!"

People respect honesty and integrity, and, with time, all mistakes will be ancient history. Take heart: Bill Clinton is the comeback kid, Martha Stewart's empire is back up and running, Richard Nixon's later books were all bestsellers, and my seminar audience laughed *with* me!

It's never too late to start anew.

*Mistakes are a part of the dues one pays for a full life.*
                                                     —Sophia Loren, actress

# Part II

# Take Care of Your Organization

# 6

## Zip It!

### A Culture of Confidentiality Is Your Goal!

---

*My only ... recommendation was to tell her that she need never feel any of her affairs would be repeated, or discussed by me with anyone. And, her reply, with that lovely smile of hers, was, 'If I did not already know that, I would never have asked you to come.'*
  —Isabella Hagner, first U.S. White House social secretary (1901–1905) on her conversation with First Lady Edith Carow Roosevelt on the first day of her job

Dear Nan:

I almost lost my job today. I let some information slip in a casual conversation, and my boss overheard it. He was furious. He said I should know better and that the rules of confidentiality were "understood" in professional offices. Nan, this is my first job out

*(continued)*

*(continued)*
of college and I'm a basket case. If I make another mistake like this one, my career will be aborted before it even begins. So, what *are* the so-called "rules"?

—Nancy in Littleton, CO

M emo to Nancy's boss: Don't assume that Nancy—or any of your other employees, for that matter—understands the nature of confidentiality to the same degree that you do. They need and deserve to have a detailed discussion with you about your expectations. Without your guidance, they will only discover the boundaries of confidentiality by tripping over them and causing problems for you in the process.

Memo to Nancy: I believe confidentiality *is* on the short list of professional job skills that everyone is presumed to simply "understand." But the devil is in the details. For that reason, the material in this chapter will prepare you for a pointed discussion with your boss about specific dilemmas related to confidentiality. If confidentiality is a "must-have" skill, this is a "must-have" discussion.

## Secrets Are in Your DNA

Humans' inherent reverence for confidentiality is ancient. Administrative professionals have inherited their roles of secret keeper, protectorate, and confidante from the earliest civilized societies in Greece, China, and Persia. It should come as no surprise that the word *secretary* is actually derived from the same root word as *secret*. Whether you're building a culture or company, nothing of consequence gets done without undertaking administrative processes based on reciprocal trust. And confidentiality is the mortar that holds these bridges of trust together.

Most administrators enjoy the pace and prestige of being the "go-to" person in their organization. Information is power, after all, and admins tend to have more information than their coworkers; they have a range of operational, strategic, financial, personnel, and personal knowledge. They have to act on some of this and pass on some; they even have to repackage some of this material, or just plain keep it secret.

"I think human nature predisposes us to want to be 'in the know,'" notes Tamra Goodall, CPS/CAP, 2012 international president of the International Association of Administrative Professionals (IAAP). "Being able to hold sensitive information in confidence is what differentiates the respected and trusted professional from the office gossip. Which would you want to be known as?"

However, administrators are not just a conduit for messages or a repository for data. They're expected to use critical thinking skills (and common sense) to determine what information to communicate and what to suppress—and from whom. They're also required to protect all that information from the "bad guys" who want to take it (it's no *wonder* admins often feel like pin cushions!) If an administrator's good judgment fails him even once, the information genie flies out of the lamp and the damage is done. You cannot "undo" or "redo" a mistaken release of information; there is no wiggle room here. A screw-up may cost someone their job—even their career. This is exactly why you and your manager must engage in an explicit discussion about what *is* and what *is not* confidential information *before* a dilemma develops.

## Nan DeMars's Up Close and Personal Confidentiality Audit with Your Manager

The following are some examples of questions to ask in this one-on-one conversation. Persist and insist that your manager make his or her answers as specific and explicit as possible. You need to feel confident as your manager's information gatekeeper.

- What exactly does your "open door" policy mean?
- Who has access to your office when you are not here?
- What materials/files/records do you value most?
- What employee/company/customer information do you always wish to know?
- If I hear gossip, what do you want me to do? (This information is difficult to predict, but the question launches the conversation).
- What documents are strictly confidential—for your and my eyes only?
- Are any items off limits to me?

- Do I have the authority to open any type of package or mail?
- Besides the two of us, who else has access to _____ information?
- What information can I share relating to current projects, and with whom?
- Do you prefer to personally approve all requests for access to restricted materials? When can I use my own judgment?
- Is anyone else allowed to use your computer? Under what circumstance, if any, would this be allowed?
- How should I handle requests from others for information, documents, computer files, and so on when you are unavailable? And, finally ...
- Do you have any particular pet peeves regarding confidentiality?

## What's the Big Deal about Confidentiality? Is My Company Hiding Information It Shouldn't Be?

Let's first determine what some of the confidential information in your organization might be. It could include inventions, trade secrets, sales projections, financial statements, new product or marketing plans, customer information, personnel documents, employee directories, e-mails, manufacturing processes and methods, acquisitions, mergers, divestitures, investments—the list goes on and on. These "slices" of information hold the key to your company's competitive advantages and the value of your company's brand.

You can imagine some unhappy scenarios that might result from the revelation of this material: Giving confidential information to the wrong people could embarrass the company, provide an unfair advantage, violate a client's privacy, put your top performers in danger of being recruited during working hours, compromise safety, start ugly and untrue rumors that hurt sales ... and that's only the short list.

Wouldn't an ethical workplace provide a more positive and productive environment? Of course. When you and your colleagues can discuss and share information with each other without worrying about the security of that information, trust—and its twin, productivity—will increase exponentially.

# But Doesn't the Public Have the Right to Know about Certain Information?

No. There are many "public" audiences, and you cannot presume that any of them will respect the information that is critical to your company. The problems stem from what others *do* with the information they know (or think they know). Just ask any candidate who has run for public office or any celebrity, sales manager, or research scientist how painful it is when others take your information and use it to put you in a defensive or catch-up position.

# Respect Your Boss's Personal Privacy As Well

Whenever I worked with my CEO in his office and he received a phone call from a family member, I always stepped out until the call was finished. He never asked me to do this, and we never discussed it, but I know he appreciated my consideration.

It's therefore a good idea to ask *your* boss about this. "If you get a phone call when I'm in your office, would you like me to leave until you have finished the call? What about a personal phone call?" I guarantee you that this kind of courtesy will *never* go unnoticed!

One admin I knew had permission to open all her boss's mail; however, she drew the line at his paycheck envelope. At her retirement party, her boss gave her high praise for her dedicated service over the years. He also added that the respect she maintained for his personal privacy was the professional trait he most appreciated. And she assumed he had never even noticed!

An assistant to the CEO of a Fortune 500 company named Carole once told me, "The most difficult task of my entire career was when I had to fire *my* assistant for a breach of confidentiality." Carole had assigned her assistant, Tina, the task of researching and purchasing an "extravagant" birthday gift for a member of the CEO's family. One month later, the CEO stormed into Carole's office and informed her that "word was out"—not only what the gift was and who it was for, but the price as well! Carole was devastated because she thought from the first day she began training her that Tina "fully understood the high stakes of the office within which we both operate. However, I (regretfully) *assumed* Tina understood that protecting our boss's professional

confidentiality also included protecting his *personal* confidentiality."
She told me, "Tina was one of the best assistants I ever hired in my
26 years of supporting this high-profile executive. Of course, I had the
'confidentiality conversation' with her during our orientation sessions,
stressing that this aspect of the job was the number one priority, but I
obviously failed to address the aspect of *personal* confidentiality." She
added, "I made a grievous mistake, which almost cost me my *own* job!"

Your boss's most confidential work products are likely to be her
current personal notes—that legal pad, those paper files, the special
notebook she keeps in her car, those 3 × 5 note cards she tucks away
or the Post-Its she plasters everywhere. Whatever her system, these
notes are probably always nearby but not backed up regularly. Do
both yourself and your boss a favor by periodically making copies or
transferring these notes to to-do lists, so that you're never in danger of
losing this "mission-critical" information. Show the same attention to
the tracking of your boss's electronic communication devices, which
are easily misplaced in fast-paced offices, by establishing a backup or
synching schedule. Your boss will be forever grateful when you save
the day during a panic.

You and your boss cannot anticipate every circumstance that
threatens confidentiality, so when in doubt, zip your lips! You will
*never* be sorry you did.

## More Unwritten Rules "Everyone Should Just Know"

- *Be discreet in all conversations, in all locations.* Cultivate self-restraint
  by asking, "Would my boss approve of this conversation if he
  overheard it?" It is surprisingly easy to make a slip during a lunch
  conversation and divulge confidential information without even
  realizing you're doing so. Haven't we all wished that we could
  retract or cover up a careless comment at one time or another?
  There was also the story of the employee who overheard in the elevator that her entire department was being laid off the following
  month! Was it true? It really doesn't matter, does it? The damage
  was done, and as a result, the whole department was thrown into
  turmoil.
- *Avoid "war stories."* It's tempting to share interesting stories with
  your peers about clients and/or coworkers. These seemingly

innocent tales, however, can hurt your career because you can never be certain who knows who. Another true story—this one from a partner in a CPA firm: As an accountant named Penny took a break at a client's office, she chatted casually with the bookkeeper. She mentioned a recent visit to an unnamed client where she had discovered an embezzlement scheme and brought it to the owner's attention. Although Penny thought she took care to conceal the client's identity, unbeknownst to her, the bookkeeper was a relative of a salesperson at the problem company. Penny shared enough details that the bookkeeper was able to determine exactly who was being discussed. The company had previously confronted the thief and worked out a quiet agreement for restitution, without the rest of the staff knowing about anything. But the salesperson talked about it with coworkers and the thief's position soon became untenable. She resigned, abandoned the agreement, and left the company holding the bag (they did not want the bad publicity that would accompany criminal charges). The company tracked the leak back to their accountant—Penny—who was reprimanded severely and lost the account. She was fortunate, however, since she *could have* (but did not) faced a lawsuit claiming damages, complaints to the accountancy board, and the risk of public disclosure of her breach of confidence.

- *Never assume someone is "in the loop."* They're probably not! Crafty individuals often hint that they're privy to a particular topic, begin asking "fishing" questions (like "What do you think of the new marketing plan?" and "What do you like best or least about the plan to move the call center?"), and soon, they become fully aware of something they have no business knowing about.

- *Discuss company business only with your boss and other authorized individuals.* This means *no* pillow talk, and excludes even your spouse, significant other, or very best friend in the world. Without you around to kick them under the table, they may inadvertently say something they shouldn't during a casual conversation—maybe even while bragging about you. It might sound something like, "My wife was working late on so-and-so's business when, to everyone's surprise, such-and-such happened. Isn't she amazing?" How can your spouse possibly know and appreciate the confidential nature of the information you have? He can't, so play it safe. What others don't know can't hurt you. Eileen Preksto, who worked in Minneapolis as an executive assistant to high-profile

Jacobs Management CEO Irwin Jacobs, followed this philosophy throughout her career. Eileen's husband told me, "In all the years she worked for Irwin, the only things I ever learned about Jacobs Management were what I read in the newspaper!" That is the highest praise for a *true* professional.

- *Speak softly—literally.* Be sure your conversation is low-pitched enough not to be overheard, both inside and outside the office. You can never assume the person in the next cubicle, seat on the plane, in line at the lunchroom, or in the next stall in the restroom (it happens) doesn't care what you are saying. That person you don't recognize could be a prospective client, a gossipy vendor, even a competitor—or their best friend.

- *Minimize your socializing with coworkers if you find the "no shoptalk" restriction difficult to observe.* Don't initiate or respond to discussions about company business if and when you participate in coffee or lunch breaks with your colleagues. Be especially wary of seemingly innocent efforts to "pump" you for information. Some of that casual chitchat may be concealing malicious motives.

- *Be especially on guard when you attend a work-related association event.* It stands to reason that the other people attending this kind of an affair are going to be interested in your business, your market, your suppliers, and even *you.* A relaxed atmosphere and the hint of a prospective job may be all it takes to turn an association networking event into an escalating arms race for secrets: "I'm an incredibly accomplished person, and I can prove it by telling you this astonishing story. ..." Response: "Oh, yeah, well I can top that story—just listen to this. ..." I know one admin who hinted to another guest "confidentially" about a pending lawsuit against the company, and the guest turned out to be a reporter! Oops.

These so-called rules will probably remain "assumed to be understood." It's not likely that they'll ever be written down (anywhere besides here, that is!) because other people's determined efforts to gain information from you is infinitely varied and relentless. You must develop your own judgment, and find the fortitude to keep mum despite the tricks and pressure others use to wheedle tidbits of information out of you.

Unfortunately, there will always be people who are not above lying, stealing, or acting in devious ways to obtain information from you. Information is what I call "portable power," so it is a commodity well worth the effort to go after. Your knowledge is valuable, so protect it. It's your job to *be suspicious* and to develop a healthy skepticism and cynicism about why you're getting all the attention, the free tickets, and the compliments. Why is this guy hovering around your desk? Your computer screen? Or that file? The best actors haven't always made it to Hollywood; they may be working with you!

"Confidentiality requires that managers hold periodic closed-door meetings with every employee," says Barbara S. Holman, an executive assistant in Spring, Texas. "Managers should explain what they consider to be confidential information and why it should not be shared, and cite various examples at these gatherings. Employees should understand that sharing confidential information affects the profitability of the company and, ultimately, everyone's pay." Well said, Barbara.

The late Thomas F. Barnum, chairman of Chicago's Everest Group management consulting firm, said to me once:

> The confidentiality aspect of my business is so significant that I discuss it with a candidate during both the job interview *and* job offer conversation. I tell them that a confidentiality infraction is the *only* area in which they will not get a second chance. If there is ever a breach of privacy, they will be dismissed on the spot. ... I repeat that statement when offering the job and ask the candidate to say it back to me in his or her own words so that there is no misunderstanding.

I support this zero-tolerance standard wholeheartedly. These company leaders take their employees at their word when they say they want to be treated—and paid—like professionals. High expectations in regards to confidentiality are an essential part of building and maintaining the ethical workplace.

The head partner of a large law firm once told me, "The number two reason for a lawsuit against a law firm is a breach of confidentiality by one of the firm's employees!" While I always wished I had asked him what the number one reason was, I *did* inquire whether he addressed the topic of confidentiality at his firm. His reply both surprised me and brought him up short: "Attorneys are always aware of this in regards to their client/attorney relationship; but no, Nan, come to think of it, we really don't discuss its importance with the rest of the staff. We assume they know!" I never forgot his words. I believe there are many executives who make the same mistake in "assuming" that their employees know their expectations regarding confidentiality; but, in reality, their employees are just guessing and making assumptions.

Maintaining confidentiality is probably the foremost occupational challenge of administrative professionals today. Since they are always "where the action is," they have to rigorously set and maintain boundaries to control that very "action."

---

### Your GOLDEN RULE OF CONFIDENTIALITY should be:

Treat everything about your job as if it is confidential—until and unless you are told otherwise!

---

## No Profession Is Immune to Confidentiality Defaults

Loose-lips behavior can cause all kinds of dire consequences. A few examples of different professions: A Minneapolis search firm partner named Roger told me of how his firm lost a major client due to a conversation overheard in an airport terminal flight club lounge in Chicago. Apparently, two of Roger's account executives were openly discussing the merits of two candidates they had just interviewed. They used first names and went into "great detail about the candidates' backgrounds and professional and personal merits." Another client of Roger's search firm was within earshot of the entire conversation—along with several others in the lounge—and "began to feel uncomfortable about these two talking so freely in a public arena and, consequently, started wondering if they were associated with the search firm *he* worked with." He purposely struck up a side conversation with one of the women and asked what firm she was with—and bingo! It *was* the search firm he was currently using to hire a new CFO. Roger told me this client immediately went to a private cubicle in the flight club and called him to terminate his search contract and all future business with his firm, and there was nothing Roger could do to persuade the client otherwise. He lost a major account, and the loose-lips players lost their jobs.

Then there was the time I was presenting at office product manufacturer Boise Cascade when an attorney in the class shared how he handled a breach of confidentiality at a law firm where he once was a partner. He was scrunched in the back of a crowded elevator going to lunch when his assistant (who didn't see him) stepped into the front of the elevator with a friend and, during the descent, "dropped the name of a client." The attorney told me he "walked off the elevator and fired her on the spot!" A tough lesson, to be sure—but this assistant's casual conversation left both the client and her employer vulnerable.

And an aide to a state legislator named Claudette was out to lunch with another legislative aide named Mary Ann when she happened to mention to Mary Ann something about a health care bill her boss was preparing to introduce. Claudette's legislator had just completed extensive research on this progressive legislation that would not only satisfy his constituents, but also portray him favorably with members of both sides of the aisle.

Guess what happened next? Shortly thereafter, Mary Ann's boss stood up in the state assembly and introduced the same health care bill, preempting Claudette's legislator and taking full credit for work that had been done by someone else. Claudette and her boss were the only ones privy to this research and the introduction of the pending bill, so you can imagine the hot water in which Claudette found herself.

Human resource professionals regularly struggle with confidentiality dilemmas, such as when they learn of layoffs, terminations, job offers, or pay reductions. Imagine hearing about impending layoffs and seeing that your best friend Bill is on the layoff list. To complicate matters, Bill recently told you he is about to purchase a new home for his growing family. You know Bill would not make this commitment at this time if he knew he was losing his job. What can you do?

As difficult as this may be, you are professionally forbidden from sharing classified information like this. Even if Bill promised to stay mum, you can never be certain of the ripple effects that might occur, and your job is on the line. Your only recourse may be to alert your manager about this situation to see if something could be done on Bill's behalf. You can take some comfort in making an effort, but, even under these circumstances, someone else is going to be upset because they didn't get the same consideration. This is truly one of those situations in which no good deed goes unpunished!

## Where Do the Threats to Confidentiality Come From?

Your position makes you a de facto clearinghouse for all sorts of information. If you are paying attention at all, you probably know quite a bit about your company, your customers, and your coworkers. Common sense tells you that most of this information is no one else's business and is therefore off limits.

But everyone wants you to bend the rules for them, don't they? I suspect you have experienced confidentiality dilemmas similar to these:

- *The boss.* She wants you to be her "eyes and ears" on both the plant floor and in the office. Any problem you hear about, she wants to hear about as well. She also wants to know what other managers are saying about her. So what do you do? Is "snitch" in your job description? How can you reply when your boss asks—or orders—you to keep a company secret about illegal or immoral acts? And how are you expected to handle private information about your boss's personal problems or secrets about his mistakes? How long, and under what circumstances, are you obligated to be a loyal team player who "knows how to keep your mouth shut"? Are you still bound by your implied or explicit oaths of confidentiality if you transfer to another department or your boss leaves the company? Do you pretend you never knew or even forgot certain information—even if it affects the company's overall well-being?

- *Coworkers.* Staying mum about a coworker's long breaks and bogus reports is the highest form of loyalty in some organizations. Lying to protect each other is considered noble, even heroic, in some "it's-us-against-management" corporate cultures. If you choose to not "get dirty" with the ones you work with, you can expect strained relationships and many awkward moments. Imagine your coworkers fill up their personal cars at the company gas pump after hours, or pilfer office supplies, or submit personal lunch receipts for reimbursement, and they fix it so the theft goes unnoticed. You declare you are not going to turn them in, but neither are you going to participate because you believe it's wrong.

    This dilemma cannot last for long; your coworkers will feel you are judging them with your silence. You reflect back to them an unflattering image of themselves. You remove the "everyone's doing it" excuse. You make them look bad by comparison.

    Because of the proximity of your coworkers, these dilemmas are usually short-lived. If they are doing something that is different from the prevailing ethical culture in the office, or if *you* are, the team is not aligned. You and your coworkers will be less effective as a team until balance is restored.

- *Other managers.* Who is allowed to see the budget? The marketing plans? The public relations program for the year ahead? What do you do when you know about or are drawn into a petty turf war that amounts to political gamesmanship? Do you sit on the sidelines and refuse to help your boss fight a political battle, and then feel bad when she loses and gets bumped down the corporate ladder? Or do you help—and fight to win? Or simply pretend you don't understand what is going on around you and naively attempt to mediate more cooperation instead of competition?

- *Corporate officers.* Imagine you are talking to a company officer who asks you directly for an honest answer to an off-base question. She's getting the run around and smells a rat, a cover-up, or a problem to which no one is willing to admit—and she wants to know what you know, right now. Whose secrets will you keep, and whose will you give up? Do you say anything about anyone who is at variance with the "corporate line"?

- *Outsiders.* Inquiring minds want to know how big the deal is, who's in and who's out, whether the company is planning to relocate, what new products are coming out and when they'll be ready, what the balance sheet will look like at the end of the quarter, who the company's biggest clients are, and how many lawsuits have been filed and why. This list of questions—and the number of people demanding answers—is unending.

## Loyalty Complicates Confidentiality Dilemmas

Geri was a church secretary whose minister told her in confidence that he was going to break his contract and resign within the next month. She agreed to keep the minister's plans to herself, and a month later, the minister abruptly left the position. The next day, the church board president called Geri into his office and asked her if she had known the minister was going to leave his position. When she admitted that the minister had told her in confidence about his plans the previous month, the president fired Geri on the spot.

Was this fair? As far as the president was concerned, Geri's first responsibility was to the church and, therefore, the board of directors—not the minister. The president believed that she was obligated to disclose *any* information she received that directly affected her employer's well-being.

In retrospect, Geri should have told the minister immediately that he was placing her in an untenable position that jeopardized her job. This so-called private information was injurious to her employer, so her loyalty to the organization trumps her loyalty to her boss. By choosing to remain silent, she effectively became a coconspirator against her employer's best interests. Geri could have extricated herself from this confidentiality-loyalty dilemma by choosing to exercise her power. She could have said something like, "If you don't say something by noon tomorrow, I'll feel compelled to talk to the board myself." Geri's Ethical Priority Compass could have guided her: First, she takes care of herself, then the organization. Her boss comes last.

Your trusty Compass will serve you well as you navigate the ethical dilemmas that confidentiality conflicts can trigger. Remember: you must protect yourself first, your company second, and your boss third against the rascals who see you as the "side door" to a cache of confidential information. Even normally ethical people are naturally curious about what is going on, especially at the top. Like it or not, one of your unwritten job duties is "vigilant, suspicious gatekeeper!"

## Inquiring Minds Do *Not* Have to Know

Colleagues and coworkers frequently expect you to play every role: confidante, communication channel to the boss, teller of secrets, early-warning system for bad news, tabloid reporter of senior management's shenanigans—and maybe even friend. And everyone becomes disappointed and upset with you when you don't meet their expectations.

Even friends are not above pushing the envelope of confidentiality with one another. Fred, executive assistant to a CEO, told me about a peer at another firm who continually pressed him to find out the amount of his salary and bonus. Fred believes his friend was simply seeking leverage to perhaps increase her own salary, since she had a comparable position. However, Fred respects confidentiality in all aspects of his job, so he routinely dodged the question (e.g., "Salaries are confidential at our firm" or "My boss doesn't want me to reveal my earnings"). But his friend persisted without ever taking the hint. Finally, Fred got blunt and said: "That is confidential information about my job, and I'm not going to tell you—ever!" *That* finally got through to her.

Most ethical dilemmas that involve confidentiality are rooted in unrealistic, misplaced, and misunderstood expectations. People are seeking certain types of information from you that they have no business seeking; yet they feel they are somehow entitled to this information merely because they have a relationship with you. It's your duty to set them straight by explaining exactly what they *can*—and should—expect from you. Be forthright and consistent in your approach to the material that you will and will not pass on. You will not satisfy them, and they may depart grumbling (this is not a perfect world), but you *will* earn their respect.

Debbie, an administrative secretary to the chief of police, Palm Bay, Florida, was privy to highly sensitive information by virtue of her position. She writes, "From the day I began my job, I made it politely clear that unless the item was discussed in a staff meeting (for which minutes are available to all employees) or reviewed in a memorandum, I was unable to answer any questions." Her standard response then became: "I hope you can understand I'm not able to share any information about that."

I like Debbie's answer best. I will forever dislike the wimpy reply of "I don't know" because I'm uncomfortable with any office professional who pretends to be uninformed when they're not. It just doesn't work for me! Feigning ignorance reflects poorly on your professional status, since your insinuation that you do not have a position of confidence diminishes your value. Besides, are you really fooling anyone anyway? The questioner knows you know the information, and you know he knows you know! Burdening yourself with a lie sends the wrong message; namely, that you will lie under some circumstances. Suddenly, your integrity seems negotiable.

**Instead, try responding to inappropriate requests with these showstoppers:**
- "I can't tell you that because it's confidential information."
- "Do you need this information to do your job?"
- "I haven't heard anything about that. You must be privy to matters about which I know nothing. Why don't *you* tell *me* about it?"
- "Please don't take this personally, but I cannot divulge that information," or "As a professional, I cannot tell you that," or "You're a professional also, so you *know* I can't divulge that information."

- And, the classic response to a probing question (even to an officer of the firm), "That's an interesting question. Would you like me to ask my boss and get back to you?"

Ann Landers always gave us two ways to field an off-base question. She suggested you should either respond (with wide-eyed shock), "I can't *believe* you asked me that!" or "Why would you *ask* such a question?" And sometimes, humor works. An admin assistant at Pacific Gas & Electric in San Francisco told me she is frequently pumped for confidential information because she works for a top officer. She always responds—in jest, of course—"I can't tell you that . . . because if I *did*, I would have to kill you!"

And then there's the approach that Kelly Adams, a property manager at Lariat Companies in Eden Prairie, Minnesota, uses. Kelly claims that her most effective way of handling persistent, rude questioners is by simply giving them the silent treatment. She just stares at them expressionlessly. If they ask it over the telephone, Kelly stops talking. In both cases, she claims it works beautifully. She adds, "The questioner becomes uncomfortable with the silence and usually retracts the question or changes the subject."

Give yourself permission to be rude if necessary. After all, the *questioners* are being rude. They *know* they are asking inappropriate questions; and don't think for a moment they aren't aware of exactly what they are doing. There are other ways to respond to invasive inquiries (e.g., "bug off" or "get lost"), but I am trying to get you to be polite! After all, you *are* a professional.

Has anyone ever approached you with the untenable words, "I'm going to tell you something . . . but please don't tell your boss"? Though this takes fast footwork on your part, this is your opportunity to throw up your hands and shout, "Then *don't* tell me! Please don't put me in that awkward position!"

## Is Firing Too Harsh?

We've discussed situations whereby the penalty for a breach of confidentiality was termination. Some may regard this punishment as a bit harsh, but this is the norm, not the exception, nowadays. These bosses were not out of line; they were just being careful. The consequences and penalties for violating data privacy laws, confidential marketing agreements, client and patient confidentiality, and the like are severe.

As soon as you cross that line of divulging confidential information, you have become a liability to the organization, and can expect—and *deserve*—to be cut loose. Most managers can attest to the fact that business is tough enough without making more trouble for ourselves with careless mistakes regarding how we handle the information entrusted to us.

## These Two Admins Knocked the Socks off Their Bosses

Eugene Nizker, chief information officer (CIO) of Custom House Currency Exchange, had high praise for his assistant, Jessica Raichl, when he said, "She guards me from problems that I will never know about." Apparently, the local police called Jessica's office and insisted that they needed to ask questions about a member of the information technology (IT) staff. Jessica's confidentiality antennae immediately went up and she became concerned about appearances. So she told the police they could not come into the office, offering instead to meet them elsewhere. The incident, fortunately, turned out to be a huge misunderstanding that caused no problem whatsoever. But Jessica's quick thinking and protective instincts obviously headed off any unnecessary gossip and/or embarrassment for her boss. Her boss was so impressed he nominated her for the IT profession's annual CIO Best Administrative Assistant Contest in recognition of the 2007 Administrative Professionals Day—and she won!

And then there is my friend, Sue Drury, who tops all honors in the confidentiality arena. Sue was executive assistant to the CEO of a major bank with corporate headquarters in the Midwest. At one point, the bank was considering moving their headquarters, a move that ultimately did not occur. But because such a departure would have involved a major employee layoff in the area, this would be an explosive media scoop were the information ever leaked. Sue told me she sat in on secret discussions over a period of several months about this potential relocation. One day, over lunch, her boss asked her, "So, Sue, what does your husband think about the possibility of moving?" Sue was shocked! She replied: "My *husband?* I haven't told my husband because all these negotiations have been confidential!" To say that Sue's boss was overwhelmed by her professional regard for the discretion of these negotiations would be an understatement. Now, *that's* a class act!

# The Best Defense Is a Strong Offense

Lest you think the rules of confidentiality are turning you into a prisoner in your own office, be clear about this: it *can* be done! A little common sense, a lot of self-restraint and self-management, and a constant appreciation for the power of the information you hold will keep your Ethical Priority Compass pointed in the right direction.

I strongly suggest you talk to your boss regularly about what information must be kept confidential. Build a reputation for tight lips, and become known as someone who has reverence for confidentiality, no matter what. Preempt prying questions by identifying yourself as a good secret keeper. Find a way to convey the message that your approach to confidential information is one that establishes the company's well-being as your filter—and do it as often as possible. When you clearly communicate that you put the organization's welfare above everything else, there is nothing anyone can say or do that will change your mind when it comes to revealing confidential information.

And, of course, you have to do all of the above without alienating your coworkers and clients, which is no easy task. It takes kindness, quick thinking, and finesse to be an effective gatekeeper and *not* be crowned the Queen Bee or King of Jerks. No one ever said these jobs are easy, but if you get the confidentiality part of your job description right, your career will grow on a solid foundation.

*Three may keep a secret if two of them are dead.*
—Benjamin Franklin, 1735

# 7

# Security *Is* Your Problem (Like It or Not)!

## *You Are the Gatekeeper of Company Assets*

---

*If you think technology can solve your security problems, then you don't understand the problems and you don't understand the technology. Amateurs hack systems, professionals hack people.*
—Bruce Schneier, author of *Secrets and Lies: Digital Security in a Networked World*

Dear Nan:

I overheard my boss's boss talking too loudly at the gym about a confidential matter, and I noticed that all ears at adjacent workout machines were cocked in his direction. I have virtually no relationship with this man (in fact, he barely knows my name),

*(continued)*

*(continued)*

but I knew I had to do something to stop his babbling. Long story short, all I could think of was to interrupt him, so I faked a pratfall into him. When he leaned over to help me up, I had just enough time to whisper, "Lower your voice—everyone can hear you!" Then I skedaddled. My boss called me in later that afternoon and said his boss appreciated the intervention, "however unorthodox." Then he put me in charge of our entire department's security! Nan, this is good because I have wanted more responsibility, but it's bad because I'm learning on the job again. My common sense may not be enough here. Can you give me a push in the right direction? We have about 50 people in the department.

—MaryBeth in Flagstaff, AZ

Lucky MaryBeth! This is yet another sign of the growing responsibilities that assistant-level professionals receive nowadays when the boss turns to them and says: "You can handle this." MaryBeth's boss is lucky, too—administrative assistants are usually well positioned to be gatekeepers, and MaryBeth sounds like she isn't shy about applying her moxie.

MaryBeth, my first suggestion is to go online and come up with some suggestions that suit you. Then, get your boss to commit to some relevant training from outside experts. There's nothing worse than being held responsible when something goes wrong and you were never provided any of the resources or authority to keep it from going wrong in the first place. This is serious stuff, and your boss has to be onboard. One of my favorite quotes comes from Dan Erwin, security officer at Dow Chemical: "The best way to get management excited about a disaster plan is for them to see the building across the street burn down."

Barbara Jary, executive assistant at Sabre Travel Network in Southlake, Texas, advises that you begin by contacting attorneys or consultants who have experience in security policy development, and warns that, "There are countless pitfalls out there. Why reinvent the wheel? The experts (found on the Internet) could save your company from major blunders and help you accomplish the task in a fraction of the time you would need if you tried to write all the policies yourself." You can also save time by connecting with local law enforcement organizations. Company resources to tap include everyone with something to protect and lose, including legal, health and safety, human resources, maintenance, and information technology (IT). AlVerta Harty, CAP, executive assistant at Bayer HealthCare in San Francisco, California, recommends that you form an in-house "security team" that represents all parts of the company to expand on the knowledge and advice of people already in your network. "These individuals will not only provide valuable insight into their particular areas of expertise; they'll also assist in conveying the security message to all employees," Harty adds.

What I offer here are some insights from your peers on the front lines. Let's first look at security as a process, then consider some specific suggestions.

## Thinking about Security Differently

Large companies have "office-land security" programs; small companies have off-the-shelf security tools. Neither approach is sufficient to stop a committed thief or enemy. No security system is perfect because security is a *process*, not an end result. It is like a cat-and-mouse game—every security measure has a countermeasure, which in turn leads to a new security measure, and so on.

The best approach to security, I think, is "defense through discouragement." This is the premise we use to defeat car thieves: make it too difficult or expensive or time consuming to rip us off, and the would-be thief will hopefully move on to an easier target. Your objective is to *not* be that easier target!

There is some truth to the adage that locks on a door will never keep thieves out; they just keep honest people honest. Most crimes are crimes of opportunity, so if you use your common sense and keep your "situational awareness" alert, you'll stop most security problems before they begin.

Thwarting the opportunistic thief doesn't stop all thieves, however; nor are thieves your only worry. Your security will be compromised somehow, someday—so another key idea to incorporate into your thinking is a recovery plan. What happens after the unthinkable happens? What can you afford to lose? What can be replaced, if stolen? And what is literally irreplaceable and absolutely essential to continuing to be in business?

The "key" (no pun intended) to effective security is to temporarily think like a thief, a competitor, a disgruntled employee, a con artist—and these days, even a terrorist. The following questions will get you started:

- Which assets (tangible property and intangible information) are most valuable? What's irreplaceable? Complete this sentence: "If we lost _____, or if _____ happened, we would be out of business forever."
- In what ways are our assets vulnerable?
- To whom is our property and/or information most valuable? Who would benefit most from our demise?

Include your coworkers in this discussion, and *write down* your answers in ways that make sense to you. This is the "stuff" your security system has to protect.

**Be sure to include:**
- Data
- Data processing equipment
- Employees' physical safety (weapons? illegal drugs? hygiene? scents, molds, perfumes, latex? after-work escorts?)
- Employees' personnel records, personal property, and identification (health records? purses? lockers? coat room?)
- Safety (insurance for slips and falls? fire? injury to customers?)
- Work-in-progress (intellectual property in files? physical prototypes under construction? ideas on flip charts?)
- Customer work entrusted to you
- Databases of customers' and vendors' information
- Bid information
- Marketing plans
- Checkbooks, charge cards, and cash
- Supplies and materials
- Telephones
- Passwords, entrance codes, and access cards
- Servers and desktop computers
- Vehicles

Consider also the main security concerns in your industry or trade. For example, a biomedical company should worry about the security of hazardous materials and research experiments that would take months to recreate, whereas a construction company is concerned about employee safety, tools, and equipment on job sites. What are the high-target temptations in your company? Is your company involved in product design? Manufacturing? Service? Do you handle cash or currency on a regular basis? Is client/patient confidentiality a priority?

## Protecting the Company's Assets

Organizations usually have three kinds of assets: *intangible assets*, like information, trade secrets, and the company's image; *tangible assets*, such as facilities, equipment, and money; and *human assets*, which include you and the other employees. (I believe the most valuable assets—the employees—walk out the door at "quittin' time." Hopefully, the human assets aren't carrying off any of the tangible or intangible assets!)

The most serious security dilemmas relate to the company's intangible assets. You can imagine a lot of unhappy scenarios: the wrong people with the right information embarrass the company or gain an unfair advantage; a client's privacy is violated; or a competitor has one of your people e-mail him your trade secrets.

Some threats to company assets are so clear-cut they pose no ethical dilemmas. Stealing inventory is obviously a crime, as is any action or condition that endangers health or safety. For example, if you're walking through the plant and you witness bullying, horseplay, liquid on the floor, or a drug transaction, you'll of course speak up and it will be remedied. Likewise, if you see someone loading supplies, inventory, or tools into his van after hours or a colleague placing a piece of equipment into her briefcase, you know what to do with your suspicions.

However, some security challenges are ethical dilemmas. They are dilemmas because "doing the right thing" is pitted against your feelings of loyalty. Think about coworkers who cut corners and assume that you'll look the other way, bosses who fudge numbers, buyers who take bribes, and employees who slip the wrong people confidential bids or plans. You shake your head and ask yourself, "What are they *thinking?*" Your Ethical Priority Compass will guide you to speak up because these individuals are hurting the company.

Your security procedures must protect everything that has any conceivable value to anyone, and the security procedures cannot impede productivity or be inconvenient!

# Don't Try to Do This Alone

"Perfect" security simply doesn't exist; remember—security is a process, not a destination. No system or set of procedures that relies on people or mechanical devices is beyond penetration or error. As they say at Homeland Security, "The bad guys just need to be lucky one time; we have to be lucky 100 percent of the time." You need to enroll all of your coworkers in the "doing the right thing" philosophy of the Ethical Office.

Kathy Sorrell, CPS, of Growing Family, Inc. in St. Louis, Missouri, stresses the importance of establishing a security policy and then communicating it to all employees:

> If you don't already have a company policy regarding security, make it a number one priority. The policy should detail specific issues and consequences in the case of violations. Have a statement available that every employee must read, sign, and file with HR to ensure that you've communicated the policy clearly.

To get your coworkers involved, you'll need to find a balance between security needs versus user convenience. If security measures are too complicated or time consuming, people tend to ignore or circumvent them. We've all heard of situations where the crime occurred when the security system wasn't turned on, doors that should have been locked were propped open or the safe wasn't closed. Walk into many offices and you will find the passwords posted on little yellow sticky notes attached to computers and keys under the mouse pad!

You cannot overcommunicate with your employees and colleagues the importance of security. Every employee has a role to play, and the company becomes safer and more secure if each takes his or her role seriously. Asking them to assist with this initiative will prompt them to help develop feasible security measures and feel invested in their success. For example, construction foremen can provide insight about the security challenges they face on job sites. Road warriors will be better able to describe the security issues they encounter when traveling with mobile devices. Do some of your employees allow strangers to follow them into a secured area without checking for a badge? Does everyone know that cell phone calls in secure areas may actually be just a ruse to take photos, or that a confidential document forgotten in the copier may leave the building in a vendor's briefcase?

A successful security policy will have guidelines for all employees that are boiled down into simple, effective, and enforceable security procedures. Senior management must visibly support and enforce the procedures; they must be communicated to 100 percent of your coworkers, perhaps at a companywide meeting. Strive to create a culture of mutual support, a feeling that "we have something valuable and important here that's worth taking care of."

## Whom Are You Most Worried About?

Why would people with malicious intent focus on your company? I think the "four horsemen" that cause most ethical security dilemmas at work are sex, money, power, and pride. Perhaps they want power or status, or a recognition or reward they believe the company owes them. Perhaps they believe it will help them get or succeed in a new job—or perhaps it is simply due to greed.

Based on feedback from my seminar attendees, here are the rascals you are most likely to encounter: hackers; penetration testers (repeat phone callers who get a tidbit like a name with every call, then use that information on the next call to pry open your operations); corporate spies (yup, there's a job description for them); identity thieves (think: dumpster divers); disgruntled employees ("I know how to hurt you!"); information brokers ("I just want to check our listing information ..."); scam artists ("Just for you—an incredible deal!"); recruiters (they poach your people); and posers (everyday people who pretend to be salespeople, government workers, students, etc.). Whew!

## Suggestions for Countermeasures
## from Your Peers

### Employee Security

- *"Identify and monitor angry and disgruntled employees; you don't want them going 'postal,'"* says Barbara S. Holman, an executive assistant from Spring, Texas. "This is why one of your prime security partners must be the human resource department." Don't hesitate to call the local police if you even *suspect* a disaster brewing. It's better to be safe than sorry.

- *Do not ever disclose your boss's whereabouts*—or the location of anyone else in your office—unless you know the person to whom you're speaking, and you are sure that it's appropriate to do so. An admin once told me of a phone call she received from someone whose voice she did not recognize. When he asked for her boss, she replied he was out of town until the following week, and her boss's home was burglarized that same day! Simply explain your boss is "unavailable," and follow that up with an offer to take a message.

- *Establish a security protocol for employee terminations.* The terminated employee is in (understandable) emotional turmoil; don't give him an opportunity to do something foolish to hurt the company. Restrict access to systems, files, and so on immediately. It is common to escort dismissed employees directly to the door after the termination interview, thereby removing the temptation to sabotage computers, e-mail themselves confidential information, or create other mischief. The supervisor (or you) is perfectly capable of packing the box of personal items for pickup later.

## Visitor Security

- *Restrict customers to "public areas" such as reception and conference rooms.* Doing so reduces the possibility that confidential information will fall into the wrong hands.

- *Be wary of service providers.* The cleaning personnel, window washer, indoor plant gardener, coffee provider, and temporary employee all have legitimate reasons for being on the premises. However, because these people are often "invisible," they are easy to overlook as security threats.

- *Control all access.* Controlling access controls thefts. Even smaller companies issue visitor name tags and/or have guests log in and out. Courteously greeting and escorting all visitors makes them feel important, with the added benefit of increasing security. Institute a system of issuing, retrieving, replacing, and otherwise accounting for door keys and access cards. Always assume that keys/cards that have left the building have been copied/cloned.

## Hard-Copy Document Security

"Don't lead others into temptation" should be your habit. Some people are naturally curious and will be tempted to at least glance at papers if you leave them in plain view. A visitor from who-knows-where, a journalist looking for story material, an insecure employee feeling threatened by a new hire—all of these individuals may be interested in something on your desk, so:

- *Keep your desk clear of any papers you consider confidential,* especially if there is a lot of traffic around your work area. Lots of people have mastered the skill of reading upside down while "hovering." Flip your papers over, even if you are just stepping away for a few minutes. If you're going to be away longer, lock 'em up. If you are working on a document that requires you to have a lot of sensitive materials on your desk for several hours at a time, avoid traffic around your desk by scheduling to work on the project during off-peak times, or by setting up camp at another workstation. Clear your desk before you leave at the end of the day. Remember that snoops and thieves are clever and persistent; they'll take every chance they get!

- *Neutralize, camouflage or "sanitize" documents when you remove them from your office.* Conceal them inside a folder or envelope, even if you are just putting them on your boss's desk or hand-delivering them to someone on the next floor. Someone standing behind you in the elevator or next to you in the hallway may be able to see just enough to begin cranking the rumor mill.

- *Never leave documents unattended.* Don't leave confidential papers exposed where people nearby can see them at meetings or steal them in public places (e.g., airports, waiting rooms, restaurants, or restrooms).

- *When snail-mailing confidential documents, seal them in an envelope that you mark "confidential."* Then, seal that envelope inside another envelope and mark that "confidential" as well. Now it's protected at the receiving end, too.

- *Make sure there are plenty of paper shredders—and use them!* Shred confidential documents, rough drafts, photocopies, and notes—any info-rich materials you aren't required to retain. *Never* dispose of these papers in a regular wastebasket or recycling bin from which they can be recovered by curious or dishonest individuals. Snoops are not above Dumpster diving for confidential gems.

## Phone Security

Phones have more features—and more security risks:

- *Use voice mail only when you don't mind being recorded.* Here's a scary story: After a particularly trying day, an employee vented her frustrations about her boss to a coworker via voice mail. Imagine her horror when she later walked into a meeting attended by her boss while her voice mail message was being replayed on speakerphone to everyone in the room! Voice mail *feels* confidential, but that's an illusion.

My friend Barbara told me another tragic story of voice mail going awry. Barbara had befriended a young neighbor and mother of four young children—let's call her Amy—who was apparently trapped in a marriage to a physically abusive husband. Amy had no skills, no way to support herself, and—understandably, due to her circumstances—suffered from low self-esteem.

Along with a few of her friends who assisted with the babysitting, Barbara helped Amy enroll in a local community college on a part-time basis so she could gain some computer skills. Their plan was a success. Over a period of time, Amy became quite a good techie, made herself employable, and blossomed into a self-assured individual who resolved to exit her marriage for her own and her children's survival. Her new friends also found her a pro bono attorney.

The plan to leave was set for a Tuesday: After Amy's husband left for work, all of his belongings were to be placed on the front lawn for his brother (deemed a safe individual) to collect. All of the locks on the house were to be changed; Amy and her children were going to a safe halfway house; and divorce papers were to be served on her husband at his workplace. A good plan!

But on Friday evening, Amy's attorney unexpectedly died. The following Monday morning, the office manager of the law practice called all of the attorney's clients to explain the unfortunate circumstances. She did not reach Amy, but instead left her a voice mail message to this effect: "This message is for Amy . . . I'm Mr. _____'s assistant, calling to let you know the sad news that he has passed away. But, please don't be concerned because his partner, Ms. _____, will now be handling your divorce case ... etc."—you get the picture.

The unthinkable happened. Amy did not hear the voice mail; her husband did. As a result, Amy almost didn't survive Monday evening. Fortunately, her husband was arrested, convicted, and is now in prison. But Amy's children were placed in foster care until she could physically take care of them again. All of this could have been avoided if the admin had thought twice before carelessly leaving her voice message. You simply never know who's going to hear a voice mail.

- *Do not presume cell phone calls are secure.* Most cellular phone conversations can be listened to and recorded with low-cost devices that are easy to obtain. Attorneys, doctors, and developers tell me they talk on their cells to their offices about schedules, assignments, and other mundane matters, but never name clients or financial figures for fear of having their conversations pirated.

- *Discarded cell phones cannot be trusted.* Selling or donating your old phone when you upgrade to a fancier model can be like handing over your purse, wallet, and diaries with a ribbon around them to someone who wears a mask. Though I'm a fan of recycling and donating used cell phones, it's tricky to do safely because these are truly minicomputers. All sorts of sensitive information piles up inside our cell phones—contacts, phone logs, appointments, task lists, voice notes and recordings, SMS messages, pictures, videos, e-mail and e-mail attachments, and application data.

  Deleting all this information is difficult. Virtually *every* refurbished cell phone selected in random tests carried *retrievable personal data*, even though they had supposedly been scrubbed of their memory. Just deleting phone numbers is not enough; neither is removing the SIM card (there's a lot of data stored elsewhere). And the "delete data" command does not actually remove data. Each phone manufacturer has a complex 8- to 10-step procedure for deleting data. If you go online or study the owner's manual, you can become the in-house cell phone security expert—and a cell phone hero.

  By the way, the average victim of identity theft spends 40 hours to repair the damage. I have a friend who is so paranoid about the information stored in his phone that he tosses his old phones into the Hudson River. (Fans of the TV series *24* would say even *this* is not safe, however.) I told him to stop polluting our rivers and do as my husband does—smash it with a hammer and then take it to a government recycling facility.

- *Texting is not secure, either.* Just ask sports figures Tiger Woods and Brett Favre, both of whom learned that their lady-friend texts were out of their control as soon as they pressed the "send" button. Even Olympic award-winning swimmer Michael Phelps's image suffered from a cell phone party scene that went viral.

- *Speakerphones are not secure.* You can never be sure who else is in the room listening. Common courtesy dictates that permission be obtained before the speakerphone is turned on, and introductions should be made where everyone says hello.

- *Faxes are not secure.* It always amuses me when I receive a fax with the word *Confidential* at the top. What is confidential about a fax? You might as well put *Read This!* If you must fax something confidential, call ahead to let the receiver know when to expect it so that they can retrieve it immediately. The good news about a fax sent via the old-fashioned, stand-alone fax machine (not fax software on your computer) is that it cannot be pirated. Though the fax's *existence* can be traced, the content cannot.

## Digital Security

Perhaps all employees today should be "Mirandized" before using *any* of today's technology—at least, *this* part of the warning:

> *You have the right to remain silent. Anything you say can—and will—be used against you in a court of law....*
> —Miranda warning (excerpt)

# Nan's Warning

I have one single mantra: quite simply, *anything* you say, tweet, text, e-mail, blog, or post can—and will—be used against you in the court of public discourse. Look at it this way: *everything* you put out there electronically is now the equivalent of DNA evidence. You can delete or erase all you want, but whatever you release into cyberspace has the potential to come back to bite you today, tomorrow, or 20 years from now—when you apply for a job or run for president.

We have morphed into a world where electronic exchanges are the norm, and any thoughts, conversations, or information exchanged via technology are tracked, preserved, and may be shared (even out of context) with anyone—at any time!

- *Adapt a "fishbowl" state of mind.* Life in the workplace was much simpler in some ways when the only form of communication was the written or verbal word. We didn't have the conveniences that came with e-mail, voice mail, texting, and instant messaging, but we didn't have the burdens, either. Although the written word would be difficult to deny (you could always claim forgery), the verbal word—short of being recorded—could be outright denied due to lack of proof! Not today! Today's threats to a company's security come from coworkers who are living in a digital fishbowl but don't realize it.

- *Remember that Big Brother owns the big browser.* All office equipment is the company's property, *period.* By extension, everything you do with that equipment is under the company's control, so you *cannot expect* to maintain *any* form of confidentiality or privacy. The reasoning goes like this: Whatever you're writing or saying is being done on company-owned equipment, using company-licensed software, by someone paid by the company. Ergo, this communication, or other work product, *belongs to the company.* And because the company is liable for its employees' actions, it has the right—truly, the *obligation*—to protect itself by tracking, auditing, monitoring, and recording all employee goings-on that occur in cyberspace. The courts have stood squarely behind an organization's right to do whatever is necessary to achieve this, including secret monitoring. Now, when your office pals call you over to their screen because "you have to see this"—or when you suspect they are using company technology outside the boundaries of legitimate business purposes—you are right to caution them. You're not being a nag; you're helping them keep their jobs!

- *Develop and be sure everyone is aware of Internet use policies.* Employees' personal use of the Internet is a no-win situation for a company, so restrictions are inevitable. In the best-case scenario, personal use is just a waste of time. Worst case is exposing the company to the viruses, malware, and worms that permeate the nonbusiness sites (sports, games, gambling, porn, shopping, photo, and humor sites are the favorites of the bad guys). Employees who engage in risky behavior (e.g., sending and receiving inappropriate texts and images, or sending/viewing pornography) are trouble with a capital T.

Your company's policy should include language that (1) company assets must be used for authorized purposes only; (2) personal use is limited to appropriate subject matter; and (3) all use must be in compliance with the company's corporate values and ethics. The words *appropriate, values,* and *ethics* help limit the company's liability and provide a rationale if it becomes necessary to show an offender the door. To avoid any misunderstandings, there should also be some specific verbiage about zero tolerance for viewing sexually oriented Web sites, gambling sites, and the like because "reasonable use" can be subjective. Are companies permitted to do this? *Absolutely.* Any organization has the right, and now it has the technology—every keystroke, click, and link can be monitored and recorded.

- *Develop and be sure everyone is aware of e-mail policies.* I opened my own Pandora's box when I asked both my column readers and seminar attendees about their e-mail problems. The constants that blanket *all* company e-mail concerns are: *No* e-mail message is private; all e-mails can be retrieved, and your company has every right to look over your shoulder. Accordingly, when crafting your own e-mail policy, I suggest you incorporate the following language:
  - There is truly no such thing as e-mail privacy or private e-mails.
  - The company owns all communications that employees send, receive, and store.
  - There shall be no use of the e-mail system that is not job related.
  - Sexually explicit, harassing, abusive, or racially/ethnically offensive e-mails are prohibited.
  - The company may monitor employee use of the e-mail system without prior notice.

Amber Dilday, executive assistant/marketing coordinator for Innovation Industries in Russellville, Arkansas, suggests this extra verbiage used at her company: "All employees are responsible for seeing that these information systems are used in an efficient, ethical, and lawful manner. The use of information systems is a privilege, not a right, which may be revoked at any time for misuse."

E-mails have become the "smoking gun" in lawsuits of all kinds. The ePolicy Institute, an organization that provides policies and resources on information security and other related topics, recently reported research that indicates that 24 percent of organizations today have had e-mail subpoenaed by courts or regulators; and 9 percent of employers have battled lawsuits triggered specifically by employee e-mail. The Institute also acknowledges that:

> Nine out of 10 business documents produced and acquired by companies today are electronic; it's no longer a matter of *if* your organization's e-mail and other electronically stored information will one day become part of the evidence pool. The question, instead, is: *When* will you be asked to produce employee e-mail as part of legal proceedings or a regulatory investigation?

With 130 million U.S. workers sending 2.8 billion e-mails *every day*, there's a substantial possibility that at least some will use company computers to send off-color or otherwise inappropriate messages. Not surprisingly, the riskiest time of the year for inappropriate e-mails is—you guessed it—Valentine's Day!

- *Practice good "netiquette" in your e-mails.* Yes, security is an issue, but we don't have to lose our civility over it. Pay attention to how *you* may be perceived. Electronic dialogues are often misinterpreted because they lack the benefit of hearing the tone of voice and/or seeing the look on someone's face. Do people cringe when your messages arrive in their inboxes? Why? Hint: No salutations? Misspellings? Incoherent or cryptic statements that create more questions than they solve? High-frequency, low-value messages? No closure? No point? Please put some effort into "writing it right." More pet peeves of mine: Professionals don't press "send" before double checking that the right person will receive this. They also check spelling, message tone (ALL CAPS LOOKS LIKE YOU'RE SHOUTING) and refrain from "Reply to All" unless it's absolutely necessary (avoiding an e-mail "storm"). And if it is clear the electronic conversation is getting bogged or dicey, *please just pick up the phone and talk to the person!*

- *Get technology working for you, not against you.* Video cameras, lighting, antitheft hardware, keystroke monitors, and many other "gee-whiz" gadgets are out there. If you can think of a problem, search for a technological solution.

- *Know your computer system's limitations.* The computer is just another tool, not a "black box" that guarantees secrecy. Your network supervisor can help you devise secure firewall settings and select antivirus software.

- *Back up and archive files routinely.* You can become your own worst enemy if you don't. One power outage could mean unhappy customers and costly downtime. You should be able to retrieve important files quickly, ensure they will be safe, and adequately remove files you no longer want in ways that render them unrecoverable. There are plenty of resources available, so there's no excuse for not being prepared.

- *Store media* like CDs, DVDs, tapes and floppy discs in a locked area so they cannot be accessed or altered.

- *Change passwords often,* and make them difficult to figure out (in other words, not your name or "password"!). Lynn Frye CPS of Decosimo Corporate Finance in Chattanooga, Tennessee, advises you to "never share your password with anyone other than the company's computer support person, and never provide your user name or password via e-mail or text message. Also, never open a message from an unknown sender. And change all passwords periodically, just in case." Well said, Lynn.

- *Position your terminal screen in a way that prevents people from reading it.* Use a "hot key" to engage your screen saver if potentially prying eyes approach your desk when you are working on confidential material. Another solution from the boys and girls in the lab: use a screen cover that makes it impossible for anyone to view what's on the screen unless they are positioned exactly in front of it.

- *Sign-off whenever you leave your terminal*—even if it is just for a coffee refill.

- *If you have the luxury of your own computer printer, keep it in a low-traffic area nearby and remove printouts as quickly as possible.* Networked printers are logically placed where everyone has easy access. Don't leave any confidential material unattended, or else you risk its being read by your office mates. While they may just be doing so unintentionally to determine whether it is their document or not—is that going to be okay with you?

- *Keep original program discs under lock and key.* Since these are rarely used after the software is loaded onto the hard drive, they may be "borrowed" and never returned—yet you won't miss them. You should register each one so that you'll avoid getting into trouble when the copy with your serial number turns up on a bootleg copy. More and more abusers are being found these days, with many companies being turned in by disgruntled ex-employees, and significant penalties are being levied.

- *Use Internet protection measures.* You must defend yourself against theft of your data from outside the company. "Cyber attacks" can be launched by a single computer anywhere in the world. Here are some shocking statistics that ought to keep you alert, based on security software company Symantec Corporation's June 2010 survey of about 2,500 small and midsized businesses with 9 to 499 employees:

  - Fully *three quarters* were hit by cyber attacks in the prior 12 months. Thirty percent of the attacks were rated as somewhat or extremely effective, and 100 percent of those targeted saw *tangible losses* in the form of downtime, theft of corporate data, or theft of personally identifiable customer or employee information.

  - Forty-two percent actually lost confidential or proprietary information in the past that caused lost revenue or direct financial loss; 24 percent had illegal losses from outside thieves; 21 percent had accidental losses from insiders; and 19 percent had illegal losses from insiders.

  - Sixty-two percent lost at least one mobile device (a laptop, personal digital assistant [PDA], smartphone, etc.) in the past 12 months, many of which had no password protection and could not be wiped of data remotely (*this* was avoidable; why didn't they have passwords, the simplest level of security?).

Other outside risks include viruses that erase your entire system; someone's breaking into your system and altering files; someone's using your computer to attack other computers; or someone's stealing credit card information to make unauthorized purchases.

Thieves use their social skills to crack security barriers, too. In a competition at Def Con 2010 (a sort of trade show for techies), 100 percent of the Fortune 500 companies contacted by a hacker group gave up information that compromised corporate security. They posed as "security auditors" and "tech support" and the like, which was enough to get the corporate employees to spill the beans. Only one employee, a female store manager at Walmart, even questioned their inquiry. I truly believe a computer's weakest security link is human.

According to Wikipedia, *phishing* is:

> The criminally fraudulent practice of attempting to acquire sensitive information such as user names, passwords, and credit card details by masquerading as a trustworthy entity in an electronic communication.

Spammers and phishers use current events ("we're calling because of the recent reports of . . .") and social engineering tactics ("I'm the tech from your manufacturer, and I just want to be sure your settings are correct . . .") to get users to give up personal and system information.

- *Remind your coworkers that "Facebooking is forever."* Is social networking a valid part of our work life today, or is it social "notworking"? Many companies limit access to social networking sites, personal e-mail accounts, risky Web sites, and so on because texting, blogging, tweeting, instant messaging, and Facebooking have become excessive drains on company time—and security risks as well. The important points to remember: Professional social networking sites should be kept free of personal information and anything that reflects poorly on the company; learn to use every social network site's privacy settings (but don't trust them—they change too frequently to be secure). What I've learned from discussions at my seminars is that the more social media contact that occurs, the greater the security risks. My best advice is for you to keep your ears and eyes open, learn how it works, and be forever and exceedingly cautious about whatever you put "out there." Remind your kids to be careful as well. I read that kids today may be as tech-savvy as Bill Gates, but as naïve as Bambi!

- *Give up any expectation of privacy.* The CEOs of Google and Facebook have predicted the end of privacy. Whatever is posted online, in any forum, stays online somewhere forever, and search engines can always troll for it. Don't post something that may prove embarrassing tomorrow, next week, or years from now. In this tight job market, more than 70 percent of employers say they do Web searches on candidates before extending a job offer. What kind of image do you project online? It may not be fair—and certainly cannot be proven—but an unflattering party picture somewhere may knock you out of a potential job competition, and you'll never know why.

## General Security

- *Erase or replace the hard drive in your copier when you turn it back in.* Didn't know your copier had a hard drive? Well, if it was manufactured in 2002 or later, it probably does, and it has kept a copy of everything you have ever copied. Be sure you verify that the hard drive is scrubbed when your lease is expires.
- *Develop a comprehensive business recovery plan.* What if the worst happens? Fires, floods, and thefts occur every day. What records are vital to your company? Developing a business recovery plan may uncover security issues that were possibly overlooked in the past. Are you as prepared as you should be?
- *Guard employee information.* Your IT and human resource personnel can help you with this one. Any documents of employee names and addresses have the potential for big-time mischief in the wrong hands.
- *Set up protocols to handle terror-related threats.* Bomb and phone/mail threats need to be reported according to your local police department's guidelines. Call them *before* any such event occurs (heaven forbid) for proper training and instructions.
- *Don't talk to any media representative without your supervisor and/or the company's public relations representative's knowledge and guidance.* You cannot ever predict or control the media, so *stay away*. Working with the media is fraught with potential slip-ups because they must gather as much timely information as soon as possible while working under extreme time pressures. To that end, they occasionally engage in ambush interview tactics that may diminish the message and the messenger. When this happens, accuracy and context suffer. And we all know that promises of confidentiality—no matter how sincerely they were once proffered—can be easily broken.

  My advice is to throw up a firewall around the company and insist that *every reporter* talk to the company's press relations or public relations individual. If the company has no such person, insist that it be the president or a designated officer. You have much to lose and virtually nothing to gain by getting your picture on the evening news. Run—don't walk—away from reporters who say they want "the real story—off the record" from an insider like you. Don't believe a word of it. "Off the record" simply does not exist; if you say it, reporters may print it.

- *Report thefts of all kinds.* Bogus expense account claims are probably the most common; so are personal items purchased by the company. Stealing office supplies is still common, too. When confronting a thief, start by giving her an opportunity to come up with her own solution. But be careful. Yes, you have to stop the behavior, but if you sound like a one-person reform team, she may misinterpret your discussion as bullying or extortion—or by others as coconspiracy when all of this comes to light later. In 99 percent of cases, the thief will immediately stop. Any hint of public disgrace or the possibility of compromising her job security by becoming exposed should be enough to reassert the reasonable standards of conduct she is expected to follow. (Of course, if it is commonplace for employees to steal in your workplace, you have a different problem altogether—one wherein a thief is likely to respond by asking, "Why are you picking on me? Everyone else is stealing a lot more. ....").

  If the thief does not respond affirmatively, back off immediately. Now you *must* talk to your supervisor. If the thief's petty larceny is more important to her than what you think of her, you may be dealing with someone who has a bigger problem than just taking an office supply or two. Do *not* let this become a point of personal conflict between the two of you by pushing further. Saying something like, "If you don't turn yourself in by Friday, then I will," creates an extremely personal conflict. It's risky—maybe even dangerous—to force someone to change her behavior just because you know something that can hurt her. The push you're trying to give her in the right direction may be a push over the edge of reasonableness, and she may retaliate if she feels threatened by you. Your health, wellness, and peace of mind are certainly more valuable than a boxcar full of staples and pens. Turning this matter over to your supervisor follows the number one guideline of your Ethical Priority Compass: take care of yourself.

- *Take office refrigerator theft seriously.* I'm not kidding; this drives coworkers crazy! Employees who don't trust each other don't work well together. I've heard of a few remedies, from taping notes and pictures to the lunch containers (apparently some thieves are deterred if they know their victim's identity), to signs on the refrigerator door ("All thieves will be hunted down and punished!"), to notes *inside* the bagged lunch with the sandwich ("I know who you are. And I know where you live!"). Good luck with this one—just don't trivialize it!

## What Will Become of Us?

I am a cheerleader for the Ethical Office, and a culture of trust and mutual support like this doesn't stand a chance if offices are overwhelmed by security concerns. You cannot drive forward by constantly looking in the rearview mirror or looking over your shoulder, my dad used to say. I worry that hyperanxiety about new technology and new threats we don't understand will make us timid and risk averse; I also worry that surreptitious monitoring with cameras, access cards, and keystroke monitors promotes a corrosive atmosphere of distrust. Monitoring with a "gotcha" attitude causes employees to feel resentment against the company. The best way to avoid this is to write security policies down, then communicate and enforce them consistently.

Today's administrative professional—like our friend MaryBeth from the chapter's opening—is a frontline gatekeeper against all sorts of rascals both inside and outside the company who place their personal interests above the company's. Your eyes and ears are often early-warning detectors of security problems. You are a target for those who want to steal or misuse your company's tangible and intangible assets, and the "side door" through which they will try to creep, simply because you possess so much of the company's information.

Like it or not—and formally or informally—you are a vital part of your company's security system. The professional's response to a breach of security is to try to stop it. If you see or learn about your company's safety being compromised or are asked to assist in a remedy, you are ethically bound to do your best to help solve the problem.

It is a compliment to you that your company depends on you to do the security work. It feels good to be trusted. But it requires psychological moxie, as well as some technical expertise. The challenge is to do your job with a healthy skepticism of others, while still expecting others to trust you—yet another juggling act.

As with all issues in the security neighborhood, "caution" should be your watchword. From the "why didn't he abide his own advice?"

file, here's a publicly disgraced politician undone by a sex scandal, thanks to the digital tracks he left:

> *If you don't have to say it—just nod. If you have to say it, only do it in person so you can always deny it. And don't ever, ever put it on paper or e-mail.*

—Eliot Spitzer (in 1992),
Former New York governor and attorney general

# 8

# Gossip Over the Cubicle Fence

## *Gossip Can Tear Apart the Ethical Office*

---

*I wish every employee in the workplace could be the target of malicious gossip just once—just once, Nan, so they would know how hurtful it is.*

—My hairdresser in Minneapolis, MN
(with tears in her eyes)

Dear Nan:

I never thought this could happen to me. For some reason, the CEO's executive assistant has never liked me. She has been with the company her entire career and perceives her position as one wherein she wields considerable "power" over many of the other employees. This has never bothered me personally; I can

*(continued)*

*(continued)*

handle anyone's ego. However, she recently started rumors about my having an affair with another employee. I've confronted her about it, but she denies having anything to do with the nasty stories (which are completely untrue). I've even talked to my boss about it, but he says he doesn't want to get involved; I'm sure he doesn't want to rattle any cages with his boss's right-hand gal. Meanwhile, the rumors continue. What—if anything—can I do?
—Ginger in New York, NY

I applaud Ginger for sticking up for herself. She has done everything right so far; she responded directly to the person she believes to be the source of the problem, and even attempted to have her boss intercede. Unfortunately, this is probably all she can do for now. The more she fights gossip, the more attention she draws to it. Eventually, people assume that where there's smoke, there's fire.

My advice to Ginger was to disregard Her Highness's gossip as best she could for the next few days or weeks, and trust her coworkers to be smart enough to dismiss it. In my experience, baseless gossip has a short shelf life and dies a natural death when it is ignored. In fact, according to Triangle Pharmaceuticals (Durham, North Carolina) executive assistant Linda E. Spruill, "Sometimes people start rumors and keep conflict going because it makes them feel powerful." So it follows that the best thing you can do is ignore such chatter. "Don't feed into the negativity," Spruill adds. "Take the high road by maintaining your own sense of confidence and professionalism. Hold your head up, show up on time, handle your work responsibly—and you will emerge the victor."

"You don't have to like the person, but you are always better off respecting her power and position," says Sandra Thorpe from Napa Valley, California. "Bridge building requires tact, imagery and sometimes even submission to another person's ego." And you never know; what you perceive as a malicious attack actually may be someone crying out for attention—even friendship. However, in Ginger's case, it seems as though something else—perhaps envy or dislike—might be the impetus.

Famed newscaster Walter Winchell once described gossip as "the art of saying nothing in a way that leaves practically nothing unsaid."

*Nothing* is true about workplace gossip, particularly if it is negative (as most is), except the following:

- You *never* hear the full story.
- As easy as it is to gossip about someone, it is even easier for that gossip to get back to that person.
- If someone gossips *with* you, it is of utter certainty that this person will someday gossip *about* you.
- Gossip is usually incorrect information anyhow; it is third-hand or even worse, embellished each time it is retold.

## All Sorts of Tongues Are Wagging

If the sins of the flesh are the world's oldest sins, the sins of the wagging tongue run a strong second. Gossip relies on "secrets," and the temptation to share a secret is always enticing. Being the source of so-called secret information elevates the gossiper—at least in her mind—at the expense of the person about whom she's gossiping. As Polish philosopher Arthur Schopenhauer observed, "If I maintain my silence about my secret, it is my prisoner. But, if I let it slip from my tongue, I am *its* prisoner."

Gossip can be defined as talking/texting/e-mailing about someone else's personal affairs when that someone cannot defend herself. Whether the information is true or untrue, it is almost always hurtful, disrespectful, and/or insulting. Gossip is bad for an Ethical Office; it causes drama, and drama erodes productivity and trust. If, for example, Ginger from Manhattan lets the gossip get the better of her, it may escalate to a point where it hurts her professional performance—and then she'll have a *real* problem.

## Why *Do* We Gossip?

Perhaps it is due to one's natural (though misdirected) desire to be accepted by others. Few among us are immune to the temptation to tell what someone else is eager to know, especially if we want to impress or please that person. Plus, we all have a tendency to want to be "in the know." Besides, we hear just enough dead-on accurate skinny about what's *really* going on in the company to stay connected to the grapevine. What's worse than being connected to the gossip net? Not being connected to it!

## What's So Bad about Gossip in the Office?

*Plenty.* To begin with, it hurts your coworkers. It can ruin reputations and wreck careers and families. Gossip destroys the culture of trust and confidentiality that knits people together in the ethical workplace. If your workplace is rampant with gossip, you will be less forthcoming with information (ergo, trust takes another hit).

Employee morale and productivity are usually pretty low in a "gossip-rich" work environment. Fear of a "gotcha" moment with a tattletale coworker dampens initiative and customer service. Employees who take sides against each other in a word war waste a lot of energy, time, and creativity dealing with divisiveness, hurt feelings, and who-said-what dramas. Additionally, an unprofessional culture like this makes it all the more difficult to recruit and retain quality employees.

And, believe it or not, gossip can get you fired! Four municipal employees from Hooksett, New Hampshire, including two with more than 20 years' experience—one of whom was just about ready to retire—learned this lesson the hard way. These four individuals were fired for spreading rumors about the town administrator's relationship with another employee. Not only did they contribute to the distribution of malicious gossip, which is harmful enough in and of itself, but, even more foolishly, their target was their *boss!*

Gossip has also been successfully prosecuted as workplace violence. Various federal statutes consider the prevalence of gossip in harassment, hostile workplace, and defamation suits. Defamation is false information that "injures" another person, and some courts have judged it as bullying. Federal law specifies three reasons which can make a person guilty of defamation: (1) you knew the information was untrue; (2) you had reason to believe that the information could be untrue, yet you did not bother to thoroughly check; and (3) the information was of such a broad, generalized nature that it simply could not be true. Sounds like gossip to me!

In short, gossip costs the company money in entirely avoidable ways. If you want to work in an Ethical Office culture, would you ever intentionally take actions that pretty much guarantee low morale, diminished productivity, defensive reactions, reluctance to initiate or take risks, or—heaven forbid—an employment-related lawsuit?

## What Can the Company Do?

If an employee continues to be the victim or perpetrator of gossip, management should have enough of an interest in this situation's impact to get involved. Informal efforts ("a word to the wise") and coaching conversations from peers or a supervisor may be enough. But if the behavior persists, the company is obligated to escalate its response through the disciplinary process. If possible, always try to find a resolution first. "Conduct" is a legitimate reason for terminating someone, and gossip fits under this umbrella term.

Many companies get a head start on solutions by making their expectations clear in their employee manuals. Even small companies can have a policy simply stating that "workplace gossip will not be tolerated," providing a reference point. There may be disagreement about what constitutes "gossip," or what gossip is unacceptable: Does a comment about someone's tendency, like, "He always arrives 10 minutes late," or "That's just the way she is," merit a response? When does complaining about someone "cross the line"? Is it "therapeutic" gossip or a guilty pleasure? You cannot say, "Stop gossiping!" too often—any discussion about what is acceptable chitchat will be a reminder that you and your team value mutual respect.

Let's imagine, however, that you suspect illegal or unethical behavior is going on in the workplace, and you confide in your coworker about your concerns. Is this gossip? No, provided you have some *basis for your suspicions* and you do not have a pattern of making negative assumptions. Always begin by asking yourself: *Is it good or bad for the company that I am speaking up?* For consequential information like this, you must immediately report your concerns to your supervisor; it is a lose-lose situation for you to sit on what you know (or think you know). Leave it up to those in charge to investigate your claims. Do make sure to document your concerns and what you did about them, just in case "gossip" escalates to "whistle-blowing."

## What Can One Employee Do?

Like Ginger, whom we met at the beginning of the chapter, we get to *choose* how we respond to gossip, just as we choose our reactions to other ethical dilemmas. Reflect again on the order established in my Ethical Priority Compass: Ginger must take care of herself first, her company second, and her supervisor third. I recommended that she make every attempt to avoid conflict with the executive assistant who doesn't like her, with the expectation that the problem will blow over. However, if it doesn't happen soon, she is more than within her rights to go beyond her boss to the human resources department or another authority figure. If she must become the squeaky wheel to end this attack, so be it.

**Here are the steps you can take should you find yourself in a similar situation:**

1. *Begin documenting what is going on, including dates, names, and verbatim recollections of conversations.* "It is of utmost importance to summarize the conversations, including the one you had with your boss," advises Valerie Weaver, CPS, Gulfport, Mississippi. "This is for your information only, and not for general circulation. Keep a copy for yourself and share one with your HR department contact when you apprise that person of your problem."

2. *Do nothing.* This can certainly be difficult. However, if you take the bait, you are giving the gossip "legs," and you'll be playing catch-up with the latest version of the story. Be the bigger person and stay above and away from the chatter if you can.

3. *Confront the person gossiping about you if you think it will resolve the situation.* Keep in mind, though, that this can be risky. To begin with, you first must determine if the person you think is the gossiper *is* indeed the gossiper—and even then, you may not be comfortable confronting the individual (e.g., perhaps it's your boss). However, if you do choose to speak with the perpetrator, be direct and factual, and keep it simple. Say something like, "I overheard you spreading stories about my having an affair with Bob in Purchasing. These rumors are untrue and malicious besides. I want you to stop—right now!" Enough said. Don't bother wasting time by getting into a dialogue with the gossiper, who will probably deny she said anything anyway. State your objection and leave it at that.

4. *If the gossiper persists, enlist your human resource (HR) contact person for objective, third-party advice.* Be sure to bring your documentation along, and make it clear that you feel strongly enough about this to get the company involved on your behalf.

5. *"As a last resort, put on your best smile and go back to work,"* Weaver adds. "Before long, one of your cohorts will have a baby, win the

lottery, or have an affair of their own, and you will no longer be center stage." Your professional behavior and decorum will always trump the gossipmonger.

I'm reminded of an ancient fable in which a grandfather tells his grandson, "I feel as if I have two wolves fighting in my heart. One wolf is full of selfishness, anger, and criticism. The other wolf is full of compassion, kindness, and love." The grandson asks, "Which wolf will win this fight in your heart?" The grandfather replies, "The one that I feed."

So which wolf will you feed? If you want to avoid the perils of gossip, here are my general guidelines to promote a more Ethical Office:

- *Remember that silence equals consent.* Run—don't walk—away from anyone who starts to gossip. Even if you don't contribute to the actual conversation, your very presence may indicate that you agree with the habit of gossiping. Instead, establish a reputation as one who won't even *listen* to gossip, much less spread it.
- *End rumors about others.* If you overhear something that you know to be untrue, step up and say so. People will respect your integrity. Best-selling author Harvey Mackay likes to relate the story of the philosopher Socrates, whose friend was about to tell him something about a friend of his. Socrates replied, "Answer three questions about this information: Is it true? Is what you are about to tell me about my friend something good? And is what you want to tell me about my friend useful?" Socrates concludes: "If what you have to tell me is neither true nor good nor even useful, why tell me at all?" Socrates may have lived 2,000 years ago, but he was spot-on! The next time the office gossiper brings up someone's name (and not in a nice way), ask, "Aren't there better things to talk about?" Of course there are.
- *Attack rumors about yourself.* Be aggressive and, if possible, determine who originated the remark (as outlined above). Always follow this with documentation.
- *Keep confidences.* Establish a reputation as someone who is close-mouthed.
- *Limit the number of personal tidbits you share about yourself—and keep them on the light side.* Too much information—and in some

cases, too little—may be blown out of proportion and/or become tempting for someone else to elaborate on.

- *Trust only those who have demonstrated and earned your confidence.* And even then, be careful what you disclose.
- *Avoid any form of belittling coworkers.* Today's mail-room clerk may very well be tomorrow's senior vice president, and you certainly don't want to make anyone feel as though their position isn't valuable. Everyone does *something* that helps your organization run smoothly.
- *Build coworkers up—don't tear them down.* If you must use the grapevine, use it to praise coworkers. Everyone wants to be appreciated, and they will remember the kind words you said about them.

I promise you that your colleagues know who gossips and who does not—and that red flags go up immediately with the former. I was once assisting a client (in finding a new executive assistant) who told me that he had interviewed an otherwise fine candidate. However, she had shared all kinds of information about her personal life during the course of the interview, offering much more than he needed or even wanted to know. As she prattled on about her broken marriages and in-law problems, all he could think of was: "If she talks so freely about these matters with me—someone she has just met—what will she someday share *about* me?" Needless to say, this client knocked her off his list of candidates in a skinny minute!

The tongue-waggers will probably always (mistakenly) believe their gossipy mischief makes them popular, mainly because they get immediate attention. And while they may be right for the time being, that momentary popularity is fragile and fleeting. One thing a gossiper *never* garners is respect. And in the ethical workplace, *respect trumps popularity every time!*

> *Gossip is like puncturing a down feather pillow. The feathers fly all over the place, out of control.*
> —Sister Aloysius (played by Actress Meryl Streep)
>                         in the movie *Doubt*

# 9

# Cupid in the Cubicle

## *Dangers of the "Triple R"*

---

*Humans have two basic needs: love and work.*

—Sigmund Freud

Dear Nan:

I'll bet you've never been asked for *this* kind of advice before! I've just graduated from college and have a brand new job. Now, I want a brand new romance! The way I see it, dating a coworker will be better than any of my previous relationships. For starters, I'll always know where he *is* and I can be certain he'll have a *job!* But I am wondering if I can get fired for crimes of the heart. Any advice for the best way to find and conduct a romance at work (and still keep my job)?

—Sally in Las Vegas, NV

Believe it or not, this question is as old as Valentine's Day. The following response to Sally is offered with my tongue *firmly* in my cheek!

Dear Sally:

You might possibly be looking for love in all the wrong places, but don't take *my* word for it. I asked I. M. Kidding, an Employee Relationship Custodian of an Unfortunate 500 company, for her advice about how to have a workplace romance. Here are her suggestions:

1. Selection of your mate: You can either …
   (a) Pick someone unlikely. The more unbelievable the pairing, the more slack you'll have. So aim low. Pick a loser; or
   (b) Aim high! Pick someone who can help you get promoted—and then make darn sure he delivers.

2. Forget about being discreet. No one pulls this off. Lovebirds always think they are fooling everyone when, in actuality, they are the last ones to know that *everybody* knows. So be adult and up front with your coworkers about your sleeping arrangements. An all-office e-mail is a great way to get the message out.

3. Show *lots* of affection at work. Flirt, bring him coffee, sit on his desk and lap, that sort of thing. Coworkers will be jealous and suspicious, accuse your new squeeze of showing favoritism toward you and providing you with inside knowledge that is beneficial to your career. And hopefully, they'll be right!

4. Find time to be alone with your guy. Work late on special projects and travel on business trips together whenever possible. There is special magic in waking up together, then going to see a client. Sharing the giggling and sly glances in client meetings just adds to the romantic excitement. And clients *really* enjoy watching these exchanges.

5. Wear the same clothing two days in a row. This always gets tongues wagging.

6. Take long lunch hours together and return to the office slightly disheveled—preferably, with wet hair.

7. Devise little signals and signs of affection you can send each other during meetings, at lunch, and while passing in the hallway. Your coworkers will enjoy trying to interpret these.

8. Better yet, use the company e-mail system to send sexy, provocative messages. Even though you know your employer has the right to view anything on your office computer, they never do—right?

9. Make company time for each other. Take time out from your busy schedules for intense conversations, dreamy "eye hugs," and even an occasional smooch behind the copy machine. If you're looking for more passionate action, hop into one of your cars in the parking lot on a break.

10. Please your man by wearing what he wants to see. Micro-mini skirts and flimsy blouses are perfect. Dress for success!

11. Finally, keep your goals in mind. At the end of the day, make sure your career gets a boost out of this relationship. If you learn he can't help you in this regard, dump him and move on to the next guy, pronto.

Sally, Ms. Kidding had more advice, but I finally told her to button it! If you do all—or even just *one*—of the items mentioned above, you'll probably have a fantastic romance with your new squeeze. However, chances are that you'll also be without a job. If you're not both canned inside of two weeks' time, it would be nothing short of a miracle. But, hey—at least you will have had a great time!

Okay, enough with the joking. On a serious note, I believe employees *are* confused, as Sally clearly was, about the wisdom of pursuing a workplace romance. They hear about office romances that blossom into marriage. Yet they also witness horror tales of love gone wrong, while destroying both personal and professional lives amid expensive litigation.

There's one thing we know for sure: work relationships that grow into intimate relationships are inevitable and on the rise. Along with various other studies, my own research has revealed that one-third of all romantic relationships begin at work. Unfortunately, many of these beginnings *end* there as well—and, as many can attest, employee heartaches can easily lead to major employer headaches.

## Employers Are Confused as Well

Workplace romances may well end happily ever after, but the odds are against it. To some employers, the possibility of unhappy outcomes makes stringent measures against workplace relationships seem justifiable. Yet most organizations employ a hands-off, "don't ask–don't tell" policy. More and more, however, are addressing the topic in their handbooks and some even explicitly prohibit dating among employees (a policy that is illegal anyhow). Human resource managers without policies say they do not want to be "cupid cops"—something they claim to be a heavy-handed invasion of an employee's private life—and I agree. As one supervisor told me, "We are also trying to avoid the possible consequences of employees' hiding their relationships." However, this often results in employers' being in the dark until it's too late—when it's no longer possible to avoid legal, morale, and professional repercussions.

## Why Is Workplace Romance on the Upswing?

It's no wonder Cupid's arrow finds its mark so often in our offices today:

- The workplace is a *safer place* to meet people than a bar or online, and there is the advantage of repeated opportunities to develop a relationship.
- The workplace provides an environment and culture you can *share*, which serves as a foundation for mutual interests and values.
- More women are *working side-by-side* in almost equal numbers to men and in the same types of jobs, which increases contact with eligible potential partners.
- The "other person" always *sees you at your best*. Your potential hook-up notices your professionalism, knowledge, business acumen, and other qualities consistently wrapped up in a nice package. In other words, you look pretty darn good to each other.
- Employees are *increasingly traveling together* and *enduring long hours*. This provides more opportunities to become acquainted and share experiences, goals, and successes. Coworker interactions lead to camaraderie, bonding, and empathetic conversations ("she's the only one who understands the stresses in my life").

## Why Do Companies Discourage Workplace Romance?

Most of us would agree that employees' personal lives should be just that—kept personal. The company is not Big Brother; it has no right to kill Cupid (thank heaven), outlaw love (I would hope not), or legislate romance (impossible anyhow) among its employees. Furthermore, the company's head honchos don't have the time or the desire to meddle in or monitor the personal romantic life of each employee.

So, why are organizations nervous about workplace romances? It's all about the money, plain and simple. Although a company cannot control matters of the heart, it *does* have a legitimate interest in the bottom line. Whereas lovers may experience their relationship as special and unique, the cynics in the human resources *and* legal departments often view these romances as tawdry clichés that can be costly, lose-lose events they would prefer to avoid. At best, workplace romance has potential to cost money in lost productivity; at worst, such liaisons can lead to ethical breaches, favoritism, poor employee morale, expensive litigation for sexual harassment claims—and even workplace violence.

## The Big Trouble: Employees Reporting to Each Other

According to the U.S. Department of Labor, merit resolutions (i.e., the amount of money paid out by organizations for sexual harassment lawsuits) has doubled between 1997 and 2007. Most often, these cases involve workplace romance between employees reporting to each other. I call this trend the *Triple R: Reporting Romantic Relationship*.

## Dangers of the *Triple R*

- *Risk to the supervisor.* If the relationship ends, the subordinate could at some point claim, under U.S. federal guidelines of sexual harassment, that the supervisor coerced her/him into the relationship. For example, the subordinate was induced or seduced with promises or threats regarding compensation, work assignments, or advancement; or they may assert that the relationship was continued unwillingly for fear of retaliation or dismissal. Thus, the company could be liable under the theory of quid pro quo sexual harassment. While this does not necessarily guarantee the subordinate will *win* such a lawsuit, it *does* ensure that the company may incur considerable expense—in addition to the harm to its reputation—defending its supervisor.

- *Risk to the subordinate.* If a subordinate wishes to end the relationship with the boss (and break the boss's heart, perhaps), how can he or she do that comfortably? Beyond the emotional challenge of such a prospect, the supervisor is in control of the subordinate's reviews, salary increases, and promotions. In some instances, more subtle damage is done to a subordinate's career, such as when a boss opts not to disclose a promotional opportunity to the subordinate for fear of losing him or her.

- *Risk to the company.* Finally, another employee not involved in the romance could make a claim against the company, alleging that the "paramour" was receiving preferential treatment, such as better sales leads, bonuses, or an easier workload. Even though these may be unfounded, *perceived* preferential treatment claims, they still leave the company vulnerable to costly settlements.

## The "David Letterman Risk"

There's one more potential risk here, as exemplified by late night talk show host David Letterman, whose romance with a direct report was revealed when a scorned boyfriend made a blackmail attempt. Even consensual relationships may jeopardize the company's survival when the scandal becomes public by a lawsuit (or blackmail scam). After the fact, its exposure has potential to create an incentive to write a revision of history. What started out as a mutually desirable romance may—to protect one's reputation or for financial reasons—morph into a "he/she-forced-me-to-do-it" lawsuit. In other words, the possibility now exists to exploit the circumstances, knowing the subordinates today have all the leverage because the romance was with the boss. However, this was not always the case.

## Equal Treatment Today

This potentially expensive vulnerability of companies today is a major departure from the time when the boss (usually male) got involved romantically with his secretary. In these *Mad Men*-esque scenarios, it was always the secretary who got fired. The old reasoning was that it was easiest to dismiss the employee who was lowest on the organization chart. This interpretation, however, no longer holds today, Instead, the new understanding dictates that companies are now responsible for protecting the *working environment*, not the "guy" or "gal" at the top. In fact, legal rulings commonly favor the subordinate because, at the end of the day, the boss has all the power—something today's courts tend to see as unfair.

## Employee Cautions

**Potential problems abound with workplace wooing:**

- Your reputation, credibility, and productivity may suffer, which will affect your advancement potential and job security.
- Your relationship may trigger resentment, envy, and even sabotage from coworkers.
- You could be accused of creating or contributing to a hostile workplace environment.
- If your workplace romance ends, you may face unresolved feelings—including hostility, vindictiveness, or even sexual harassment charges—when working together, even long after the affair is over. Your former lover may also hurt the kind of work assignments, raises, or advancement opportunities you receive.

Thus, conventional wisdom would advise that the best course of action to follow when it comes to a workplace romance is simply to not have one.

## Viva Romance!

However, I am aware that at times, love does conquer all. So if you must proceed, by all means—*keep your romance out of the office!* Some people actually accomplish this, and coworkers discover their secret only when the wedding announcements arrive. However, this is the exception, not the rule. Usually, the couple thinks no one knows about their romance, when in actuality, our friend Ms. Kidding is right: they are the last to know that *everyone* knows!

Should you find yourself in this situation, here are a few guidelines to help you keep your head in the game around your new romance:

- *Don't look up—and don't look down.* Don't even consider a romance with someone to whom you directly report, or someone who reports to you (even if layers exist between you). Following a seminar, I had dinner with the human resource director of a major company in the Midwest. That day, we had discussed the company's policy forbidding "romantic reporting-to relationships." I asked him, "What do you do, then, if one of your supervisors becomes involved with someone who reports to him or her?" He replied: "We don't fire anyone—but we do split up their working relationship. And, Nan, 'off the record,' from that time on, neither is promoted again." Strong words, and maybe not fair. But it's an unwritten policy that's certainly not provable—and it's how seriously this company takes the infraction.

- *Be realistic.* Know your temperament. Ask yourself the following important question: If I get involved with this individual and the relationship goes south, can I still go to work each day and see him or her? Some of you would say "no problem"; others know that they'd have a major problem.

- *Don't ever date because you are afraid to say "no," and don't ever* imply *a promotion to get a date.* Both are time bombs for potential lawsuits. You will only do harm to yourself and your colleagues by dating a manager or making an employee feel as though they should date you in order to advance their career.

- *Keep in mind at all times that you must keep your professional and personal lives completely separate.* Then, and only then, will you have any kind of a chance to have your relationship work.

- *Keep the relationship private* until you are ready to publicly announce that you are a couple.

- *Stay professional at all times.* Let professional manners and courtesy guide your actions and conversation in every single situation, and don't ever engage in public displays of affection. Make sure as well that both you and your partner are on the same page in this regard. Do not let your relationship diminish your productivity (e.g., leaving x-rated voice mails and/or flirty e-mails or texts).

- *Be sensitive to your coworkers.* Don't discuss your relationship with them. Believe it or not, coworkers are not particularly enthralled when they find themselves in the middle of your relationship drama.

- *Limit the number of people with whom you share confidential information.* This will prevent the gossip that is certain to follow any romantic disclosures.

- *Never go behind closed doors* (your offices or conference room) for extended periods of time together or leave work together during office hours.
- *Never carry on romantic discussions or electronic communications, flirt, or display physical or sexual behavior on the job.* This behavior will always be inappropriate—whether you both consent or not—because it affects your coworkers and has potential to be perceived as a harassment situation for them.
- *Don't ever bring your domestic arguments or involved discussions to the job.* Enough said. This will only make others feel uncomfortable and distract everyone from the work upon which you all need to focus.
- *Always get your work done.* Make certain the quality of your work doesn't suffer because you are distracted by your significant other.
- *Never engage in sexual activity at work.* This includes empty offices, stairwells, and the parking lot.
- *Don't show or request favoritism.* Benefits do not extend to work assignments, raises, promotions, or company perks.
- *Do not use company funds to entertain your partner.* Even a lunch out here and there can be perceived as unfair and favoritism by other colleagues.
- *If the relationship ends, don't use other coworkers and/or company grounds, equipment, or time as a forum to express your hurt and anger.* Just as you should not use work time to engage in romantic activities, neither should you use it to try to win back your ex or engage in retribution.

## Cupid Cops and Love Contracts

In the "believe it or not" category, I have heard of some companies that have appointed "Cupid cops" to monitor office romances and nip them in the bud before they bloom into a potentially explosive lawsuit. The latter is accomplished by changing any "reporting-to" relationships of a couple and/or encouraging them to make this change themselves. I have also heard of organizations that have asked employees to reveal their dating relationships with fellow employees as soon as they begin (a policy that smacks of invasion of personal privacy, even though there are few laws that promise workplace privacy in the private sector); and

companies that have gone so far as to require employees to sign documents (known as a "dating waiver" or "love contract") acknowledging
that their relationship with a coworker is consensual and that either
party can break things off at any time without fear of reprisal. My
advice? Tread carefully before developing or signing any such waiver
or contract. These contracts protect the company, not you, and are of
questionable enforceability—especially since a person might take the
position that entering into the contract was never truly consensual. You
should sign such a document only after fully considering the circumstances and other policies maintained by the company. For example,
does the company have a policy expressly stating that it will protect an
employee's privacy rights?

The above-listed skittish efforts—dating waivers, Cupid cops, and
love contracts—ultimately reflect the concern and confusion that companies endure regarding workplace romance. The bottom line is that
your company has questionable rights (legal or otherwise) to get involved in your workplace romance if it is not a "reporting romantic
relationship." If it *is* a Triple R, however, the company can intercede
in the interest of preventing a potential harassment lawsuit. In other
words, if you get fired (or disciplined) simply for having a workplace
romance with someone to whom you do not report (or vice versa), you
should consult legal counsel to assess whether possible claims exist,
especially if such policies and practices are not consistently enforced. If
it is a Triple R, though, the company has every right (and obligation)
to get involved.

## The Potential "Hostile Environment" Claim

Companies today also are taking steps to prevent a "sexually charged"
situation, an interesting twist on the "hostile environment." For
example, after a six-year battle, the California Supreme Court is-
sued an eagerly anticipated decision pertaining to sexual harassment
claims brought under California's Fair Employment and Housing Act
(FEHA). The justices held that widespread sexual favoritism in the
workplace creates a hostile work environment that demeans other
employees.

Edna Miller and Frances Mackey (latter now deceased) were employed by the California Department of Corrections (CDC). The
two claimed that prison warden Lewis Kuykendall was having affairs
with at least three subordinates, and that these women were receiving

preferential treatment. In 1999, Miller and Mackey filed a lawsuit against CDC alleging sex discrimination and illegal retaliation, claiming they were "forced to work in a hostile work environment where women got ahead and were promoted if they performed sexual favors for employees of CDC."

Miller and Mackey's lawsuit got stalled in the lower courts for some time because everyone involved in the affairs said they were consensual. And Miller never argued that the warden directly harassed her. However, the courts eventually ruled in Miller's favor by stating that a sexually charged atmosphere, if sufficiently widespread, created an actionable "hostile work environment" and qualified as a type of sexual harassment. That's when sexual tensions are so intolerable at work that they would affect any normal person's ability to do a job.

This lawsuit cranked up the accountability for all workplace romances a notch, since it focused on consensual sexual relationships in the workplace that were found to affect other employees who were not in any way coerced to have sex.

## Managers' Alert

As you can see, workplace romance is fraught with problems for managers. An organization walks a fine line between ensuring a productive workplace and interfering in their employees' private affairs. Managers want staff members to perceive them as advocates for their well-being and high morale, not as the rule-making, interfering, systematizing arms of management.

An organization cannot ban employees from having relationships, nor should they even attempt to do so. Stuff happens. But organizations *can* properly manage them by establishing the following practices:

- *Have a written policy* that prohibits employees from dating direct subordinates or bosses (my Triple R's) and that clearly states the consequences of failing to comply. Remember, however, that a company is still vulnerable to charges of discrimination and harassment—regardless of whether it has a written policy in place against such practices. Have a legal professional review these policies to ensure compliance with federal, state, and local laws.
- *Alert employees to this policy*, and inform them of the reasons for its enforcement. If employees understand the potential harassment

pitfalls involved in the Triple R, they'll be less likely to feel that their employer is being unreasonably restrictive.

- *Unconditionally and uniformly enforce this policy.* Document every-thing.

- *Encourage employees to promptly report any harassment* they experi-ence or observe, and follow your company's procedures for re-porting and dealing with sexual harassment complaints. Don't retaliate or allow any of your employees to retaliate against em-ployees who file any sort of complaint related to a workplace romance.

- Finally, if managers exercise *good judgment and common sense* in their personal relationships with employees, they can make sure their employees' romances don't have the potential to deteriorate into a lawsuit. Such vigilance can also limit the possibility that those love-struck employees don't eventually strike out against each other—or worse, the company.

## A Word on Adulterous Workplace Romances

Unfortunately, employees do, on occasion, witness workplace affairs in which one or both of the individuals are married. I have three simple rules for such situations:

1. Stay out of it! It's their affair, not yours.
2. Try hard not to be judgmental. Easy to say, but difficult to do. But, remember—none of us live in other people's lives.
3. Take a stand only if they try to involve *you*. In other words, if asked, tell them you will not lie or cover up for them, nor do you wish to hear about the affair.

Adulterous affairs in the workplace can be damaging because they present a threat to organizational effectiveness by workplace behavior that is "job affecting" to other employees. Often, just the disruptive gossip surrounding such affairs lands under the "job-affecting" slot. Extremes of any such behavior can morph into the "hostile environ-ment" and leave the company vulnerable to a potential harassment lawsuit leveled by other employees.

# Major Sea Changes

Along these lines, the firing of Boeing Company's CEO Harry Stonecipher reflects a significant transformation in the matter of workplace romance. Stonecipher was brought out of retirement to clean up the company's image after a damaging Air Force procurement scandal, the loss of important government contracts, and the jailing of two former top executives. Shortly thereafter, however, Boeing's board requested the CEO's resignation after it was disclosed that Stonecipher, who was married, was having an affair with a female Boeing executive. Boeing's code of conduct (imposed by Stonecipher on all Boeing employees) did not prohibit affairs between employees (which, as we know, you cannot legally restrict anyhow). However, the board determined that a CEO brought in to restore an aura of integrity to the company clearly lost credibility when that kind of behavior came to light. This was a case where the company fired an individual to restore their reputation.

Another example of this sea change in management accountability is the volunteer resignation of Hewlett-Packard CEO Mark Hurd, following a sexual harassment probe (which sent shockwaves throughout Silicon Valley). The resulting investigation concluded that H-P's sexual harassment policy was not violated per se, but its standards of business conduct were.

# Workplace Romance: The Final Verdict?

The long and short of it is that companies should be concerned with office romance and should formally restrict "reporting-to" liaisons in their workplace. They should also stay on top of situations that create a potentially hostile environment, especially if the hostility takes the form of an uncomfortably flirtatious or sexual atmosphere. Taking these protective steps is simply good business practice.

There are both perks and drawbacks to a workplace romance. The benefits might include: (1) you get to see each other all the time, (2) you have someone who understands and can discuss your work situation, and (3) you get to know that person outside of their personal life (which can be insightful into their personality). The drawbacks could be: (1) you're always together, and this kind of constant closeness may breed friction (remember what renowned advice columnist Ann Landers once said: "Marry him for better or worse—but *never* for lunch!");

(2) you may lose some mystery or anticipation because you see each other so much; and (3) you can be distracted or even annoyed—and your work may suffer.

The heart will always remain a vulnerable organ. So, for you romantics who are ready to tackle a workplace romance with integrity and responsibility, not to worry. A company today can legally prevent romantically involved couples from working *for* each other but not *with* each other. As long as that is the case, Corporate America will never truly be able to ban Cupid from the cubicle!

> *Temptation is certain to ring your doorbell. But you don't have to invite it to dinner!*
>
> —Grandmothers everywhere

# 10

## Party Up—or Party Down?

### The Worst Hangover May Come with a Lawsuit!

*The only thing I don't like about office parties . . . is having to look for a new job the next day!*

—Phyllis Diller, Comedienne

Dear Nan:

Lucky me! My job description was just expanded to include two major all-company events: The summer picnic and the annual holiday party. I'm actually excited about these new responsibilities (I love parties), and I want to use my unlimited budget to plan

*(continued)*

*(continued)*

two splashy events. But I've heard of past events where some "unprofessional" behavior occurred, so I wish to avoid any such disastrous circumstances or morning-after lawsuits. I know the rules have changed a lot from the lampshade-on-the-head office parties of yesteryear. Can you give me some advice that won't land the planner (me) in hot water or have me labeled as a "wet blanket"?

—Randy in Altoona, PA

Good for you for choosing the high road, Randy. Your caution may spare you and your coworkers a lot of grief. It may also save your company the cost of lawsuits filed by the victims of party "fun" and the expense of recruiting new hires to replace those who quit in disgust or embarrassment.

To see how far we've come in these matters, rent the 1950s flick *The Apartment*, in which Jack Lemmon plays a fledgling accounting clerk in a New York City advertising company, and Shirley MacLaine plays the "elevator girl." In the midst of the turmoil experienced by executives (all married males, of course), who are sleeping with the secretaries (all single females), there is a blowout holiday party where no-holds-barred partying takes place on the company premises! Such an activity today would keep the lawyers busy throughout the following holiday season!

Fast-forward to today: You did not see mistletoe at your last holiday party, and you will not see beer kegs at the summer picnic, either. They've been Grinched. "It's too dangerous," the human resource people say—meaning the former may cause you to kiss people you should not kiss, and the latter may cause you to misbehave in ways that are even worse. Cleaning up after an office party should not include settling expensive harassment lawsuits or paying for driving accidents. For the same reason, you won't find gag gifts under the tree, open bars, or lampshades that can be used as headwear.

The "anything goes" company party of years past has evolved into a networking function. While you can certainly plan to have fun, don't do or say anything you wouldn't want to show up on the cover of the company newsletter. Keeping misbehavior out of the office now extends to all company-sponsored social functions, even those that are held "off campus." The company's liability for any activity that can be construed as an organization-subsidized event has the potential to be expensive trouble.

Now, there are dress codes, codes of conduct, new rules of engagement, and "expected outcomes." If, for example, you express your romantic feelings to a coworker or tell your boss what you *really* think of her, you will likely find yourself sheepishly apologizing the next day, avoiding certain people—or even resigning. In short, professional etiquette trumps unrestrained fun at corporate social events. Here are some tips for planning and attending social events at the Ethical Office.

### If you're the planner:

- *Rethink the concept of the event itself.* Do you even need to host one? A lot of companies are eliminating these kinds of events altogether. With the ever-increasing pressures on employees' personal and professional lives, many work-weary staff members may prefer to skip the entire thing. Might employees instead jump at a check for $100 apiece to take their families out for a private "appreciation outing"? Or perhaps you could offer to make a donation in their name to a charity of their choice. Consider a company-sponsored holiday or summer concert, theater outing, or family afternoon party with entertainment. A block of seats at an event (e.g., amusement park, sporting event, dinner theater) is usually a safe bet, as is a professionally organized theme party.

- *Try to anticipate and eliminate any potential risks,* including transportation home for those who have overimbibed. If, like Randy, you are new to the party-giving game, have a flexible budget—you may wish to get some support from a professional (e.g., party planner or special events coordinator). If your budget is tight, call on your friends and coworkers for help and advice.

- *Eliminate the word party from the event's title.* This communicates it is a business function with the expected protocol. "Employee Appreciation" is a popular description. And stay away from religious themes or titles (aka "Christmas" or "Easter" events) unless 100 percent of employees are like-minded.

- *Communicate with a clear, detailed invitation specifying the hour it begins and ends.* Include a dress code. Employees appreciate knowing what is expected of them so they do not, for example, come over- (or under-) dressed and/or arrive too late to hear the boss's welcoming remarks.

- *If possible, serve no alcohol.* If you do, avoid an open bar; a cash bar will slow down consumption. Supplying drink tickets and limiting these to two per person will also deter overconsumption. Hire a professional bartender who knows how to measure a drink and refuse service to an inebriated employee. Be sensitive to nondrinkers by providing plenty of nonalcoholic beverages, and stop serving an hour before the official end of the event. Make sure that you offer taxi service for anyone who wants it.

- *Encourage everyone to bring a guest.* Office parties that exclude spouses and friends can be a nest of potential behavior problems. If the event is appropriate for children, encourage employees to bring their families as well.

- *Skip the dancing.* Some people do not like (or know how) to dance. Some will feel obligated to dance with others (the boss, for example), and some will have no partner to dance with and feel left out.

**If you're the attendee:**

- *Be a team player and show up!* Even if you abhor party functions, make an effort to attend, at least for a while. Whether it seems fair or not, others will note your absence, and it will reflect negatively on you. Try to arrive within 15 minutes of the start time.

- *Keep in mind that a company party is an extension of the office.* So be on your best professional behavior because your conduct will be observed, measured and—you better believe it—talked about the next day. Remember, you represent your company; so, make management proud of you!

- *Don't use this as the chance to have a candid chat with any of your colleagues.* This is not the perfect time to "clear the air" with your boss or coworkers. Too many margaritas do not mix well with "the truth"—or continued employment.

- *Dress appropriately.* Leave the "real you" in the closet (or in the car) and save the sexy look for a party with your real friends who love you in spite of yourself. If you're not sure what to wear, consult a long-time employee on correct attire. Rachel wrote that she fretted over her attire for her first-time company holiday event due to the professional, dark-suit protocol of her conservative employer. Upon arriving, she became nervous about her "sleeveless, but modest, gown . . . I was uncomfortable about having my arms and neck out there for the world to see." She had no cause to worry, however, when "one of the youngest new hires showed up wearing little more than a belt! Her curve-hugging, high-hemmed dress with the plunging neckline—combined with her appreciation for brightly colored martinis and dancing—was the buzz at the office for weeks!"

- *Don't drink—or at least watch your consumption.* Feeling too embarrassed (or sick!) to go to work the next day is a surefire sign that you had too much to drink the night before. I know of one woman who exceeded her wine limit and spoke in detail to another guest about a sensitive company lawsuit. Alcohol free, she would have known better. It was especially unfortunate that the guest turned out to be a newspaper reporter whose story soon ran on page one—full of her attributed comments.

- *Watch your frisky date's or spouse's behavior and consumption as well*—and don't bring a "first" or a high-maintenance date. The former could result in disaster, and the latter could prevent you from circulating appropriately. The employee who brought her blind date to the company's summer picnic was surprised when he overimbibed, and then mortified when he "hit on" the boss's wife. There's really *no* recovery here!

- *Socialize.* There are always employees who are new, shy, or alone and not good mixers, and the same is true for the guests they bring. They will forever remember and appreciate you for making them feel at home and comfortable. Others, such as your boss, will also notice and value your kind efforts.

- *Finally, go home at the expected time.* Remember, this is the end of the workday, so treat it as such. Relocating the party to the pub down the road will cause eyebrows to rise and tongues to wag.

- *And ... writing a thank-you note* to the boss/host (whomever appropriate) is always appreciated.

It *is* possible nowadays to plan a company event that will not result in your staring down a potential lawsuit the next day. And, it *is* possible to have a good time attending such an event and not have to launch a job search Monday morning. Remember to have fun, but to do so in a way that *boosts* your career, rather than trashes it. In other words, don't ignore the "office" in "office party"!

Think of Benjamin Franklin as your date. He once said, "A reputation is like fine china. When broken, it is difficult to restore."

**Top 10 questions to determine if you had *too* good a time at your company office party (with apologies to David Letterman):**

10. Are you in jail?

 9. Are you in a treatment center?

 8. Were you subpoenaed this morning?

 7. Did your associate or assistant call in and resign?

 6. Is a particular coworker not talking to you?

 5. Is *any* coworker talking to you?

 4. Did you have to call and apologize to anyone?

 3. Has your spouse or significant other announced he/she is boycotting *all* such future events?

 2. Are people smiling at you—or snickering?

And the number one way to tell if you have misbehaved at your office party . . .

 1. Was your name removed from the voice mail, the locks changed on your office door, and all your belongings tossed on the front steps of the building?

*Regard your good name as the richest jewel you can possibly possess. The way to gain a good reputation is to endeavor to be what you desire to appear.*

—Socrates

# 11

## Trick or Treat

### *Vendors Can Be Tricksters, and They Wear Many Masks*

---

*Doubt means don't!*

—Oprah Winfrey

C onsider how you'd react to the following scenario: An office supply vendor has offered you free tickets to a concert and you're dying to go. All you have to do is throw a little work her way, which you would probably do anyway. No one would ever know; these purchases are "below the radar" of anyone else. Is it okay to accept the tickets?

What you mean to say is that no one *else* would ever know. But the two of you will know forever after that your business can be bought. And as much as you love to rock, it just isn't worth the trouble!

You might recall the case of Ann Copland, former aide to Mississippi U.S. Senator Thad Cochran, who was charged in the bribery scandal of lobbyist Jack Abramoff. According to court documents, Copland took gifts from Abramoff and other lobbyists, including thousands of dollars' worth of event tickets and meals. Prosecutors claimed that the gifts were given in exchange for her help getting favors for Abramoff's top client—the Mississippi Band of Choctaw Indians.

Did the boss know his staff person was apparently for sale? Once they learned her price, it almost didn't matter; the influence store was open, and favors were for sale. The damage was done. This example is a reminder that once you cross the no-gifts-from-vendors line, you are sliding down a slippery slope.

A tight economy or hypercompetitive marketplace increases the likelihood that vendors will use gifts and freebies to attempt to unfairly tip the scales in their favor. As the pressure on suppliers to nab the deal—and on buyers to get the most bang for their buck—increases, ethical behavior will be tested. How you handle these temptations is a test of your organization's ethical mettle.

Just like purchasing agents, meeting planners are constantly being pursued by suppliers for their business. Jennifer, a new member of the hospitality industry, wrote me after one of my seminars:

> As a meeting planner for our company, I am continually being wooed by vendors. Their inducements are not trivial, and many times include my family. For example, I often receive gifts, tickets for concerts and events (even to my favorite New York Knicks), as well as excursions and weekend packages to "experience" the surroundings, food, etc.

Jennifer goes on to explain:

> Part of my job is to tour facilities, because heaven forbid I schedule a meeting at some dump I haven't previewed. So in a way, I *have* to accept their hospitality, but I feel guilty enjoying myself. That's just my simple naïve self overthinking the situation, right?
>
> I once made the mistake of telling a vendor my family name was Czechoslovakian—and bang! Within a month, I had an all-expenses-paid offer to go to Prague, a trip my husband and I had dreamed of for years. The vendor had misinterpreted my casual comment as a request for a bribe. "I pretended I was offended but, wow—was I tempted! The vendor backed down and we patched things up—he was an important vendor—but I still "had" to accept a gorgeous (and costly) table book of Prague.

My company has only vague policies on what perks are acceptable versus unacceptable; it's pretty loose-goosey. I've noticed my boss doesn't even adhere to them (and doesn't seem to care if I do either). But I feel uncomfortable about the entire process, as though our company's meeting business is for sale to the highest bidder; only I get the goodies, and the company pays the bill. If this keeps up, I'm going to be shopping for myself—who's got the best "incentive"—and not shopping for the best value for the company. So how and where do I draw the ethical lines?

Jennifer is at a crossroads. How she decides to handle this dilemma will doubtlessly affect both her reputation and her career. The hospitality industry is known for its freebies, and the questionable practices described here persist for the simple reason that they are often effective.

Similar *quid pro quo* (meaning "something for something" or "favor for favor" or "I'll scratch your back if you scratch mine") practices occur out of sight in other functions of other businesses, too. And a tough economic climate for either the buyer or seller is often just enough to degrade an otherwise professional relationship into a nerve-wracking conspiracy of secrets, embarrassment, oblique wink-wink messages, and stress.

Jennifer's instinct that "something is wrong here" is correct, and she has accurately predicted the end game: Is she going to ultimately be taking care of herself or her company? Initially, the best thing for the company happens to benefit her as well; however, this is a happy coincidence that is the exception. Before long, Jennifer will be faced with the option to accept gifts for herself, provided she buys venues that are only "just good enough"—and she will have to choose whether she is working for the company or for herself.

What to do, what to do . . . maybe accept just one gift and then no more? From the outside, it looks easy to stop, right? But some vendors are masters at guilt-free seduction. They are also not stupid; they are well aware of the internal dialogue a person undergoes when making an ethical choice. Saying yes to one bribe and no to another does not signal ethical maturity; it merely shows that you are an unethical person who has particular preferences. Jennifer is betting her professional reputation and her career that she'll never be held accountable for her purchasing decisions. This game will continue until it ends badly.

Most of us have equivalent temptations. In Jennifer's case, gaming the system is just not who she is—that's probably why the company trusts her to do her job in the first place. Lose that trust, and say bye-bye to the job.

# The Pit-of-the-Stomach Rule

Why are vendors' gift-giving practices so troublesome? Because rather than using a gift to say "thank you," some vendors use gifts to say "choose me, choose me." It may not always be that explicit, but that's what they mean. How can you tell? Because, unlike other thank-you gifts, this one comes *before* you have ever done anything.

Trying to win influence over the people who make purchasing decisions works often enough to perpetuate the practice. A bottle of wine, a trip, a box of steaks, gift certificates, and so on are obvious inducements (spelled b-r-i-b-e). Less obvious are the promises to make an introduction that will help your spouse, write a letter for your son's college application, or provide a lead on a new house or job. These are highly personal in nature and out of your boss's sight. No matter what the nature of the enticements, these are all intended to facilitate a shortcut to getting your company's business. They're good for you and bad for your employer.

Can you ever accept gifts without stepping over ethical boundaries? Usually not, though it depends on the gift's value, the true motivation behind it, the expectations attached to it, and your existing relationship with the vendor. For example, it may be appropriate for a hotel to offer a free or reduced rate as an inducement to have you sample a venue; however, it would be inappropriate for that same hotel to try to buy your favoritism with a "promotional" flat screen or digital camera. Likewise, gifts offered by new vendors differ from those offered by vendors with whom you have had a long relationship. Remember that old saying, "Gifts ought to come with ribbons, not strings"?

When trying to decide whether or not to accept a vendor's gift, follow this advice, using the "pit-of-the-stomach" rule:

- Consider the word *uncomfortable*. If you feel the least bit uncomfortable about accepting a gift, don't do it!
- Consider the word *compromised*. If you feel the least bit compromised by such an acceptance, don't do it! And if you feel you may be perceived by others to be compromised, definitely don't do it!

Kris Pool, CAP, executive administrative assistant for Pentair Water Treatment in Sheboygan, Wisconsin, has been creative in solving her vendor perk problems. Pool's company does not have any established guidelines, so she "puts all gift baskets (notes attached) in the office lunchroom for all to share. Larger gifts (tickets, weekend hotel stays, etc.) are used for employee raffle prizes and drawings. This not only benefits all our employees; it also saves on the company's budget for buying prizes for employee events."

Racine, Wisconsin, All Saints Healthcare secretary Stacia Y. Stokes says that Jennifer—and the rest of us who sometimes give up too soon—ought to be reminded that the *perception* of ethical behavior (or lack thereof) is readily noticeable to those both inside and outside the company. This argues for a clear, consistent policy, even though it may not be perfect. Stokes explains: "You can suggest tightening up your company's 'loose policy' on accepting perks. Be sure that these guidelines cover what all employees in your company—from the CEO to the maintenance crew—can and cannot accept from vendors, and be as specific as possible."

Jennifer's boss may not truly be as indifferent as he seems to the inherent ethical dilemmas of vendor relations; he may simply be overwhelmed or unsupported by senior management. Resignation and defeatism are merely a shortcut to more problems, though; one actually has to be seen *trying* to do the right thing.

# Establishing and Documenting Company Guidelines

Employee handbooks are the ideal communication tool for conveying specific guidelines relating to vendors. You can document acceptable and unacceptable practices here, and eliminate any mystery as to how employees should conduct themselves. I am seeing increasingly more specificity in these guidelines, such as "only gifts with a nominal value of less than $10 may be accepted" and "when dining with a vendor, our employees must always pay for their own food and beverages."

The objective is to avoid the mere *appearance* that preferential treatment is for sale. You don't want a vendor walking away wondering "if only"—if only, for example, he had crossed *his* ethical boundaries and offered you a kickback or other inducement, then he could have had your business. You want the vendor thinking about how to better serve your company, not considering whether he should have offered you a larger TV.

Employees actually appreciate this clarity. They don't worry that their employers suspect they can be bought for the price of a drink; rather, they use the rules (usually with some humor!) to stop the situation from becoming awkward before it starts: "Bob, I don't want you to pay for dinner—what I want is better service and free shipping!"

Unambiguous guidelines are essential for meeting planners like Jennifer. Any business will benefit, however, because wherever buying and selling occurs—which it does for every business—there are risks for ethical lapses. A few examples of specifics that need to be addressed:

- *Gifts.* Most government entities and organizations that have government contracts operate under a zero-acceptance policy. If your company strategy does permit the acceptance of gifts, make sure you clearly cite the maximum dollar value. Must the gifts be reported to a compliance officer? Good idea. Can gifts be "solicited"? Bad idea. If your company does international business, make an allowance for local customs: "The giving and acceptance of gifts is acceptable as long as it comports to local customs and traditions."

- *Familiarization trips/site inspections/pseudo-conferences "for educational purposes."* Are these bona fide business trips? Qualify who can go where, and for what purpose. These "fam" trips can include everything from free rooms, complimentary golf/spa visits, and countless other luxuries meant to woo decision makers. All of these appear ethically vague and questionable. You need to decide upfront whether you or the company is permitted to keep the reward points and frequent flier miles.

- *Social invites.* Determine where and when one can accept, and reciprocate the offer whenever possible.

I recommend a question-and-answer format in an employee handbook. This allows you to easily update the guidelines as each new dilemma is discussed and resolved.

## Nan DeMars's Vendor Ethics Audit

Finally, when struggling with these ethical dilemmas, a quick Ethics Audit might be helpful:

- Would I feel uncomfortable explaining my actions to my boss, the CEO, or the media?
- Could others possibly perceive a conflict of interest?
- Could my behavior appear unfair and/or seem to undermine the effectiveness of my work?
- Has my ability to make an impartial and objective decision been compromised or forced to be biased in any way?

And the real zinger:

- Would I feel uncomfortable accepting this gift and *not* giving the giver my business?

If you answered "yes" to any of above questions, then you need to rethink your decision.

Should temptations from vendors influence your purchasing decisions? Of course not. Your professional commitment to do your best for your company is not for sale for any price.

> *Integrity is not a conditional word. It doesn't blow in the wind or change with the weather. It is your inner image of yourself, and if you look in there and see a [wo]man who won't cheat, then you know [s]he never will.*
> —John D. MacDonald, American novelist

# 12

## Copyright or Copy Wrong?

### *There Are Boundaries around Intellectual Property*

---

*I think copyright is moral and proper. I think a creator has the right to control the disposition of his or her works—I actually believe that the financial issue is less important than the integrity of the work, the attribution, that kind of stuff.*
> —Esther Dyson, American scientist

Dear Nan:

My boss and I worked up a pretty great sales presentation. But what helped make it great, I think, is our use of about a dozen photos for which we did not obtain permission. My boss literally said (with a wink-wink), "Go steal something off the Internet"—and so I did. This can't be right, can it? How much trouble am I in?
> —Regretful Pirate, Bismarck, ND

Your instincts are correct—you *are* a pirate. Arggggh, copyright is treacherous! You may not receive a nasty-gram this time from the owners of those images, but if your sales presentation goes viral, or lands in front of prospects who see lots of presentations, you may wind up with some explaining to do.

I'm no substitute for up-to-date, expert legal advice, so I can only wish to give you the most basic guidelines regarding copyright law. This will show you what to watch out for—so that you can keep your boss and your company out of an embarrassing and/or expensive dilemma. More important, however, I want to keep *you* from being forced to walk the plank!

This is yet another area to which the personal responsibility of employees today applies. Because administrative professionals and other assistants are most offices' unofficial defenders of documents, they make countless decisions about what to put in—and what to leave out. For that reason, let's see if we can help clarify the line between copyright and copy wrong.

## Copyright Basics

U.S. copyright laws exist for two major reasons: (1) to protect the creator's right to obtain commercial benefit from his or her original work, and (2) to protect the creator's right to control how a work is used. The "creator" can be anyone who produces a written work, published or unpublished (from e-mails and blogs to the Great American Novel), to someone who records a piece of audio, or designs a pictorial, graphic, or sculptural work—and limitless other examples. And, yes, even Facebook photos and YouTube videos are included, as are any graphics or photos lifted from another Web site and used in a sales presentation (I'm talking to you, Regretful Pirate!).

Web-based encyclopedia Wikipedia.com defines *copyright* as:

> The set of exclusive rights granted to the author or creator of an original work, including the right to copy, distribute, and adapt the work. These rights can be licensed, transferred, and/or assigned. Copyright lasts for a certain time period, after which the work is said to enter the public domain.

So while a piece of writing, a recording, or an artwork isn't protected indefinitely, it does fall under this category for a certain amount of time, and that's when you have to make sure you're taking the appropriate steps.

## Intellectual Property Law Basics

Copyright is one of the four major intellectual property laws in the United States and Canada, which include:

- *Copyright law.* This protects original "works of authorship."
- *Patent law.* This protects new, useful, and "nonobvious" inventions and processes.
- *Trademark law.* This protects words, names, and symbols used by manufacturers and businesses to identify their goods and services.
- *Trade secret law.* This protects valuable information not generally known that has been kept secret by its owners.

Employees are most often concerned with copyright law. Many of you might be responsible for generating Web content, training manuals, and other internal documents. In such situations, the temptation to spice up a dreary piece of writing with a cool photo or graphic might sound familiar to you. Just be aware that your habit of "clicking-copying-pasting" an illustration from here or some text from there is likely going to require that you obtain permission from the proper sources.

## Requesting Permission

Let's imagine you have found something you want to copy, either printed on paper or on the Internet, but it's copyrighted. Getting permission (and perhaps paying a nominal fee of $10 to $500) is not difficult; however, it typically takes a few weeks or months to obtain. You'll need to send a request to copy a copyrighted work to the permissions department of the work's publisher, or the Web site's owner/producer. Permission requests should contain the following information about the work:

- Title, author, and/or editor and edition
- Exact material to be used, providing chapter or page numbers, or URLs
- Number of copies to be made

- How you're planning to use the copied materials
- Form of distribution (classroom, newsletter, blog, etc.)
- Whether the material is to be sold

Some organizations will have forms (electronic or hard copy) on their Web sites that may ask for additional information from you as well.

Though this part might sound somewhat complicated, keep in mind that copyright protects against copying the "expression" in a work, not against copying the work's "ideas." The difference between "idea" and "expression" is one of the most difficult concepts to understand in terms of copyright law. However, the most important point to appreciate here is that one can copy the protected expression in a work without copying the literal words (or the exact shape of a sculpture, or the precise look of a stuffed animal). When a new work is generated by copying an existing copyrighted work, copyright infringement exists if the new work is "substantially similar" to the work that was copied. The new work need not be identical to the copied work. Always keep in mind here that it's better to be safe than sorry; if you think it's "close," then err on the side of caution.

## Cubicle Copyright Myths

What you don't know that you don't know—or what you think you know that is actually false—will probably be the source of any copyright headaches. However, you shouldn't feel alone. Copyright laws cannot keep up with the online world; for that reason, they tend to remain vague, rarely providing concrete lists of do's and don'ts. The following are a few myths I'd like to dispel for you:

*Myth 1: Things are not protected by copyright unless and until they are registered with the U.S. Copyright Office and/or carry the © symbol.* Wrong. Since 1989, almost all things are *automatically* copyrighted the moment they are created—and no copyright notice is required.

*Myth 2: I can protect my copyright with a Poor Man's Copyright; I can simply mail myself a copy of the work and make sure the postmark is legible, thereby establishing the date I created it. If challenged, I'll just open the envelope in front of the judge.* This tactic is absolutely *not* effective. As clever as it may sound, it has never worked—for too many reasons to enumerate here. Yet this myth persists, and by doing so, it gives people a false sense of security. If you determine that registration is, in fact, desirable because you anticipate legal action, seek another alternative to a full registration that *is* effective. Better yet, invest in a good lawyer.

*Myth 3: If it's on the Internet, it's "public domain" and copyright free.* Nope. Things do not become public domain (and therefore copyright free) until a certain time has lapsed after the death of the creator. The works of William Shakespeare are in the public domain, and so is *The Wizard of Oz.* However, the novel you purchased that just came out last week certainly is not.

*Myth 4: I didn't make any money off the stuff I stole. No harm, no foul, right?* Wrong. You've still violated copyright whether you charged (or made) money or not.

*Myth 5: I gave the copyright holder full credit for the work I copied. Again, no harm, no foul, right?* Nope, wrong again. The owner of a copyright has *exclusive* rights to control the work. It's up to him or her (or the institution) to allow you to reuse it. And this will often be contingent on your citing them as a source in your new work.

*Myth 6: Okay, let's say that I just tweak someone else's nonfiction work, or make up my own stories based on someone else's fiction work. Then my new work belongs to me, right?* No. U.S. copyright law is quite explicit that the making of what are called *derivative works*—works based on or derived from another copyrighted work—is the exclusive province of the original work's owner. You might be wondering, "But in the real world, isn't most work derivative, *not* original?" Aren't there just so many ways to write an employee policy manual or photograph a bowl of fruit or draw a circle? And if you had to reinvent the wheel and start from scratch every time you took on an assignment, then wouldn't you be fired for your low productivity?

Most so-called creative tasks do not merit the time, budget, or audience of completely original work. In my humble opinion, it is perfectly acceptable to learn from and build upon others' products. In the real world, it's okay and even preferred to draw background, context, ideas, and even inspiration from the public discourse, provided you remain sensitive to where someone else's work leaves off and yours begins.

But be honest with yourself: are you copying-and-pasting from someone else because you are stumped for an idea, or are you just being lazy? Are you screen-grabbing an image and tweaking it with Photoshop because you need it as a place to begin, or are you just too unprofessional to get yourself organized to have time to do it ethically? "Jumping off" from someone else's work is an "it depends" dilemma.

*Myth 7: If I hired a Web designer to develop our Web site, we must own the copyright.* Probably not, unless you contracted in writing that the design was on a "work for hire" basis, in which case you would own the copyright.

*Myth 8: The Internet is big, and my theft of copyrighted material is so small, no one will ever know.* Don't be so sure; just a few minutes with Google or Yahoo! can reveal all. As search engines like these improve, piracy—and the pirates—are becoming increasingly easier to identify. The latest trend toward "semantic search" returns results based on the meaning and the context of the words in the query. This makes whatever you stole—and where you stole it from—much easier to trace.

And while there might not be "copyright police" who catch you, your coworkers will. Once you are "outed" as a pirate among those whose opinions matter to you, *all* your work will become tainted. Colleagues, supervisor, and clients will question from that point forward if your work is really your own.

"You shouldn't have to be ashamed to tell your boss that you found usable information on the Internet," says Katharine Lewman, CPS, an administrative assistant for Milliman USA Inc., in Indianapolis, Indiana. "After you let him or her know what information is not original, your company may or may not contact the original writer(s) to get permission to use the material or remove the text if they so desire. You are more likely to get in hot water for *not* 'fessing up.'"

*Myth 9: I used only a little of the other guy's stuff, so I'm protected under "fair use."* Maybe. "Fair use" allows you to use material such as commentary, parody, news reporting, research, and education *about* copyrighted works without the author's permission, so that readers can freely express their thoughts about another's work. Passages are usually short, and are always attributed to the source. Intent and damage to the commercial value of the work is considered very important. In one famous case, 300 words from Gerald Ford's 200,000-word memoir reprinted in a magazine article was ruled as *not* fair use, in spite of its being very newsworthy, because it was the most important 300 words: an explanation of why Ford pardoned Nixon.

*Myth 10: Okay, I get it—everything is off limits, right?* Unfortunately, it's not readily apparent. Consider the following:

- The predominant business model on the Web is called "freemium," whereby the site owner uses free information to attract traffic, then sells advertising on the Web site. These owners *want* you to come to their site and make the most of their stuff, because advertisers pay for traffic—and more visitors equals more ad revenue. This is serious business, with revenue totals topping $25 billion in 2009. With money like this at stake, no wonder these Web sites offer their content for free. They usually assume (rightfully so) that people wouldn't pay for it anyway, since someone else is likely providing it for free.

- Many Web sites *cannot* charge for their content, because *they* have stolen it from someone else! They don't generate original content; they just "chew" what they've appropriated from someone else. Some hilarious instances have occurred where the victims of this pirating have intentionally "spiked" their content with typos and other errors in order to prove they were being ripped off because the pirates didn't even bother to fix the errors!

- Paid content is becoming more common as people wise up to the fact that you get what you pay for. High-value content, like original research and reportage, may be valuable enough to command a subscription or nominal use fee. But what copyrights do you get for your subscription fee? You have to read the Web site's fine print to find out. This is the most dangerous material to pirate, because you deny the copyright holder a demonstrable financial benefit when you "surf away" with the goods.

## Copyright Offline

Dilemmas related to piracy also surface when a company considers making additional copies of software, videos, music, and other copyrighted intellectual property. We've heard these rationalizations before: "I've already paid for one overpriced copy, so it's okay to make another one," and "No one gets hurt if I make a copy; it's not like I'm depleting an inventory." My personal favorite from the Lame Excuse Department is, "In fact, by making another copy and showing off the artist's work, I'm actually doing the creator a favor; he should be paying *me* for publicizing it for *him!*" This is a very weak justification; after all, it's doubtful whether your exposure of the work will add to its value, and in any case, the owner of the copyright is the only one who can decide whether to grant permission.

Imagine your manager returns from a seminar and drops the course manual on your desk with instructions to "make copies for everyone." What do you do if the workshop materials carry a copyright notice? Is it okay to make copies if your company has paid for at least one person to attend the workshop? Permissions vary with the workshop presenters' fee agreement, so it's best to check. Extra copies are probably available for a minimal fee, which is inexpensive (and well worth it!) insurance against future trouble. You may have to (gently) explain to your boss that copying the workshop materials is a violation of copyright law. If she doesn't believe you, suggest she visit the local copy shop and try to get them to reproduce it in spite of the © notice; chances are, she'll get a quick lesson in the finer points of copyright law.

Bottom line? *Never* use someone else's intellectual property— ever—unless you are certain you can do so without incurring a liability. Because the laws relating to intellectual property are so vague and vary from case to case, err on the conservative side and consult your legal adviser.

## When You *Don't* Need Permission

**You may freely copy and report works that are:**
- In the public domain (the copyright has expired and is no longer protected)
- Government documents
- Facts (no one can claim originality or authorship for facts like, "The sun rises in the east," and "There are 50 states in the United States")
- "Fair use," which you can determine based on these four tests:
  - *Test No. 1: Purpose and character of use.* When the use is noncommercial, the copied work is more likely to be found to be fair use. Transformative uses (where the work is physically changed) are favored over mere copying. Noncommercial uses are also more likely to be judged fair use.

- *Test No. 2: Nature of the copyrighted work.* A copied work is more likely to be judged fair use if it is factual rather than creative.
- *Test No. 3: Amount and substantiality of the portion used.* If only an inconsequential amount of the protected work is used, it is likely to be found to be fair use. If what is used is small in amount but substantial in terms of importance, such as the excerpt from President Gerald Ford's memoir cited earlier, a finding of fair use is unlikely. Keep in mind that a work does not have to be *identical* to infringe on the copyright of another piece. The legal test of infringement is "substantial similarity," which translates (roughly) into whether a work is copied in whole or in part from an earlier one.
- *Test No. 4: Effect on the potential market for, or value of, the protected work.* For example, if the copied work deprives the copyright owner of sales revenue, it will not pass the fair use test.

## Finally, Some Good News

A growing amount of material on the Internet is being made available at no charge through something called a "Creative Commons" license. If the work you want to use carries the Creative Commons notice, you are free to share (copy, alter, transform, build upon, distribute, and transmit) and/or remix (adapt) the work—provided you attribute it in the manner that the author or licensor specifies (but *not* in any way that suggests they endorse you or your use of the work).

If you use a work under the provisions of Creative Commons, you must also make your resulting work available under the same, similar, or compatible license. See www.creativecommons.org/licenses for the best way to do it.

## Err on the Safe Side

There aren't many rules that can be applied broadly when it comes to copyright enforcement. Every copyright holder and infringement case is different—and to make matters more complicated, the rules are still evolving. Very little is stable or decided in terms of legality, technology, and the social sphere. The best thing anyone can do is take an honest look at his specific situation and decide on a strategy that best serves his needs.

At the end of the day, your safest course of action, particularly if you have any doubt, is to remember the following: *Do not copy a work for which others own the copyright unless you have permission.* Instead of risking your reputation (or even your job), use clip art, software libraries, and other sources of materials that are sold for the purpose of being copied. Keep in mind, however, that even these have limits (e.g., a CD of clip art may be used in printed works, but the license may forbid digital distribution).

And, if all else fails, why not create a new work altogether? The world needs more expressions of ideas in all artistic forms in all media. You can produce something yourself or hire someone else to do it—knowing with confidence that when the shoe is on the other foot, federal laws will protect *your* work from copyright pirates, too.

This chapter's discussion reminds me of the application of the Hippocratic Oath in the medical profession, which states, *primum non nocere*: "To not knowingly do harm." None of us can promise we will always do good for others (no matter how hard we try). All we *can* honestly promise is that we will not knowingly do others any harm.

The chain of accountability of your Ethical Compass is exercised once again: You owe it to your boss, your company, your customers, and *yourself* to not knowingly do harm. There are huge risks and consequences today to stealing or "borrowing" intellectual works without permission, which reminds us once again that it's *our* responsibility to help maintain the ethical workplace.

*Why do we educate people? We educate people to become good persons . . . and, good persons behave nobly.*

—Plato

# 13

## To Blow or Not to Blow

*If You Blow the Whistle, Blow Wisely!!*

---

*During times of universal deceit, telling the truth becomes a revolutionary act.*

—George Orwell

On August 1, 2007, a major interstate bridge in Minneapolis, Minnesota, the city where I work and live, collapsed during the evening rush hour.

This tragedy resulted in 13 deaths and injured over 100 motorists. Two months later, Minnesota bridge inspector and union official Bart Andersen told Congress that the state lacked the staff and funding to adequately inspect its bridges and guarantee public safety. Minnesota Department of Transportation officials immediately tried to discredit Andersen's testimony as "inaccurate." They then attacked his personal integrity and accused him of being "a union troublemaker." So much for trying to do the right thing! It seemed to be the kind of situation to which German philosopher Goethe was referring when he said, "No good deed goes unpunished."

The term *whistle-blower* has become a catch-all description for any employee who learns of any illegal, unethical, or incompetent activity and reports it. Speaking up may be the right—and even heroic—thing to do; however, it will almost *always* have a negative affect on the whistle-blower's career. Whistle-blowing involves taking on an enormous risk—to both your reputation and your livelihood. You always have to ask yourself, *is doing the right thing always the right thing to do?*

Whistle-blowing is rife with ethical dilemmas and personal risks because it is where the high-minded Public Good collides with trade secrets, corporate egos, and greed. I am inclined to encourage you to seek less destructive or "nuclear" options, as long as they accomplish the same goal.

The job security risk is acute for an employee who does not have much clout or power within the organization, but who is sitting on a time bomb of technical information, inside knowledge, or the "dirty truth" about a particular situation. Ironically, it's often the people at the bottom who find themselves with a bird's-eye view of office shenanigans, illegality, gross waste, mismanagement, abuse of authority, or "substantial and specific danger" to public health or safety.

I asked my *OfficePro* column readers to weigh in with their experiences, and they shared their stories generously. Interestingly, most of them said that they did *not* regret blowing the whistle. Yet, paradoxically, most also stated that if they were in the same scenario in the future, they would handle it differently. They claimed that they would proceed with more forethought and caution, or *might not proceed at all.*

The mere act of "speaking up" can put into play a series of events that are almost impossible to fully anticipate. Your job, family, and even your health may be drawn into the whirlwind. On the flip side, turning a blind eye may cause tremendous guilt and remorse. It's a difficult choice for anyone to make. You must carefully consider the decision to act, and ensure that your family (and attorney) are fully engaged in your decision. As much as I want to encourage you to speak up whenever you see something amiss in the workplace, I also want you to keep yourself financially and professionally safe.

I was thrilled when *Time* magazine named whistle-blowers Sherron Watkins (Enron), Cynthia Cooper (WorldCom), and Coleen Rowley (FBI) 2002's "Persons of the Year." All three were also honored with Mike Oxley and Paul Sarbanes (authors of the Sarbanes-Oxley Act or SOX), which is also known as the Corporate Criminal Fraud

Accountability Act. I agree with those who believe SOX ought to be renamed the "Sherron-Cynthia Law" as a reminder of the very real people behind exposing these corporate high jinks.

Unfortunately, these people are among the small number of winners in the lottery of whistle-blowing, as are the few hundred whistle-blowers who benefited from the $1 billion paid out under the False Claims Act, one of the laws designed to protect these individuals. However, few whistle-blowers end up with a lucrative settlement, a book deal, or the prestige that comes from being on the cover of *Time*. In fact, most whistle-blowers *see their careers end*—despite a patchwork of more than 50 federal whistle-blower and antiretaliation laws, such as SOX, the False Claim Act, and the Whistleblower Protection Act. There are also common-law provisions for wrongful termination at the state level. Alas, it's a crazy quilt of protection, full of overlaps and holes—one that doesn't protect everyone. The people most at risk are those who work in an at-will employment state, and/or work for a privately held company that does not sell to the government.

## Lessons from Other Whistle-Blowers

"You risk everything when you do it," states Jim Alderson, who endured years of exhausting and expensive lawsuits after being terminated for squealing on the nation's largest for-profit hospital chain for Medicare fraud.

Despite the growing body of laws designed to protect employees who raise legitimate concerns, retaliation still occurs—frequently. Just ask the two courageous Federal Aviation Administration (FAA) employees who testified before a congressional committee regarding the FAA's lapse of safety inspections within the airline industry. Both said they were badgered simply for doing their jobs. This brings to mind the admission by U.S. Senator Charles Grassley (R-Iowa), who has cosponsored whistle-blower protections, "Whistle-blowers are as welcome as a skunk at the company picnic."

Retaliation can take many forms: harassment, discrimination, pay cuts, reassignment to bureaucratic Siberia, being buried in paperwork, demotion, declines of all requests for time off—the list goes on and on. Once you blow the whistle, you are marked as a "troublemaker" or "not a team player"—and you have to watch your back.

"This was the most difficult thing I have gone through in my lifetime," said former vice president of internal audit at WorldCom,

Cynthia Cooper, who informed the company's auditor of improper accounting practices. "There were times when I was scared to death." Cooper exposed one of the biggest instances of fraud in corporate history, and in the process, faced years of personal attacks and struggles with depression. Yet she still encourages people to use their personal power to make ethical decisions, however difficult. She emphasizes that "we all have the power of our ethics. No one can take it away from us."

Senior staff administrative assistant at ExxonMobil Development Company, Debbie Bartelsmeyer, wrote:

> I worked for the same company for over 30 years and found myself in a role as a whistle-blower seven or eight years into the job. It certainly had a short-term effect on my career—and possibly a long-term one, too.
>
> When two female geologists filed a sex discrimination complaint with the EEOC [Equal Employment Opportunity Commission], I found myself in the center of the investigation because the EEOC requested an interview with any female employee who had 5–10 years with the company. I was candid with the EEOC representative about the disparities in salary offers that existed—even with the same or similar qualifications—automatic low rankings or salary recommendations for females at salary meetings, and the tendency to give women employees less challenging work assignments. I also cited comments I had overheard my bosses make about female employees. Because of this "inside information," the big boss was immediately kicked off the salary committee and was forced to retire about a year later. The women who introduced the complaint were both transferred to other jobs, and I was promoted out of the group.
>
> The downside was that the job into which I was "promoted" was not a desirable one. I was also blatantly excluded from the big boss's retirement party, which created some awkward moments for a day or two. But even though this chain of events probably had some effect on my longer-term career, I maintain that the benefits exceeded the costs.

Though Debbie did not start the EEOC action, she had the guts to tell the truth when her turn came. Would she do it again? "Sure," she says, "because it was a fight worth fighting."

There are unsung heroes everywhere who struggle anonymously in the trenches of ethical dilemmas every day. Though it's certainly different, a more publicly known hero of mine is Coleen Rowley, the FBI whistle-blower who I am proud to say worked in my home city of Minneapolis. Attorney and long-respected agent Rowley reported on the FBI's failure to act on agents' preexisting information and investigation of terrorist suspect Zacarias Moussaoui after 9/11. Rowley's memo to FBI Director Mueller in May 2002—followed by her blunt congressional testimony to the Senate Judiciary Committee—captivated the nation. Based on her experience, Rowley suggests there are three steps to consider when thinking about whether to blow the whistle:

*Step 1: Discern what the right thing to do is.* This is relatively easy when a contemplated action is clearly criminal (e.g., illegal drugs), violates a clear ethical mandate (e.g., lying), or when the action is right because it's legal and beneficial (e.g., helping others or following the Golden Rule). However, there is a gray area between right and wrong where competing interests sometimes result in "ethical dilemmas" (such as problems involving moral relativism). Rowley believes we should be willing to devote enough thought and reflection, if need be, in consultation with other authorities to make the gray area of moral relativism as thin a line as possible.

*Step 2: Act to do the right thing.* This takes courage because you may have to buck peer or familial pressure, such as when Unabomber Ted Kaczynski's brother contacted law enforcement. However, despite its difficulty, these actions ultimately result in the best outcome for everyone.

*Step 3: Act openly in a constructive manner.* Seize any and all opportunities for constructive action and "teachable moments" in a transparent manner. For example, in the midst of an expensive mistake in a food company (say someone substituted substandard ingredients, which forced the company to issue a product recall), ask, "What have we learned here?" This memorializes the lessons learned while getting people to stop the blame game, and then encourages them to start focusing on the future instead.

As a result of her continued activist actions, the FBI forced Rowley into early retirement. Both Watkins of Enron and Cooper of World-Com lost their jobs when their companies crashed. However, *all three women say they would do it all over again.* But Watkins adds two caveats:

She reports that she would go *directly* to the board of directors at Enron with her concerns instead of going only to Enron chairman Ken Lay. She also adds that she would "never act alone again." It can take some time, Watkins asserts; but in her opinion, it is worth it to find one or two fellow employees to endure the process with you. She states that she "failed to grasp the seriousness of the emperor-has-no-clothes phenomenon. I thought leaders were made in moments of crisis, and I naïvely thought that I would be handing Mr. Lay his leadership moment. I honestly thought people would step up. But I said he was naked, and when he turned to the ministers around him, they said they were sure he was clothed."

## Protection for Whistle-Blowers Is Sketchy

Just being right is not enough these days. Sadly, there are no guarantees you will prevail, or assurances that you will not suffer reprisals. I suggest you immerse yourself in the work of the Government Accountability Project and other nonprofit whistle-blower protection groups. I also suggest that you do the following:

- Exhaust *all* reasonable possibilities of working within the system.
- Obtain legal opinions from attorneys specifically trained in this new subspecialty of employment law.
- Before taking any irreversible steps, talk to your family or close friends about your decision (without revealing specific details about your situation).
- Be alert and discreetly attempt to learn of any other witnesses who are upset about the wrongdoing.
- Develop a plan, such as the strategically timed release of information to government agencies, so your employer is reacting to you, instead of vice versa.
- Maintain good relations with administration and staff.
- Keep a careful record of events as they unfold. Try to construct a straightforward, factual log of the relevant activities and events on the job, keeping in mind that your employer will have access to your diary if there is a lawsuit.
- Identify and copy all necessary supporting records beforehand.
- Don't become isolated. Seek a support network of potential allies, such as elected officials, journalists, and activists.

- Do not embellish your charges.
- Engage in whistle-blowing initiatives on your own time and with your own resources.
- Don't wear your cynicism on your sleeve when working with authorities.
- Recruit others to help you fight the good fight whenever you can.
- If you experience retaliation, do not delay to make a claim, as some of the laws protecting you have time limits as short as 30 days (your attorney will know specifics here).

## Doing the Right Thing for the Right Reasons

I believe we must persistently advocate for a more ethical workplace, even though we may not win all the battles. In my mind, whistle-blowers acting in good faith—*and with the right motivations*—are the heroes of the workplace today. These are the people who see sins of omission or commission and have the courage to take action by speaking up. And isn't this the heart and soul of the Ethical Office?

Ilja Kraag, assistant to David Lerman, MD, JD, in Pasadena, California, says:

> I have been and will be a whistle-blower again, if I need to be. These people have a big heart for the company and are the watchdogs that prevent or interrupt anything that can hurt the organization. That can range from colleagues stealing supplies, supervisors claiming nonexisting expenses, lying to customers, falsifying records, and similar misbehavior. A whistle-blower does not look for petty information to use to get even with colleagues or supervisors they don't like.

Ilja raises an excellent point here: for every hero who is motivated by advancing an ethical workplace, there are, unfortunately, those who are motivated by the wrong reasons.

This is why you must be certain that your motives are above reproach. If you are due for a poor performance review, are competing for a promotion, or are about to receive your final bad-conduct notice, your self-interests compromise your ethical stance. Honestly, is your conscience clear? Expect to be asked if you have participated in conduct similar to that you are complaining about, and to be quizzed on whether you have an axe to grind because of a promotion recently denied or pending allegations against you. Expect to be challenged with the charge that you are filing a false claim.

Finally, consider these four criteria to distinguish "tattletaling" from "whistle-blowing":

1. *The issue must be significant.* A classmate telling on another classmate about a stolen pencil may not be an ethical imperative, but a Columbine-type situation of overhearing a classmate threaten to bring weapons to school certainly qualifies.

2. *Your statement must be truthful and essentially right,* despite the fact that in many cases there is no way of anyone having perfect intelligence or completely objective knowledge of all of the pertinent facts.

3. *Your motivation must not be to promote self-interest, but to promote the interest (safety, etc.) of others or the public.* Coleen Rowley confirmed this point when she and I watched President George W. Bush's former press secretary, Scott McClellan, testify at a congressional hearing together. I was presenting a seminar in Boston with Coleen, and we saw his testimony on TV in our suite before going down for the session. McClellan was being called a "whistle-blower" at the time. Coleen turned to me and said, "Nan, he is *not* a true whistle-blower—because he has written a book which he is selling (and promoting) for profit!"

4. *The action taken must be done in the most constructive, positive way for all involved.* No personal vendettas or attacks. If the matter can be resolved without anyone's taking a serious fall, then that's all the better.

## Final Considerations: The Big Picture

More often than not, whistle-blowing takes a toll on our professional, personal, and family lives. It is shocking to discover the extent to which companies will go to protect their interests. You will be bruised by the process—and possibly by retaliation.

Another thing that makes whistle-blowing so challenging is that it involves taking a rigorous personal moral inventory. You're forced to ask yourself: "Can I live with myself if I choose to do nothing?" You must then ask yourself if you are willing to take the risks and pay the price—and you may well answer "no" or "not now." My advice is to acknowledge this and leave it at that. Don't try to rationalize your unwillingness to move forward by whitewashing the original cause of your concern. In other words, don't try to justify your unwillingness to act by painting a wrong as a right. That will simply erode your own ethical standards. I believe doing the right thing is its own reward—and that may be all the reward you need.

*Bridges in America should not fall down!*
                                    —U.S. Senator Amy Klobuchar

# Part III

# Take Care of Your Supervisor

# 14

## The Trouble with the Boss—Is the Boss!

*When the President does it, it's not a crime!*
—President Richard M. Nixon in a 1977 interview
with TV host David Frost, defending his involvement
in the Watergate scandal

### That Was Then; This Is What Happens Now

In a workshop for law firm administrators, a group at one of my tables debated how they would rein in a partner known for his "colorful" but inappropriate language. Employees who complained to the administrators did not feel that the partner was directing his behavior toward them individually; they were simply upset about having to constantly overhear such offensive language.

The legal administrators at this table agreed on the direct approach: tell the partner about the complaints, and ask him to clean up his act—pronto. Case solved.

Suddenly, one of the administrators at another table was on his feet. "Nice idea," he said, "but what if he's the *rainmaker?*"

The next thing we knew, all you-know-what broke loose!

The *rainmaker* is the term that many individuals and corporations use for the primary moneymaker—the person who brings in the most profitable clients. Rainmakers are revered, sometimes even coddled, because without them the company may fold!

Once the melee settled down, the administrators unanimously agreed that you *still* have to sit down with Mr. Rainmaker to explain that employees are complaining about his bad language, how it is affecting their work, and how this situation—if not curbed—might result in a costly and hostile environment lawsuit. Remember to follow your Ethical Compass: First, protect your job by doing the right thing in spite of this individual's privileged status. Second, try to protect your company by averting a potential legal problem. Finally, third in line, you can at least attempt to protect your boss from himself!

Yes, this is a special case because the rainmaker is involved; however, his actions should receive only special scrutiny, not extra leeway. The rainmaker is an obvious target because courts today favor the person with the *least* amount of power, and the rainmaker has all the power. After all, he *is* the boss!

## Ethical Dilemmas with Your Boss

You and your boss have a unique relationship that can be described accordingly: (1) your boss is capable of being wrong, just like everyone else; and (2) because of (1), you have more power than you think you do to affect your boss's ethical (or unethical) decisions.

Your boss is actually the very first person you should talk to about an ethical dilemma in your workplace. While honest, open communication between supervisors and their employees does not necessarily guarantee a good, productive work team, there certainly isn't a prayer for an effective working relationship *without* this kind of mutually candid interaction. John Gardner, president of the nonprofit organization Common Cause, put it this way: "There must be not only easy communication from leaders to constituents but, also, ample *return* communication—*including* dissent!"

You need to learn how to talk to your boss about your ethical dilemmas; it's required for you to be successful in your job. You must also give your manager a fair chance to respond and help you with any conundrum in which you find yourself that you cannot solve. And return the favor by watching her back; don't allow her to be blind-sided with an ethical problem that's headed her way. Instead, grant her the professional courtesy of having a "heads-up" conversation with you.

## The Unique Boss/Assistant Relationship Is Unique to Its Own

I've heard about the following dilemma in one form or another many times, usually in a private conversation in the corners of one of my seminars. It captures the essence of the personal and nuanced relationship of trust that can exist only between an assistant and boss:

Dear Nan:

I am the executive assistant for Mr. D, the CEO of a successful company with about 400 employees. Mr. D is a well-respected businessman within our organization and the community. For the past 15 years, we have developed a professional working relationship based on trust and mutual respect. My job description includes responsibilities of a personal nature: for example, handling his personal financial records, appointment calendar, personal and professional travel plans, along with duties related to his commitments to outside boards and trade and civic associations.

Mr. D told me in confidence about six months ago that he was planning to divorce his wife. He did not even have to ask me not to share this information with anyone else; he knows our professional relationship would preclude such an action.

I have become concerned, however. Within the scope of my assistant responsibilities, I have assisted him in the transfer of titles of ownership of several major assets. I have also helped him open new bank accounts, and set up trust accounts for his children and several other people with whom I am not familiar. I've even arranged a storage locker for him.

While all of these activities appear to be technically legal, I am getting a "gut feeling" that Mr. D may possibly be in the process of hiding his assets in preparation for his impending divorce. I've applied your Ethical Compass and your common sense tests,

*(continued)*

*(continued)*

and have concluded this situation is a bona fide ethical dilemma that is affecting my work. I know my best way to resolve this is to talk directly to Mr. D about this, since no one else can help me—but I don't even know how to start. Can you help me?

—Lauren in Middleton, CT

Lauren, you are correct. This requires a thoughtful, calm, one-on-one conversation with your boss; you owe him that. However, your biggest problem here is that you don't even know if there *is* a problem; at this point, it's merely a suspicion on your part. If you started a discussion about this dilemma in an unplanned, emotional way—and your boss is completely innocent in this activity—you could be essentially (and incorrectly) calling your boss of many years a liar, a thief, and a scoundrel of a husband to boot—none of which sounds too good! Or let's say that you stormed into his office and confronted him with your suspicions, and his intentions *have* been unscrupulous. He is quite likely to respond with anger, defensiveness, and denial, and may well challenge you by asking, "What in the world are you talking about?" Needless to say, your working relationship would go south in a big hurry.

Therefore, here are a few suggestions of actions to take before Lauren—or anyone—engages in such a confrontation:

1. Make a detailed list of all the transactions and similar activities you have handled that have contributed to your suspicions. Amass as much evidence as possible that provides reasoning for your concerns. When the person you're confronting asks why or challenges you on this, you'll have the answers ready and can hopefully avoid feeling (too) flustered.

2. *Protect yourself legally by sharing the list with your attorney (not his, and not the company's).* If your attorney determines that your boss is indeed asking you to do something illegal, then you have a different problem altogether. Follow your Ethical Compass and do what you must in order to take care of yourself before you go any further out on a legal limb for your boss. As good a boss as Mr. D may be, he is unlikely to put your best interests before his own in this situation.

If counsel's advice is that there is no problem with your activities, then proceed as follows:

3. *You can choose to simply do your job, keep mum and let the situation unfold.* You *always* have this choice. However, it can be risky since you are "bothered by the situation."

4. *Pick a good time and sit down with your boss to discuss the fact that "something has been bothering" you.* This has to be a thoughtful, calm, one-on-one conversation. Set your frustration aside and give him the benefit of the doubt until you learn how he wants to deal with your ethical dilemma.

5. *Show your boss the detailed list you made, as instructed in Number 1.* This is important because sometimes people get so caught up in their personal drama du jour that they don't realize they are drawing other people too far into their plans. You are simply pointing out your (critical) involvement.

6. *Say something like this:* "Mr. D, you have told me you are planning to divorce your wife some time in the future. I have kept this confidential, and will continue to do so. However, you have asked me to handle the following list of transactions over the past few weeks. These activities are starting to make me feel *uncomfortable*. I'm aware that assistants are often subpoenaed as a witness in divorce proceedings and, if I ever were, I would be bound to reveal these activities. I'm worried and distracted by this situation, and it's starting to affect my job performance. Can we talk about this?" I guarantee that a lightbulb will go on in your boss's head; he'll back off and pull you right out of the equation.

7. If he still persists and/or plays the "but I really need you now" or "it's in your job description" cards, you have to push back and insist you remain out of his personal situation. Your reason again should be "because I may have to be held accountable some day."

Note that you haven't actually accused Mr. D of anything in the above process, nor have you judged him. You have not been confrontational, but merely said you are "uncomfortable." You've presented the facts as you see them, which are an ethical dilemma for you: that your accountability may be at stake. Your feelings of vulnerability, guilt, conflicted loyalties, and so on are *your* feelings, not his. Therefore, it's unreasonable to expect him to change his behavior just because you feel badly. But he will most likely disconnect you from the circumstances if you "package" your dilemma as an unnecessary risk to his interests. When you extract yourself from this situation, you have achieved your goal. If you later decide you no longer respect this man as a person, and can no longer work for him, then you can move on with a clear conscience.

## Power versus Ethics

A conversation about ethics should be the logical starting point for resolving a dilemma. But if it's done carelessly or thoughtlessly, it could also be the beginning of the end of your relationship with this person. And the stakes are even higher when "this person" is your boss. Always keep in mind that *you run a high risk of offending the other person when you initiate a discussion about ethics, and consequently jeopardizing your working relationship along with your job security.*

We know intuitively that however we couch our language or tiptoe around the point, the core message of a discussion about ethics will come through loud and clear: "I have a problem with your behavior, and I'm talking to you because I want you to help me make this problem go away."

Though you may not like it, your success on the job largely depends on the success of your interpersonal relationship with your boss. If you work well together, great; but if you don't, you are probably both miserable.

You cannot change the fundamental power relationship with your supervisor; it's just a simple reality. The good news, though, is that the interpersonal dimension of your relationship is elastic. You can improve it by changing how you talk to, treat, and work with each other.

## Only *You* Can Launch the Ethical Conversation

I suggest you have this kind of conversation with your new boss while you're still in the "honeymoon days" of getting to know each other. Before any conflict arises, say something to your boss along the lines of, "I would like us to have an honest and direct style of communication with one another. I hope to have the kind of relationship whereby we both feel free to compliment and constructively criticize each other. I want you to let me know when I have done something well, and I want you to tell me when I have not met your expectations. I would like to hear these things right away, instead of saving them all up for my six-month performance review. This kind of continuous feedback helps me get better at my job on a *daily* basis. Likewise, I would appreciate it if I could give *you* feedback about when we are and are not working well together. ..." You get the idea. What manager *wouldn't* want this kind of high-quality communication?

## Truth-Telling Discussions Are Not Easy

"Right versus wrong" discussions are difficult to keep on point; they're full of words that everyone defines differently and plagued by the syndrome of "let's-hurry-up-and-get-this-over-with." Ethical issues can be so volatile, so explosive, that once we've started the discussion, we have to finish it—however messy and destructive it becomes. We can't very well say, "Oops! Sorry, boss. On second thought, and after observing that you're not taking this very well, why don't we just forget that I brought this up?" Sorry; you've already opened Pandora's box, and now your boss is having all kinds of (probably erroneous) thoughts about your questioning his ethics.

Ethical discussions are difficult. This causes us to avoid them, which in turns causes them to remain difficult. That's why we hold back and fail to confront the issue, and why we sometimes continue too long in our role of "supportive helpmate." When we finally get to the point at which we're boiling up inside and absolutely *have* to say something, we're rarely as rational or as professional as we need to be. And "mind reading" is not a reasonable quality to include in a job description!

## The Trouble with Talking to Your Boss

In a perfect world, genteel conversations would be all that were required to solve all our ethical dilemmas. All bosses would be nice, logical, and reasonable people who shared common values with you, and who were just as interested as you are in doing the right thing.

In the real world, however, your boss may be part of the problem. Because you work so closely—and she's higher on the office food chain—it's likely that many or most of your dilemmas will actually *come from* her. For example:

- *Your manager starts the problem* by either behaving unethically and/or asking you to do something unethical.
- *Your manager tolerates the problem,* thereby making it worse. Here are a few such responses:
  - "It's not your job to worry about this."
  - "It's not my job to worry about that."
  - "The law does not require us to be concerned with that."
  - "I can't because _____ (fill in the excuse)."
  - "I'm paid for getting the right results, not using the right process."
  - "I don't want to rock the boat; let's go along to get along."
  - Or the classic, "This is just the way we do things around here." And its close cousins, "We've always done it like this" and "It's just the way it is."
- *Your manager ignores or minimizes the problem* by pretending it doesn't exist. This response is one of denial and/or attacking the messenger (which would unfortunately be *you*).

This sounds like:

- "I don't believe you."
- "It's not that bad."
- "If it's such a big deal, let human resources handle it." Translation: upward delegation, or passing the buck to anyone else.
- "I don't even know what you're talking about."
- "Are you sure you're not overreacting?" Or its twin, "Are you sure you're not imagining this?"
- And the most hurtful, "Why are you making such an issue of this anyhow? What's *your* agenda?"

*Your manager sets a bad example.* We all pay attention to the explicit and implied cues that those with whom we work send out. We naturally look to managers for guidance about what is and is not acceptable. Their actions communicate the behavior that is expected in the workplace and let us know what it takes to get ahead. We tend to mimic the patterns that managers set because these examples are stronger than any written policy or set of notes from an ethics program. If ethics are genuinely important to management, it's likely everyone else in the organization will care about this issue as well.

However, when a manager denies her responsibility to be an ethical leader and standard-setter, she abdicates her authority and turns her back on an opportunity to create a positive ethically professional environment. I often hear from employees who claim to have quit a job they really liked solely because their ethics clashed with their boss's. They usually add the words, "And I knew it would always be that way." People notice what managers do and don't do about ethics violations.

## Why Do They Do It?

No surprises here; while managers are not ignorant of their influence on the ethical environment, they get trapped, pressured, and tempted just like everyone else. My surveys reflect these responses as the top reasons they compromise their ethical standards.

**They claim that they do it to:**
- Meet schedules
- Meet overly aggressive financial or business objectives
- Make *their* boss look good
- Beat their peers
- Defeat the competition
- Keep their jobs
- Get a good performance review

Do you think an informal discussion with your boss will be sufficient to resolve a dilemma of which he or she is a part? Hopefully! Judd Ringer, the one and only boss I've ever had, always said, "Nan, don't ever come into my office with a problem unless you also have a solution!" And I always followed that rule! He didn't always take my suggestions, but I was able to air—and ultimately solve—my problems. He taught me well to be proactive.

In some cases, however, you may need a more formal and structured process to follow. Fortunately, I've designed and provided one for you.

# Nan DeMars's 12-Step Program to Keep Your Boss Ethical

Imagine that your boss has asked you to do something you believe to be unethical. Take the following steps in order to "manage upward" and resolve the dilemma:

*Step 1: Pick a good (meaning convenient and comfortable for both of you) time and place to discuss your disagreement.* Just as you wouldn't schedule a meeting with your boss about an ethical problem the same day she just lost her biggest client, you also wouldn't have such a meeting out in the receptionist area either.

*Step 2: Thank your boss for taking the time to meet with you.* Tell her how much you appreciate her willingness to continue your effective working relationship and how much you value the open relationship the two of you have developed.

*Step 3: Define your ethical expectations again.* You (hopefully) did this at the time you were hired; now, do it again, clearly and simply. Remind her of the earlier agreement you made to tell each other when something is bothering you about your working relationship. You can acknowledge that, while her standards may differ from yours, you wish to have her respect for your parameters as well.

*Step 4: Lay out the dilemma in clear, simple terms without being accusatory.* Always keep in mind that this is the situation *as you see it*, which may not be how she sees it or even the concrete facts.

*Step 5: Give your boss a chance to retract her request.* Replay the request accordingly, "Am I to understand you wish me to tape a telephone conversation this afternoon with a client without the client's knowledge?" In other words, clearly state your understanding of her unethical request "so that there is no misunderstanding." Seeing her request through your eyes may be a wake-up call for her, and enough to cause her to back off and save face. ("No, I didn't mean that . . . oh, never mind.") This enables her to think twice about what she's doing and gives her the opportunity to change her mind without embarrassment. If taking these steps does not solve the situation, it is time to up the ante.

*Step 6: Tell your boss you are concerned about this dilemma* because your goal is to protect her reputation and that of the company.

*Step 7: Say "no" to the request you find objectionable and state your reason, the best being: "Because I may have to be held liable."* This not only puts you squarely in the accountability loop; it also puts the dilemma on hold and reopens the discussion. Remain firm in your decision despite any difficulty. Chances are that if you had to proceed this far, your boss will probably become angry and uncomfortable—after all, you're challenging her authority. However, you won't be asked again until this is resolved. Your objective is to use this opportunity to declare your position and negotiate a resolution to your dilemma, even if you have complied with her unethical requests in the past.

Just saying "no" is not enough, however. You can be fired for insubordination unless you clearly and credibly base your refusal to obey her instructions on the foundation that to do otherwise would violate the law or your religious beliefs. However, most situations will not be that clear-cut. So, follow up immediately with the steps below; these are likely to result in a win-win outcome.

*Step 8: Reiterate your wish to protect her reputation as well as the company's.* After all, this is the very reason that this dilemma is concerning you. Again, keep it simple, and try not to be accusatory.

*Step 9: Ask questions.* Acknowledge that you may have misunderstood the situation, and give her ample opportunity to provide an explanation or clarify the details. Again, it is possible you don't have all—or even the correct—information. For example, you may think your boss is feeding the company's insurance business to her best golfing buddy when, in actuality, this buddy is providing special service as well as competitive rates.

*Step 10: Suggest a solution that is agreeable to both of you.* This is your time to become proactive. Your boss may never have thought of your brilliant solution to the problem and be delighted to accept it. Case solved!

*Step 11: Be sure to ask for a commitment to action.* You don't want to walk away from the meeting wondering where you stand or what's going to happen next.

*Step 12: Always thank your boss* for listening and making an effort to work together on this matter of mutual concern.

## How to Keep Your Job *and* Your Relationship with Your Boss

One of the most difficult tasks an office professional has is making the boss realize that "no" is a complete sentence.

You have to keep trying. You have to believe that your boss can change her mind. Even if earlier attempts to "talk this thing through" yielded only unhappy consequences, a few of your arguments just might have gotten through. Maybe your boss has reconsidered and tempered her position, or maybe there are sufficient incentives—like the threat of a lawsuit by another person due to a similar dilemma—that will cause your boss to return to the discussion and try to work out some sort of an understanding. Whatever your reasons, I applaud your efforts to persist. I wish I could personally pin a medal on each and every one of you who continue to fight for what is right.

Did you comply or not comply with her request? Did you clam up and do it, divorcing yourself from the act with some rationalization like, "No one is getting hurt anyway, so why not?" or "I have to do it to keep my job"? Close your eyes and let her rip off the company knowing that questioning her actions would cost you your job? Use your knowledge for leverage in the future? Or did you challenge her to get her act together and do the right thing? Attempt to "fix" her, or save her from herself or rehabilitate her? Turn her into the ethics police in your company?

What hurts most in these situations, of course, is that she asked you to do the deed in the first place. The act of making the request communicates volumes; it tells you that she apparently doesn't understand you, which means you've misjudged the relationship, or her—or both. Does she perceive you as a coconspirator, a person willing to do these things without a second thought? Does she think you don't care or won't notice? Does she think you're too dense to catch on? Or maybe she views your opinions and concerns as unimportant?

The reality is that you may have to do the distasteful deed (providing it's not illegal) "one last time" to avert a company crisis, operating under the agreement that your boss will work with you to resolve the dilemma at the earliest opportunity. You are not saying "no" just to be difficult; rather, you are using this incident to get her attention and begin a discussion. So when your boss wants to know why you won't do what she's asked you to do, grab this chance to tell her. This is the time to redefine yourself in your boss's mind—starting by covering the basics again (e.g., you're committed to helping her succeed by building an ethical office). Who knows? Maybe she was distracted or simply didn't have time to listen when you said it the first time, or she didn't take you seriously. Stuff happens.

## Now, a Few Tips about Your Style

**You can make your discussions with your boss more effective if you:**

- *Avoid becoming defensive or emotional.* If you find this happening, you may have to take a "time out" and arrange another meeting. Emotions can hinder the potential for an objective discussion and may cause your boss to take you less seriously.
- *Avoid getting sidetracked.* It would be easy for you and your boss to spend a lot of time talking about other aspects of the business, but now is not the time. Stay focused on the dilemma about which you're concerned.
- *Avoid sounding "holier than thou."* Example: "I would never *think* of doing something like that" is a bit intemperate; perhaps "I wonder if that's the best thing to do" is gentler.
- *Never give the impression that you do not care* or that ethical compromises can be made. You now are personally involved in developing your company's reputation for ethics and integrity. You *do* care; that's why you're sitting there!
- *Avoid using the word you in an accusatory way.* You are not the judge and jury, so frame your statements in neutral terms when you can. Example: Instead of saying, "You are handling the client poorly," it would be more constructive to say, "Would it help if we handled the client differently? How about this way?"
- *Avoid using judgmental words,* such as *should, have to, wrong, always,* and *never.* Example: "You should never have done that. It was wrong." Scolding the boss or accusing him of being unethical triggers defensiveness on his part. Like most of us, when your boss feels like he is being judged, he is likely to dig in his heels to defend his actions, even though it's irrational to defend the indefensible. Then, you waste time trying to persuade him to agree with your judgment. It is not necessary that you see the situation exactly the same; just focus on a solution.

- *Avoid using emotionally charged words*, such as *hate, furious, fed up*, and so on.
- *When you've finished pleading your case, stop talking!* There's a famous story about U.S. Senator Bob Dole, who once stood up on the Senate floor while a fellow senator was delivering an unbelievably lengthy oratory on why his bill deserved support. Frustrated, Dole simply said, "Would the respected senator please sit down—while some of us are still *for* your bill!" In sales, you quit talking when the customer is ready to buy.
- *Remember, your objective is to continue to build trust and a sense of teamwork with your boss.* You are demonstrating that you can address, discuss and even resolve tough dilemmas in a professional way with no lingering hard feelings.

Finally, if you absolutely must end your relationship with your boss, do so in a professional manner by stating your reasons honestly. However, resigning should *always* be your last resort.

## Sara's Story

Here's a true story that comes from Sara, one of my seminar attendees. I don't make this stuff up, folks; I hear everything. . . .

Sara was administrative assistant to the president/CEO of a medium-sized printing company. One day, her boss asked her if she would take over the payroll supervisor's responsibilities while he was on vacation for two weeks, and Sara accepted the responsibilities. When the day arrived for her to handle the payroll tasks, she observed that several of the firm's officers (including her boss) had listed their home addresses as being in a neighboring state. Since Sara knew these individuals resided year-round in the town near the plant, she questioned her boss the next day about the bogus addresses. He quickly brushed it off as a trivial matter that was not even worth discussing (ever been there?). Sara thought about the situation further and soon returned to press the issue. She had decided she was ready to get to the bottom of this, no matter what. Her boss sheepishly replied, "Well, you know the tax situation in [the neighboring state] is much more lenient than it is here."

Clang! Sara's ethics alarm sounded loud and clear. She was now privy to something her officers were doing that "was probably illegal."

Though she hadn't wanted to get involved, like it or not, she now knew about the tax evasion scheme. She said she went home and worried all night about the situation. She also shared with me that she was "the breadwinner in my family" and could "not afford to lose my job."

Nevertheless, Sara bit the bullet and did the right thing for herself. She went into her boss's office the next day and tactfully but firmly forced her boss to discuss this dilemma. (She also added she wished she had had my guidelines at the time because she had to just "wing it on my own.") I was proud of her for taking such action.

Though her boss bristled and huffed and puffed, in the end, he said there was nothing that Sara could say or do that would cause the officers to change their practice. He informed her that doing so would cost them all huge sums in back taxes and penalties (no kidding!), not to mention the humiliation (bad press) and expense that would come along with admitting and correcting their scheme. Sara chose not to blow the whistle on them—despite the fact that she certainly had a case—because, as she told me, "My reality at the time was that hurting the company would have had a direct, negative impact on my personal livelihood." But she also told me that because she was aware of this illegal practice, she refused to be involved with the payroll responsibilities anymore.

Sara's boss didn't fire her; instead, he simply removed her from the payroll responsibilities (she thinks he took them over himself for the two-week period). In a perfect world, Sara would have taken an active role to bring her bosses to justice. But, as we well know, this isn't a perfect world. She did not call the authorities. Sara had lost respect for her boss (and the other officers involved), though, and eventually left the company on her own volition. I was proud that Sara got out of there, even though I personally worry that she still may be asked to testify about her knowledge of this illegal activity at some time in the future.

## Summary

The trouble with the boss will always be that he (or she) *is* the boss! So, like it or not, this person has a lot more power than you do. Your job satisfaction, quality of work life, advancement opportunities, job security, compensation, and benefits depend on how satisfied your supervisor is with your performance. This relationship will always be the centerpiece of your job.

For the obvious reasons of authority, access to information, contact with others, and so on, the manager sometimes appears to be the only one in the office who can raise or lower the ethical standards. This is not true, however—and *you* are not without influence! You and your boss still have the power to positively impact each other. Your boss communicates his feelings about company rules, courtesy, fairness, honesty, respect, and integrity by his example—and *you do too*. You also convey your feelings by how you respond to his directions. Acknowledging this is a good starting place.

Sometimes, an informal discussion about a particular situation's ethics will regrettably not be enough to resolve it. The situation may escalate until your employer-employee relationship is at risk. This chapter looked at informal and structured approaches you can use that may lead to a satisfactory remedy of your dilemma. Each step in these processes comes with a price, however, as each one extracts an increasingly greater price from you—and there is never a guarantee that it will all be worth it in the end. Though moral victory is sweet, you can't put it in the bank, and you probably don't want to put "troublemaker" or "ethics enforcer" on your resume.

This is my empowerment message: You have some power in this situation, probably more power than you believe you have right now. Be bold! Okay, so maybe you are not as powerful as your boss, but you are not completely power*less*, either. You can choose to move either toward or away from a more ethical working relationship with your boss simply by deciding how you are going to act and react. You have the choice, so you have the power to change this partnership for the better. The trick (as always) will be to do it in a professional and not self-destructive manner. And I promise—this fight is usually worth it! In almost every case where I have seen an otherwise confident and competent colleague back away from an ethics fight, she or he came to regret it. Again, German philosopher Goethe got it right: "We become that which we tolerate."

> *A no is a no is a no. And couching it in pretty talk doesn't change it to yes, correct, or affirmative.*
>
> —Gertrude Stein

# 15

## The Dog Ate My Laptop

### *Lies, Lies—and More Lies!*

---

*A lie gets halfway around the world ... before the truth has a
chance to get its pants on!*
> —Winston Churchill, prime minister of England
> (50 years *before* the Internet)

---

Dear Nan:

Help! I have just come from a management meeting I attended
with my boss, a project manager. He received many questions
about a project in which we are involved, and he fudged on every
single answer. Worse than that, he outright lied in response to
some. He is not only lying to the team, but also to his boss,
the company president. He is trying to cast a good light on the
progress of the project by saying we are further along than we

*(continued)*

> *(continued)*
>
> are. However, I also know I cannot continue to work with him when I know he has been so deceptive to our teammates. Should I just mind my own business? After all, he is the boss!
>
> —Bob in accounting, Philadelphia, PA

According to my ongoing surveys, lying for the boss continues to be the number one ethical dilemma employees face in the workplace today. The good news, however, is that the problem is diminishing as a result of both diminished requests *and* compliance.

In response to the question above, virtually 100 percent of my readers declared that they would never lie for their boss, and reiterated their belief that "honesty is always the best policy." We all know desperate times often make people push the ethical envelope, so I commend these individuals for refusing to compromise their ethics to keep their jobs—especially during this economic downturn. Make no mistake: you do *not* have to lie to stay employed.

## Let's Face It: A Lie by Any Other Name Is Still a Lie!

I have yet to hear a justifiable reason to ask an employee to lie for his or her boss, and I have never heard an employee satisfactorily explain why she or he absolutely *had* to do so. Even the "white lie" about the boss's whereabouts can be circumvented with a simple reply of, "She's unavailable," followed by an offer to pass on the message (and if you recall, for security reasons, you don't want to disclose her location anyway!). I believe the adage: *If you tell a lot of white lies, you soon become color-blind!*

However, with mounting fears over job security nowadays, many employees may be more ready to cover for the boss despite what their moral compass tells them. Their logic dictates that protecting their boss's job may, by default, safeguard their own.

But a lie is only a short-term fix. It's a bad habit that causes even more trouble and an illusion that serves no one well. Randy Cohen, author of the *New York Times Magazine*'s Ethicist column, states that even the small lies you brush off can snowball and eventually damage your reputation. Cohen explains that, "It's seldom you get an explicit deal from the devil; these things tend to 'creep up' on people. I'm sure that for the most part, these lies are extremely minor and easy to justify, but once you kill the first guy, it's not so hard to kill the second."

All lies—whatever they are, and whatever your reason for telling them—are *intentionally deceptive* messages. They are explicitly intended to mislead. There are two primary ways to lie: to conceal and to falsify. *Concealing* requires that the liar withhold information without actually saying anything untrue. When *falsifying*, the liar goes one step further and not only withholds information, but also presents false information as if it were true. Bob's boss is doing both!

What *is* the truth—and whose version of the truth is it? Truth telling *can* be a minefield of contradictions, excuses, vagueness, justifications, and self-deceptions—but it usually isn't. Most liars know exactly what they are doing, even when they're confused about why they are doing it. Once you take away the honest misunderstandings due to dropped cell phone calls, misused words, and other broken communications, what you have remaining are intentional efforts to mislead, confuse, or divert. And no matter what you call 'em, they're still lies.

## So What If I Lie? Does It *Really* Matter?

While I do not believe that *all* lies are inherently or automatically evil, I am strongly biased against them for several reasons. First, I believe lying almost always produces negative consequences. Furthermore, I believe the truth will almost always serve personal and organizational needs better than a lie. Truth, as I am using it here, is the moral truth that is specific to the context and content of a conversation between two people and limited to the question: is someone deliberately misleading another person with false statements?

Consider the negative consequences of lies just in the case of professional communications. The lies themselves cause all sorts of mushrooming mischief and damage, such as poor decisions based on incorrect information. In addition, the liar is constantly worried about getting caught because if he is, his reputation will suffer. Even if he doesn't get caught, he must frequently continue to lie in order to conceal the original deception. Worry and anxiety about being discovered—and subsequent energy to cover up the first lie with supporting deception—can take a horrendous toll on a person's and organization's productivity.

I am sure that most of us would agree that truthfulness is generally preferable to untruthfulness. My favorite philosopher, Aristotle, articulated the "doctrine of the golden mean." Good ole "Ari" preached the virtue of moderation in all things, arguing against the application of one-answer-fits-all rules. He gives us the basis for our common-sense ethics test, aka *the test of reasonableness.*

Lying undermines relationships by undermining trust, and trust is what forms the foundation of our professional, cooperative relationships. Less trust means less constructive communication, and that means less of everything that is good and productive. In short, there is a direct connection between lying and a negative impact on the organization's economic health. These negative outcomes make lies very difficult to justify. So does it matter if you lie? You *bet* it does!

## Is It Always Morally Wrong to Lie?

No, not always. (Now how's *that* from Ms. Ethics?!) I believe there are at least two situations in which a person is morally justified to lie—in other words, when their lies can be defended as just, right, or proper by providing adequate reasons. If a lie is morally justifiable, a liar can take comfort in the judgment that he did nothing ethically wrong. This is a tough standard to meet, however; thus, the list of justifiable lies is short.

Generally, the only lies deemed morally free of blame and guilt are the very *trivial* and the very *serious* lies. Everything in between is a violation of society's ethical code to "always tell the truth." This was Aristotle's view and that of many other philosophers.

## Is a Lie Ever Justified?

To give good reason for lying, the person doing the deceiving must be able to explain his lie in such a way that other *reasonable people* would agree with him that a lie was the best solution to a particular dilemma. This is the "publicity test" whereby *the reason for the lie is judged to be reasonable by reasonable people.* For instance, most reasonable people would find it justifiable to lie to a gunman holding hostages in a bank lobby. "If it saves some lives, tell him whatever he needs to hear" would be a rational reaction that falls under the category of "whatever it takes." Additional justification would be: Lying to a liar doesn't count! Moral absolutists, however, would argue that it is still morally wrong, no matter what the circumstances. These people would contend that "the absolute truth" will always be a better solution. In the case of the hostages in the bank lobby, absolutists might make a case that the gunman is mentally unstable, and that any attempt to lie—should the gunman detect it—would result in even more people being killed.

I'm on the side of the "reasonable" argument. I find public scrutiny to be a reliable and useful way to link personal moral behavior with the community's standards. It is, in my opinion, the best way to identify deceptive practices and separate the justifiable lies from the indefensible ones.

Justification for a lie *cannot* be a discussion between the liar and his conscience. The liar's perspective is distorted, and his evaluation will be flimsy and self-serving. Of course, he would quite naturally attempt to trivialize the impact of his lie or attempt to blow it out of proportion by presenting it as "the only possible way" to save innocent lives from a horrible fate. For this reason, any justification must involve other reasonable people who can more accurately mirror the community's values and morals. Let's reiterate a few public disclosure questions with *reasonable people*:

- Is there any behavior or action taking place in the office that you would be embarrassed to see reported in the media?
- Are you being asked to do something contrary to your industry's professional standards?
- Is there anything going on in your workplace that you would feel uncomfortable explaining to your mother-in-law? Your kids? How about your grandma?

If you can't justify a lie to these reasonable people, then your lie is unethical. That doesn't mean you aren't going to do it, and it doesn't mean you don't have a good reason to do it that satisfies *you*, at least. However, you must be aware that your lie is probably unethical according to community standards. Maybe just knowing that you are stepping over the boundary of ethical behavior is enough to cause you to change your behavior; maybe not. But at the very least, *you should be fully aware of what you are doing.*

## Little White Lies

What about this oft-defended category of deceit? Like the lie to prevent serious harm, I believe that many of these are morally justifiable, too. My definition of a "little white lie" is pretty narrow, though. The lie must really be "little"—meaning that it's about something of trivial or no consequence, and causes absolutely no harm to anyone. However, the level of "harmlessness" is always open to debate. A liar will often downplay the harm he thinks his lie may cause, and might sometimes even try to couch it as something beneficial. You can test a lie's justification by asking one simple question: *How would the person being deceived feel about the lie?*

Telling "little white lies" or "fibettes" is sometimes necessary to save someone from embarrassment or social discomfort—in other words, to be polite. This happens all the time when, for instance, someone asks, "Do you like my new haircut?" and you say "Yes," even though you are really thinking, "Why would you ever do *that* to yourself?" While lying to spare someone's feelings or extricate yourself from an awkward situation isn't always nice, it can be expedient and justifiable. A "little white lie" is also different from a "regular lie" because of the liar's motive. The former is told with good intentions, while the latter is told with selfishness. Again, reasonable people will disagree about where that line is and whether the liars can accurately discern their true motives; for example, are they lying to their boss out of kindness, or are they "sucking up" to ingratiate themselves for favors later?

I can also defend minor lies when I believe that they can protect others from harm, especially the emotional kind. At the risk of being deemed "Minnesota Nice," consider what life would be like without the social graces that these trivial fibs make possible. The hostess would know exactly what we thought of the evening's meal; the mother would get the unvarnished truth about her not-so-cute baby; the child would hear the so-called truth about his or her would-be athletic abilities—just imagine the resulting self-esteem problems! Life would be rougher than it already is, and relationships would be much more difficult to maintain.

## Serious Lies

At the other end of the spectrum is the lie that we can defend because it prevents serious harm. The test here is to ask the question: *Does this lie protect the greater good?* For example, a thief comes up to your drugstore counter and demands to know if there are any other employees in the store. There are three hiding in the back room, but you say "no." The justification for this lie, of course, is it's okay to lie to a liar! And you're clearly guarding your employees' safety, so there's no question here.

## "White Lies" via the Telephone

Now, let's return to a workplace-specific situation. We are familiar with the "telephone white lie," which requires that we tell a caller someone is "out of the office" when they are clearly "in the office." This everyday dilemma remains a pesky challenge for 63 percent of my survey respondents. But I hope many of you have learned (and now practice) the priceless word *unavailable*. Stating that someone is unavailable—which is the truth, even if they are standing in front of you—and offering to help or take a message is an honest as well as effective answer to this age-old conundrum.

I know, I know. There *are* those bully callers who still may push you to answer the question, "Then, he/she is not there?" Just give the same answer, period.

Here's a trick to field those pesky calls when your boss *is* in but available only to certain people. Your response is, "I'm sorry, but Ms. Olson is unavailable at the moment. Could you please give me your name and number and I'll see that she gets your message?" Then, if the caller identifies himself as someone your boss has informed you that she *wants* to talk to, you can always say, "Oh, I *know* she would like to be interrupted to talk with *you!*" When you put that call through, your caller feels on top of the world—and *you* are the hero! Please note as well that you *still* did not have to lie.

Another important item to remember: *Never make a promise for your boss, either.* She may *never* return the caller's phone call, and you will be left with egg on your face. The best response is simply, "I will give him/her the message." Again, you are telling the truth!

Of course, there's a big ethical difference between lying to callers by telling them your boss will get back to them when you know he won't and, say, keeping mum about fudged numbers on a budget report. But the space between them is a gray zone. Remember, if you choose to lie for your boss in *any* situation—no matter how minor you think it is—you have implied to your boss that you're willing to "negotiate" the truth. Don't be surprised when he comes back to you later and asks to you lie again.

Jane Pauley asked me during my *Dateline* interview, "What should assistants do if their bosses ask them to lie for them?" I responded: "Tell your boss you will never lie *for* him; but he should also know you will never lie *to* him." This response translates into immediate respect. I have had candidates in job interviews say these words to their potential boss and always receive a positive response. One client told me, "Her directness was refreshing, and I hired her on the spot!"

## What Do I Do If I Am Asked to Lie?

What if you have a boss or client who hints, expects, or explicitly asks you to lie for him?

I have found that calling a lie exactly what it is—*a lie*—deters most requests. The challenge, of course, is to do this tactfully without shaming your boss and thereby creating a rift between you. I suggest you find a way to use "uncomfortable" in your protest, because it's not a judgmental or confrontational term. You could simply say, "I'm uncomfortable with this request." This gets the conversation started and safely launches you into taking the following steps:

- *Repeat the request back to him or her.* It's up to you to see through your boss's tactics and put it right back into her lap clearly and succinctly. Ask the simple question: "In other words, Susan, you wish me to lie to the client for you?" Or "In other words, George, you wish me to alter these figures on this report for you?" This will be a wake-up call for them, because you have accomplished two things: (1) Your boss will realize that you fully understand what you are being asked to do and that you recognize it is an unethical and/or illegal request. You have made it clear to him that he is overstepping boundaries. (2) You are giving your boss the opportunity to withdraw the request and save face, thereby solving your problem without having to go any further.

  But what happens if your boss does not back off and presses on with: "Yes, I want you to lie for me"? Then, you have to take a definitive stand as the professional you are.

- *Say "no," and give a rock-solid reason for it.* Explain exactly what makes you so uncomfortable with the request: that you believe it to be wrong and you do not want to be held accountable some day. These are powerful words because you easily *could* be. There is no comeback to this professional, respectful defense. Though your boss may go elsewhere for a coconspirator, at least it won't be you!

- *Document the entire incident, in detail.* Include what your boss asked you to do and how you responded. This is vital for your personal protection.

This may take care of the entire issue, as you have clearly signaled to your boss you will not compromise your ethics. Whether the two of you can continue to work together is yet to be determined; but at least you have established your working relationship under *your* terms by drawing an unmistakable boundary.

But what if your boss presses you even further by threatening to fire you, or says something such as, "Do this thing for me or else ..." or "If you can't or won't do what I've asked, I'm going to have to let you go and get someone else in here who can"? That's when you must take the following actions:

- *Try to generate a creative alternative for this poor person who can't imagine any other option.* If you cannot, this is probably the end of your relationship. Call your lawyer to see if you have any recourse for wrongful termination—and count your blessings that you managed to escape this toxic work environment.

  If your boss's request was regarding *illegal* activity, forget about making efforts at tact and niceties. You need to protect yourself *immediately*.

- *Contact appropriate personnel and request an immediate, confidential meeting.* Relay your boss's illegal request and everything that occurred in relation to it. And of course, document *this* meeting as well.

What happens if and when I say "no" to a request to lie? If you refuse to perform an unethical or illegal request from Ms. Boss, you can expect a few responses:

- *Your refusal will make the person upset.* Depending on how you worded your response, the person who made the request will feel embarrassed and ashamed, relieved that you are clear-headed enough to take a stand for what's right, or furious at your insubordination.

- *She will understand why you are saying "no" (even though she probably won't accept it as a valid reason).*

- *She will respect you for saying "no" (again, probably not acknowledging this).*
- *She will never ask you to do it again.* You've established your ethical boundaries and solved the problem as well—a clear win-win.

You have to take care of yourself. My readers came through loud and clear with their urges for you to protect yourself from others' ethical lapses. CarolAnn Smallwood, an executive assistant from Stratford, Connecticut, writes: "If you lie for an unethical boss, you lose your self-respect." Teri K. Seybti, Internet administrator for Ducane Gas Grills Inc., Columbia, South Carolina, states: "To me, [keeping] a job is not as important as losing your self-worth and self-esteem in order to please someone else by lying." And Gay Oswalt, an executive assistant at Randall Publishing Company in Tuscaloosa, Alabama, adds: "Lying is never right. The truth always comes out. And if you've lied, you have lost your integrity, which is difficult to get back."

These are powerful words threading through their comments, all of which define one's sense of personal professionalism: *integrity*, *self-respect*, *conscience*, *self-worth*, and *self-esteem*. They certainly define today's ideal businessperson.

## Can Lies Ever Be Excused?

This is entirely up to you and your coworkers. You have to work with each other the day after you lied to each other, and how well you work together depends on mutual trust, respect, support, and all the other qualities that go into making relationships work well. If deception creeps into your professional interactions, you have to be ready to deal with all of the negative consequences that may (and probably will) occur.

Every chance I get, I personally counsel people to always take the high road and *do everything they can possibly do to avoid lying.* I think this is a key component of workplace professionalism. If our coworkers, managers, clients, and employees sense that they cannot trust us—if they perceive our truthfulness as negotiable rather than absolute—we will achieve only a fraction of our potential effectiveness in our job, and we'll never earn the respect our profession deserves.

Another way to look at it is to consider that you're saving yourself some serious effort; after all, lying is a lot of work! You have to forever remind yourself of your lies so you don't trip up and give yourself away. I love President Abraham Lincoln's words: "I'd make a terrible liar because I have a terrible memory!"

This leads me to the final most common question about lying....

## How Do I Avoid Being Trapped by Lies?

This is simple: don't tell 'em, don't listen to 'em, and stop 'em whenever you find them. You should not have to lie for anyone in the workplace, for *any* reason. If you think about it, you can always find ways to avoid situations where you have to deceive—for either yourself or someone else. As your office becomes more ethical, you should encounter fewer and fewer lies or reasons for doing so.

## Aren't I Legally Protected If I Lie for My Boss at His Request?

No, no, *no!* Consider the similarities between your own and other professions. It is generally agreed that when a client gives information to certain professionals, this information merits a certain level of legal confidentiality protection. This authorized shield recognizes that in these unique relationships—as with those between husband and wife—a person can expect certain secrets to remain private. However, like these other professionals, we are *all* bound to *not* lie on behalf of a client or anyone else. Do not confuse an expectation of confidentiality with lying; there's a big difference between keeping silent and uttering a falsehood. You have no immunity against lies, and, if asked, you will have to tell whatever you know under oath in the courtroom.

## The Military Gets It Right

All branches of the military have a great response to an inappropriate question: "You do not have a need to know." End of report, and no lying!

When it comes to lying is this culture, there is *no* wiggle room whatsoever. My friend, retired Air Force Brigadier General Dennis

Schulstad, shared some comments about the consequences of not telling the truth in the military:

> They have an honor code at the Air Force Academy that reads, "We will not lie, steal, or cheat, nor tolerate among us anyone who does." This code is enforced by the cadets, and anyone caught breaking it faces removal from the Academy. The honor code serves as a basis for each cadet's personal code of ethical behavior.
>
> Case in point: Some years ago, an exceptional young lieutenant was selected to be the first female pilot of an Air Force bomber that could carry nuclear weapons (today, there are many women flying all types of Air Force planes in combat). This lieutenant received significant national media attention for this groundbreaking assignment. However, just after the announcement, she was caught in an adulterous affair with the civilian husband of an enlisted woman. The officer's commander immediately ordered her to end the relationship.
>
> The lieutenant lied to her superior officer saying it was over; but, instead, she continued the affair. Disobeying the order of her commander and continuing the adulterous affair, while wrong and potentially damaging to her career, probably would have resulted only in an official reprimand. However, at the end of the day, the serious crime that got her instantly discharged from the military was the fact that she lied to her commander.

Schulstad added that, "In the military, trust is of upmost importance—and lives depend upon it. In this case, it was betrayal of trust and her outright lie, not the sexual affair, that ended this Air Force lieutenant's extraordinary career."

## What about Poor Bob, Whose Boss Is Lying at the Opening of This Chapter?

Your boss's job performance *is* your business; this is what makes Bob's dilemma too significant to ignore. Bob's boss's failure to respond truthfully in the meeting, compounded by his lying to the team (including to the president—who is also his boss) to cover his tracks, impacts the company's employees and customers, and therefore Bob, too. Bob is in the ethical hot seat on this one and is honor-bound to take action. Any inaction on his part would imply complicity.

## How to Proceed

A workable solution to Bob's dilemma requires that he have a potentially difficult conversation with his boss, while keeping the following items in mind:

- *People often lie because they feel powerless.* Liars believe that the unvarnished truth diminishes them in the eyes of the people with whom they work. Haven't we all been tempted to put a favorable spin on a message to avoid appearing foolish, incompetent, or inadequate in front of people we care about? When we lie, we're trying to retain control of a situation so we can maintain our sense of self-esteem and status in the group.

- *Truth depends on trust.* A person who fears rejection, shame, and blame for telling the truth will become a messenger of only good news. Since Bob didn't say anything about his boss lying habitually in the past, let's assume his behavior in this circumstance is an unusual occurrence. It may be a last-resort strategy to conceal something because the boss believes the team will somehow punish him if they learn the truth about his shortcomings.

## Should Bob Speak Up or Keep Quiet about His Boss's Lies?

This is an easy answer: Bob must communicate the truth about the situation. To remain passive and silent without protest while his teammates are deceived would be committing a lie of omission. What Bob fails to say is as hurtful as what his boss says out loud. Bob's might even be the more serious offense because he can see all sides of the situation, while his boss may be trapped in his anxiety and the lies he is telling himself. Therefore, Bob *must* speak up.

This is where Bob must utilize his Ethical Compass:

*Take care of yourself.* If you are to remain true to your own ethical standards, you must stay free of your boss's risky lies that may strip you of your honor, your good reputation, and your self-esteem.

"I got caught many times in my boss's lies because he would commit them in front of me," says one anonymous contributor in Lake Washington, Washington. "I realized I was getting to the point where I couldn't even look in the mirror at night. My own ethical beliefs were being compromised every day."

*Take care of your company.* It's in your best interests to keep your company healthy. If a dilemma has a negative effect on the company, it will have a negative effect on you. Remember, when you protect your company, you protect yourself!

*Finally, take care of your boss.* Loyalty should not be confused with morality. Bob can be loyal to a boss with lower moral standards than his, as long as he can manage to keep himself separate from his lies and other misdeeds. This is not easy, however. His discussions must be held in the context of loyalty, not "I'm right and you're wrong."

## To Whom Should Bob Talk?

Bob should start with his boss, even though this is the most difficult conversation. By voicing his concerns to his boss before anyone else, Bob gives him a chance to come clean on his own terms.

## What Should Bob Say?

Bob must assume that he may not know all the facts, so he should start the conversation with his boss by asking questions. Is the project really as far along as he stated in the meeting? It might be, and Bob is just not aware of the progress. Next, he needs to challenge the information that does *not* ring true. It is very important that this part of the discussion stay focused clearly on the situation's facts. Bob should not judge his boss or take an accusatory tone, as this will only make his boss more defensive and confirm his irrational belief that he cannot share bad news with the team. Bob's boss is probably feeling a lot of stress and frustration in the situation, hence his reason for lying in the first place. Bob's job is to help him solve his problems in the most constructive way possible. He should be sympathetic and supportive but clear about needing the truth in order to be helpful.

In a perfect world, Bob's boss will quickly come to understand that this conversation with Bob is probably his last, best chance to tell the truth. He should respond positively, perhaps saying something like, "I don't know what I was thinking, but I really oversold the project," or "I really screwed up. The real situation is this...." This gives Bob an opportunity to be constructive and helpful. For the sake of loyalty, he should do his best to help his boss out of the pickle into which he's gotten himself. However, under no circumstances should Bob allow himself to be implicated, blamed, or held responsible for his boss's problems.

## What If Bob's Boss Gets Angry and Defensive?

This may happen, and the situation may even accelerate. Bob's boss may demand that he lie to support his own lie, manipulate or fabricate paperwork, or worse. In essence, his boss may up the ante in a high-risk game of bluff and hide. Bob never agreed to play this game, so this is where his loyalty ends. His boss no longer deserves Bob's support.

There are several ways for Bob to tell the boss he is now on his own if he chooses to continue in the same false direction. One way is to restate his implicit request without any sugarcoating by saying something like: "Am I to understand you want me to lie for you to both your boss and our project team?" Challenge him by clearly stating your understanding of his unethical request. Seeing it through the other person's eyes may be enough to cause the boss to withdraw his request.

If he still doesn't get it, Bob must tell his boss he will *not* lie for him, period—nor will he lie to his boss and his teammates. If Bob's boss needs an explanation, Bob can say that he wants people to trust him. If his boss perceives Bob's truthfulness as flexible, he will never earn the professional respect he deserves.

## "Just the Facts, Ma'am"

In order to fully protect himself, Bob must document his entire conversation with his boss in writing and talk to another supervisor about it (or the human resources administrator, preferably someone at or above his boss's level). Bob should tell this person that he needs to have a *confidential* conversation, and then reveal the entire occurrence with his boss. Bob must be absolutely professional in his presentation. He has to stick to the facts and focus on the dilemma and the potential consequences to the company, without getting into a discussion about personalities and turf wars. Again, Bob needs to document the date and substance of every conversation.

Bob's refusal to support his boss's lies may be interpreted as disloyalty and may signal the fact that his relationship with this boss will soon be forced to end. This is probably the inevitable outcome with ethically impaired managers, anyhow, and Bob is certainly better off working for someone else.

Of course, we always have the option of resigning our job at any time, even though it is not fair that we have to give up a good job with benefits because someone is acting unethically. Margaret H. Caddell, CPS, of Tuskegee, Alabama, reminds us that "there will always be ethical issues in the workplace. You'll likely encounter similar ethical dilemmas at your next job, so it's best to learn to resolve them."

Here are a few more dilemmas relating to lying.

## Can I Slide around It?

> Dear Nan:
>
> My boss, who travels a lot, has asked me to lie for her and say she's out working the territory when she is actually at home (where she tells me she is working). No one would think twice about whatever I said—but I still don't feel quite right about it. What should I do?
> —George in sales, Waconia, MN

Tell your boss from the get-go that you will not deceive others on her behalf. This is simply a matter of self-preservation. And the reason you must give her, of course, is that you may have to be held accountable some day. Don't worry; she can't win the accountability argument. This kind of a lie is one you can't get away with for very long, anyway. And if you choose to lie for her, guess who she'll take out with her when she comes falling down (and she will)? That's right—you!

> Dear Nan:
>
> I can't decide which is less unethical: lying to my boss or lying to my coworker. I know, I know; the optimal situation is neither, but believe me—I'm going to have to lie to someone. What should I do?
>
> —Carla in Kalamazoo, MI

I'm sorry, Carla, but I *don't* believe you—no one *has* to lie in the business world. Besides, doesn't it hurt your head to keep all those lies straight? Of course, you should tell the truth, especially to those with whom you work. You're probably not fooling anyone, anyway; the human ear is amazingly acute when listening for the truth. The nose is remarkably sensitive, too—and this one doesn't pass the smell test.

---

Dear Nan:

I love my job as assistant to the VP of sales. My boss travels a lot and enjoys a well-earned reputation as the "star performer" within our company. Lately, however, he is frequently "forgetting" to call in, leaving me with no way to reach him. I know his customers are getting frustrated because they tell me about it! Worst of all, yesterday he directed me to tell the company president (should he call) that he's working in another city—when I knew for a fact that he was home. I'm wondering how I should react to my boss's strange behavior. Or should I just mind my own business?
—Letitia in Newark, NJ

---

Your boss's failure to stay in touch affects you because it affects your company's customers. Your boss has also asked you to lie to someone else in the company (the president, no less) to cover his tracks. Letitia, you don't just have one huge problem—you have *two*! Below are the steps on what you should do:

*Step 1: Tell your boss privately that you are concerned about his new pattern of "forgetting to call in."* Make sure he understands why this is a problem. Talking to him first gives him the benefit of the doubt and demonstrates your loyalty and confidence in him. He deserves that much.

While it is not your responsibility to judge your boss, it *is* your responsibility to look out for the company's best interests. Even a personal crisis of some kind is not a good enough reason to disappoint his customers or break trust with you and the company. You can't help him keep things under control unless he tells you the truth about what is going on.

*Step 2: Suggest alternatives that empower you to help him.* Be proactive. Calling in less frequently is okay, for example, as long as you have a complete itinerary or a call-in schedule you can count on. Perhaps you can redirect customer calls to other company resources. And "unavailable" is all that most people need to know about his whereabouts, anyhow—followed, of course, by an offer to take a message.

*Step 3: You have to tell your boss you will not lie for him.* You have no way of assessing the significance of your boss's deception (i.e., he may be playing company politics, hiding a romantic interlude, or even interviewing for another job on company time). Though his reasons are none of your business, it *is* of your concern that being asked to lie to your boss's boss on his behalf places *you* in the role of coconspirator—something that is entirely unacceptable.

Start by telling your boss you are "uncomfortable" with his request, and repeat it back to him without any sugarcoating: "Do I understand you want me to tell the president, should he call, that you are in New Orleans, even though I know you are not? In other words, you wish me to lie to the president on your behalf?" This approach gives him the opportunity to alter or withdraw his request (and perhaps even save face).

If matters do not improve, document the instances and how you handled them, and involve someone in a higher authority in the situation. This is one problem that cannot be allowed to continue; and you are the only one in the position to remedy it.

---

Dear Nan:

My boss, a production manager for a specialty printing company, lies constantly to customers about shipping dates to "keep the customer happy"—and he insists I give the same untrue answers. Then when we default on those falsified deadlines, he blames the shipper. No matter how you cut it, we are both just plain lying. I've tried to be proactive and suggest ways to tell the customer the truth (I believe they would appreciate it), but he will have no part of my input.

—Lissa in production (for the time being), Paducah, KY

---

Lissa, I commend you for trying to repair your ethically impaired boss, but it looks like you've hit a brick wall. You can try one more card—the "reputation" one—by explaining to your boss that your company will eventually become known as one that doesn't keep its promises. This tag will filter on down to future customers and those customers' suppliers and, sooner or later, will reach the entire business community. Follow the above advice to Letitia, but be careful to stay focused on the fact that you do not want to be a coconspirator in his lying. (*You* have a reputation to maintain as well).

## Lies Will Always Be Ethically Wrong

Lies should be rare exceptions to your standard ethical conduct. Though they may occasionally be excused, they cannot be justified unless they are little white lies or lies to prevent great harm. They are ethically wrong, risky, and don't always (or even usually) work. In my opinion, choosing to use deception to get from here to there is like climbing out on a skinny branch in the false hope that the branch is a shortcut. That skinny branch never gets thicker and more stable, and it doesn't go anywhere you want to be (just the opposite, in fact). Choose to lie if you must, but be prepared for the negative consequences because they will be forthcoming.

Lies are just shortcuts to immediate feel-good benefits. They temporarily take the pressure away from a discussion where the truth may be acutely embarrassing or hurtful. But they are merely that: delays. Ultimately, the conversation will occur and the problem must be confronted. The day of reckoning comes sooner or later. The trap, of course, is getting caught up in multiple lies in the hope that you can rescue the situation *before* your deception is discovered.

Lying is a habit with virtually no brakes, which makes it a truly loose cannon on a slippery slope, ethically speaking. The more lies you tell, the easier it becomes to tell more (just ask Bernard Madoff—if you can access him in his prison cell). It is a difficult habit to break away from. There are no thought police or truth squads to monitor one's lies, so however often a liar tells lies—and the matters about which he is willing to lie—is between the liar and his own conscience. Once deceiving others becomes a habit, it's difficult to stop; and it's even more difficult to recover the trust of those to whom you told repeated falsehoods.

*Marge, it takes two to lie! One to lie . . . and one to listen!*
—Homer Simpson

# 16

## The XXX Files

### The Workplace Is No Place for Porn!

---

*Reputation is character minus what you've been caught doing.*
—Michael Iapoce, *A Funny Thing Happened on the Way to the Boardroom*

Dear Nan:

My boss is an otherwise great guy, but I accidentally discovered that he has been downloading pornography off the Internet and storing the files on his computer. His computer is in his office, and no one else normally has access to it. I would never have known myself had he not called from a client's office and asked me to look something up for him. That's when wham—I came across all these embarrassing images. On one hand, I am thinking that this is his private business and I should just forget about it. However, our company has strict policies against such risky activities. I like my boss a lot, and he has always been appropriate in his dealings with me and the rest of the staff. He doesn't know I know about these files. What (if anything) should I do?

—Susan in Houston, TX

Houston, we have a problem! (I've always wanted to say that.) I think we can all agree that viewing pornography at work is a potential harassment lawsuit. So should your boss be engaging in this behavior on company time with company equipment? The answer is a resounding *no!*

That's the easy response to the simpler part of this situation. The more difficult question is: what should you do about it?

## Is Porn at Work Really a Problem?

Big time. The Nielsen Company, which tracks media statistics, reports that 21 million Americans accessed adult Web sites on computers at work in March 2010. That's 29 percent of working adults in a typical month. Some more alarming problems:

- Seventy percent of traffic to porn Web sites occurs *during the work day*.
- About 65 percent of U.S. companies attempt to block employees' access to inappropriate sites, but frequently fail because of the widespread use of portable devices like laptops and cell phones.

You may ask, "What's the harm?" The same-old, same-old: money.

First, pornography is clear-cut evidence of sexual harassment (that's why most employers have a zero-tolerance standard today). Enough employers have been financially stung for tolerating it to make this an easy policy decision.

Second, information technology (IT) managers report that adult Web sites are frequently the source of computer viruses, malware, and spyware—all of which have the potential to degrade the company's network security. Personnel managers state that they often become aware of a porn problem simply because a person's computer crashes so often. "We have a tough enough time keeping the bad guys out," says one IT executive. "When someone inside the company is actively trying to disable or work around our security measures to get to porn sites, our job becomes much more difficult—and the damage is much more expensive to fix."

Back to our problem in Houston . . .

Even though Susan is not at fault, she has to deal with this. Because her boss is using company equipment on company time, and exposing a company employee—Susan—to pornography, the company is at risk. Your Ethical Compass helps sort this out. Take care of yourself first: Susan seems willing to excuse her boss's behavior because he has kept this little habit to himself, but she's still at risk because she is obligated to report that she has become aware of a situation that is potentially damaging to the company. Take care of your company second: this could hurt the company legally and compromise data security (that's why this is a big deal). Third, take care of your boss: he could lose his job.

Susan *must* take action, and do so pronto. How Susan proceeds depends on her company's policy, starting with good documentation ("on this date, I saw this because my boss asked me to do that"). If your company has no relevant guidelines, this is an opportunity to spearhead the development of an up-to-date policy.

I would give Susan the following advice:

First, familiarize yourself with the company policy and how this could have happened in spite of your firewall.

Then, if you are comfortable doing so, discuss the existence of these computer files with your boss. (If you are not comfortable discussing it, move on to a human resource principal).

Begin the conversation with your boss by reporting that you stumbled upon the objectionable files, and that you are concerned because of the risks to the company. Be careful not to sound judgmental; you are simply explaining the facts.

Ask him if he is aware of the files. Giving your boss the benefit of the doubt is important. And who knows? Sabotage, viruses, and after-hours use by the cleaning crew are possibilities. Stay focused on your concern that this puts the company at risk. A positive discussion of this kind will be well received, as long as your boss doesn't feel as though you are judging or threatening him. You want to give the impression that you're only trying to help both the company *and* him. Making your boss feel embarrassed, guilty, or shamed will only put him on the defensive, so avoid being sidetracked.

Your boss might attempt to diminish this incident ("a little porn is no big deal"). Don't back down, Susan. Explain the risks to him. When this catches up to him later on (and it will), do you really want to be the one who has to admit: "Yes, I knew about it, but I chose to look the other way"? Despite your efforts, however, if your boss becomes angry and stonewalls you, you need to immediately end the conversation and discuss the situation with a higher authority.

Hopefully, this won't occur and you can wrap up the conversation by reiterating your company's policies, such as removing all objectionable material from his computer and self-reporting his actions to appropriate personnel. This part isn't too tough; you simply outline your company's procedures, and let him draw his own conclusions.

Explain also that you are documenting this conversation for your own protection and planning to report it accordingly. This is a *key point* to make, since it's entirely possible that your boss will promise to follow through and not do so. However, that's *his* problem, not yours.

Again, be sure to document the entire conversation, whatever the outcome, in order to protect yourself. Immediately summarize or recap verbatim everything you can remember about your discussion, then write the date and time on the page and store it in a secure place outside of the office.

And, of course, it may be too late. The company may already know about your boss's proclivities and be preparing his termination papers. Organizations nowadays are increasingly using software tools to track employees' Internet use; if they want to, they can track every click you make. Companies sometimes even assign a staff member to review information that has been downloaded by employees.

## A Word about Child Pornography

This chapter has focused on adult pornography, which—whether one likes it or not—is a legal expression of free speech in the United States. I often receive a darn good question related to this topic in my seminars, however: what should an employee do if ever confronted by child pornography in workplace situations? Child pornography in both the United States and Canada is illegal, period—whether in the workplace *or* the community. It makes no difference where you observe it; you must *immediately* take action.

If you are ever exposed to child pornography of any kind on any computer site, authorities will tell you to "freeze" immediately (i.e., don't leave the Web site or allow anyone to touch it)—pick up your phone and call the local police! You must do this even if it occurs in your home. Police Chief John Luse of the City of St. Louis Park, Minnesota, advises: "From that point on, do not touch anything until the police arrive. Then, turn your computer over to them."

*Snap Quiz:* Our company policy restricts "inappropriate e-mail," whatever that is. Some of my coworkers tend to circulate e-mail that is humorous, in their opinion, but sometimes borders on objectionable smut in my eyes. I have made my personal objections clear, so I am not on the list serve for "fun" (that's what they call it). I'm neither a prude nor a tattletale, but I can tell that they're distracted from their jobs when they all gather around a monitor for a good laugh. Should I just button up my objections?

Your coworkers are holding a slippery pole here. Explain to them why your company has such a policy (e.g., to protect itself from harassment lawsuits, viruses, and malware). If they don't stop their antics, talk confidentially to your human resource people about the situation because they are making the company vulnerable. Besides that, they are playing Russian roulette with their jobs!

> *You have brains in your head. You have feet in your shoes. You can steer yourself any direction you choose. You're on your own. And you know what you know. And YOU are the guy/gal who'll decide where to go.*
>
> —Dr. Seuss

# 17

# Abuse in the Workplace

## *If It Hurts, It's Abuse—and If It Happens More than Once, It's Harassment!*

*Those who can, do. Those who can't, bully.*

—www.bullyonline.org

I always encourage my ethics workshop attendees to openly discuss their concerns without fear. That's the beauty of face-to-face discussions about ethical dilemmas—what gets talked about in the room stays in the room!

After introducing one particular session in this way, a lady leaped to her feet and blurted out, "Great! I want to discuss my explosive, out-of-control boss!" All of a sudden, several other attendees shouted out, "Me, too!"

And so we did.

Abuse in the workplace is a particularly sensitive subject and, un-fortunately, a *common* one. It has many faces: the explosive boss who causes you to jump when he speaks; the domineering, in-your-face coworker whom you try to avoid as much as possible; or a jealous peer who attempts to undercut your every achievement. No workplace seems immune, and no profession is beyond it or above it. And surveys (including my own) indicate about half of you (49 percent) have experienced or witnessed workplace abuse, and you report it was caused almost equally by your bosses and your coworkers. What's going on here?

## We're Still Misbehavin'

Dear Nan:

I am a VP at a smallish company (about 25 employees), and I got the short end of the straw when we divvied up the administrative tasks. I'm now in charge of EEOC compliance, which means it's my job to see that everyone plays nicely together so the company avoids lawsuits. I have my work cut out for me because these are a few of our current dilemmas:

- From the hallway, within earshot of a dozen cubicles, an employee explodes with profanity peppered with racial slurs while referring to the newly elected U.S. president. This employee has never done this before—and everyone who heard (including me) was stunned into horrified silence.

- One of the "old guard" in the sales department routinely flirts with the clerical staff. He tells off-color jokes and hugs a lot. No one has complained, but not as many of the women (or men) are laughing these days. He proudly claimed ownership of a provocative (but not obscene) calendar recently hung by the copier, noting that it was a fund raiser organized by the cheerleaders of his favorite NFL team.

Nan, my company doesn't "get it" at all. How do I even begin to clean up this mess?

—Cheri in White Bear Lake, MN

Cheri can start by explaining to her coworkers the fundamental business reason for an Ethical Office: Ethical behavior makes money and helps the company succeed, which incidentally ensures that everyone's paychecks continue. Unethical behavior costs money and puts those paychecks at risk. Besides, ethical behavior is the right thing to do—I come from the camp that believes virtue is its own reward, and it is happily, coincidentally, good for business as well. Cheri can expect the perpetrators to protest. "But I'm not hurting anyone," "Get over it!," "What's the big deal?," or the classic putdown: "Where's your sense of humor?" She will have to be prepared to explain a few legal points, such as:

The U.S. Equal Employment Opportunity Commission (the EEOC mentioned in her letter) enforces the laws that make it illegal to discriminate against someone (applicant or employee) because of that person's race, color, religion, sex (including pregnancy), national origin, age (40 or older), disability, or genetic information. It is also illegal to retaliate against a person because he or she complained about discrimination, filed a charge of discrimination, or participated in an employment discrimination investigation or lawsuit.

Seems perfectly clear, right? Essentially, the laws that the EEOC enforces forbid discrimination in every aspect of employment, ranging from job advertisements, recruitment, and hiring to pay, benefits, discipline, disability, religion, and conditions of employment—you get the idea.

The challenging part of the law is determining when violations become more than an ethical problem and graduate to being legally actionable. This distinction is important for employees, who want to know what they can do if they have been victimized, and managers like Cheri, who are often the deciding factors on whether or not the company is liable.

In Cheri's case, the profane and racist outburst was, well, profane and racist. It should not be ignored, and qualifies for a reprimand of some kind. But because it is an isolated incident (assuming that this person does not behave this way normally), it does not, by itself, rise to the level of illegal discrimination or hostile work environment.

That's not to say, however, that somebody might not make an issue of it (which argues for some other disciplinary action). "This kind of inflammatory remark by a coworker falls into the category of 'unlawful harassment' when the harassment is directed to someone in the above protected class category," says Stacey A. DeKalb, who heads the employment law practice at the Minneapolis, Minnesota law firm of Lommen, Abdo, Cole, King & Stageberg, PA.

Cheri's other dilemma is a sexual harassment case in waiting. This is a lawsuit just begging to hatch, but it isn't actionable yet. No one has apparently made it clear to the salesperson that his salacious behavior is indeed offensive, so he has not yet been allowed to change his behavior. Sexual harassment includes a range of behavior from seemingly mild transgressions and annoyances to actual sexual abuse or assault. It can come in the form of unwelcome sexual advances and requests for sexual favors, and it may include intimidation, bullying, or coercion and other types of harassment.

In some (but not all) contexts or circumstances, sexual harassment may be illegal. To be legally actionable, sexual harassment must be judged to be a form of illegal employment discrimination. The law does *not* prohibit simple teasing, offhand comments, or not-as-serious isolated incidents. However, harassment *is* illegal if it is so frequent or severe that it creates a hostile or offensive work environment (which means it affects the employee's productivity) or if it results in an adverse employment decision (such as the victim's being fired or demoted).

## Let's Hear It for Common Sense—and Common Courtesy

This is the time for Cheri to get involved—to tell the guy to cool his jets, take down the calendar, and keep his hands and limericks to himself! As a management representative, she is obligated to speak up to try to remedy the situation. If she witnesses something she believes is wrong but does nothing, the company will be vulnerable.

I suggest that if managers like Cheri (and the rest of us) *speak up sooner*, we can stop bad behavior before it becomes a legal problem. Yes, I'm serious as a lawsuit: just speaking up can cause someone to change their abusive ways and head *off* that lawsuit.

Case in point: A VP of sales of a trucking firm once told me his top producer had extremely salty language. Though her clients didn't "seem to mind," the administrative staff sitting outside her door objected to hearing her colorful language on the phone. The astute VP realized that "as soon as the first admin complained to me, I had to take action because her language falls under the harassment guidelines." His solution made me chuckle. He sat down with the VP and told her to clean up her act. She responded: "How can I *do* that? That's why I'm so successful with my clients; I speak their language!" The VP firmly replied: "Then, I have one solution, Fran, *shut the door!*" And so she did! Problem solved.

# Is It Abuse or Harassment or Bullying or Something Else?

Frankly, my dears, it doesn't matter. Most organizations have ceased to make a distinction among different types of abuse—what's more important is recognizing a *pattern of abuse* that constitutes harassment. If a coworker is hurting another coworker in any way, you know everything you need to know. Whatever you call it, it has to stop.

I group all types of abuse, bullying, harassment, and other bad behaviors together when I discuss harassment as an ethical dilemma, since they are all wrong, hurtful, and disrespectful. Regardless of how they are categorized, these behaviors have a common negative impact on the office's ethical climate and the victims' job performance. Also, two or more types of harassment may overlap in an incident, such as verbal harassment accompanying emotional and/or sexual abuse. Let the lawyers quibble about the wording; your focus should be responding immediately to an occurrence so the situation does not morph into a "hostile, intimidating, or offensive work environment." Bottom line: establish a pattern of abuse and you have grounds for a harassment lawsuit.

# The "Job-Affecting" Standard

The following statement is my short and simple filter to identify abusive behavior: *If another person's behavior has a negative affect on your ability to do your job, you may have a problem with harassment.* I call this the "job-affecting" standard.

**Legally, a behavior is generally considered harassment if it is:**
- Not welcome, offensive to the employee, not asked for, not mutual, and not reciprocated
- Objected to by the employee in such a way that allows the individual(s) offending the employee to correct their behavior
- Affecting the terms or conditions of employment, including the work environment and the capacity of the employee to perform his or her duties efficiently and in a responsible manner.

**Harassing behaviors tend to be combinations of the following:**
- *Sexual harassment* is described as unwelcome sexual advances, requests for sexual favors, and other verbal or physical conduct of

a sexual nature. To be legally actionable, sexual harassment (and other forms of harassment) must be judged to be a form of illegal employment discrimination. The law does *not* prohibit simple teasing, offhand comments, or isolated incidents. However, harassment *is* illegal if it is so frequent or severe that it creates a hostile or offensive work environment (which means it affects the employee's productivity). Harassment, sexual or otherwise, is also illegal if it results in an adverse employment decision (such as the victim's being fired or demoted).

- *Verbal harassment* is yelling, profanity, public humiliation, excessive criticism, personal insults, and all other forms of demeaning or disrespectful comments and conversation.

- *Physical harassment* is pushing, shoving, touching, horseplay, or other conduct that intimidates and/or threatens safety.

- *Emotional harassment* is abusive or disrespectful conduct that manipulates, coerces, humiliates, and/or intimidates; this also is sometimes called psychological harassment, and it can be done by a group (this is called *mobbing*); this is difficult to prove because the only evidence is the victim's complaint.

## The Costs of Harassment

Among the negative effects of harassment are higher stress, lower self-esteem, and poor productivity among the abused, which in turn damage the organization's effectiveness, stability, productivity, and profitability. The costs of rudeness, insensitivity, disrespect, and other types of unethical behavior are even higher if victims fight back because the employer allowed the situation to exist or persist.

Consider how you would respond to the pick-pick-pick of emotional and verbal harassment that sounds something like, "Did you do that again, Jane?" or "What's it going to take, Rick, to teach you to do this *right?*" Denver-based consultant coach and trainer Ben Leichtling, PhD, calls this "bullying below the radar."

The effects are equally damaging for sabotage, badgering, pestering, hounding, persecution, teasing, molestation, bashing, humiliation, and denigration (look at how many ways we can hurt each other!). However you characterize it, abuse has a cancerous, corrosive effect on productivity and profitability. When abusive behavior dominates an office, fresh ideas are eliminated and employees are reduced to "yes people" who keep their heads down and their mouths shut.

**Other consequences of harassment:**
- Management delivers a demoralizing message that the company doesn't really care about employees and/or actually condones bad behavior.
- Employees find ways to retaliate against management.
- Employee morale is reduced to zero.
- Increased absenteeism and employee distraction due to stress cause productivity to plummet.
- Creativity and innovative thinking tank.
- Employee turnover increases, compromising stability.
- Costs to avoid legal retaliation arise.

One more real "biggie": the "I quit, but I forgot to tell you" syndrome. In other words, employees show up for work physically, but "check out" mentally and emotionally. These employees no longer care about the company and perform accordingly. Productivity and profitability hit the carpet.

Consequently, the company is damaged from the inside out by chewing up its people. I believe "Dr. Phil" (Phillip McGraw) gets this one right: "Being subjected to abuse changes who you are." You believe you don't deserve to be abused, and yet you are—does that mean you are actually a "bad" person who is undeserving of respect? Are you weak or foolish to tolerate the abuse? Why is this happening to you? The mental stress caused by an endless loop of questions like these is exhausting.

# Are You Being Harassed, Abused, or Bullied?

Do not go crazy asking yourself questions with no answers. Ask yourself instead if you are being harassed. This isn't always clear when you're in the middle of the day-to-day drama. If you can put a label on what is toxic about a situation, you have a fighting chance of surviving it with your reputation, sanity, and job intact.

# Nan DeMars's Workplace Harassment Audit

Use these questions to determine if you are being bullied, harassed, or subjected to other abusive behavior.

- Describe the behavior that you find objectionable.
- Are you the sole target?
- Does the person behave in the same way toward others?
- Is the behavior deliberate?
- Have you told the person you find his/her behavior bothersome?
- Have you asked him/her to stop?
- Has the person repeated and continued the behavior?
- How does the behavior make you feel?
- Do others who receive this same behavior feel the same as you do?
- Is there a chance that you're overreacting and/or being overly sensitive?
- Is the behavior welcomed, encouraged, asked for, returned, or reciprocated? Does the person acting in this way think it is?
- Is the behavior affecting your job performance? In what way(s)? Is this behavior making you feel reluctant to go to work?
- Is the behavior affecting your well-being? (Are you intimidated? Fearful? Stressed? Angry? Losing sleep?)
- Have you discussed your concern with a neutral individual outside the company (e.g., a counselor, spouse, clergy individual, or friend)? Does this person agree with your assessment?
- Would a reasonable person find the behavior objectionable, offensive, or otherwise not socially acceptable?
- Has the person explained his/her behavior to your satisfaction? Would he/she be able to explain the behavior to their spouse? Daughter? Mother-in-law? Boss? The company attorney? A reporter? A jury?

# What Can You Do before You Call the Lawyers?

Assuming you are reasonably certain you are being harassed, you must make a good-faith attempt to stop the behavior in the most constructive way possible. The good news: if all your efforts to remedy the situation fail, you can always quit.

But quitting your job is the last resort. I rarely suggest that one leave a job due to someone else's behavior, but this may be one of those occasions you have to toss in the towel for your own preservation. Sadly, abuse dilemmas do not respond well to logic or appeals to fairness. An abusive boss may have deep-seated anger issues, for example, so you may have to acknowledge the fact that you are not equipped to handle his or her dysfunctional behavior. You are not a therapist, scapegoat, enabler, or whipping post. Before you remove yourself from the situation, though, please consider again that the angels are on *your* side in court today. In fact, legal rulings in harassment cases commonly favor the subordinate because the justice system sees these as power issues where the person with less power deserves more sympathy. (Memo to Dagwood: Mr. Dithers would be in *big* trouble in today's courts.)

## How to Get Harassment to Stop

Dear Nan:

My boss has a dreadful temper. It is known throughout the company that he blows his stack now and then, lets loose with four-letter words, and even once threw a stapler across the room in my presence. He has never directed his explosions (or staplers) at me personally; however, he often addresses me in a demeaning and condescending manner. I know I'm a good assistant, but his actions make me doubt myself. I thought I could get used to his temper tantrums, but I'm more unnerved every day. I like (and need) the job otherwise. Is there anything I can do about this?

—Martha in Tampa, FL

In addition to enrolling in an anger management class, Martha's boss needs to grow up.

The popular 1980s movie *Nine to Five* served as an eye-opener to abusive, over-the-top bosses. A more recent flick, *The Devil Wears Prada*, starred Meryl Streep as an equally outrageously demanding boss in the high-fashion industry. Both put faces on the "Boss from

Hell"—and depicted an all-too-real, painful reality for many. The former told the story of an abusive boss who got his just desserts when a group of secretaries—played by Jane Fonda, Lily Tomlin, and Dolly Parton—*literally* strung him up. In the latter, we cheered our heroine assistant when, after selling her soul to the devil of fashion for a year, she walked off the job with lessons learned.

Do harassing bosses really believe that their browbeating intimidation tactics achieve legitimate business objectives? Unfortunately, I believe some do.

### Before Martha gives up on her boss, however, I suggest the following:

- *Don't take your boss's behavior personally* (easy for me to say, right?). But remember the mantra of Al-Anon (the Alcoholics Anonymous support group for family members): *Their behavior is not your fault!* You are not the problem. He is.

- *Recognize that your boss will abuse you only to the limit you allow it to happen.* Since the way in which you *react* to his treatment of you is all you can control, this is what you should focus on.

- *Start documenting objectionable incidents.* In this journal of your boss's behavior, note how you felt after each incident. The point you want to make is this: if you are intimidated or otherwise diminished, he (meaning the company) is being deprived of your peak performance. It's a situation in which no one wins.

- *Talk with your boss about his behavior.* Your boss deserves to hear firsthand from you that you are offended—and affected—by his behavior. State in clear, firm language that you do not work well with his verbal and emotional abuse. (And, no, there is *nothing wrong* with calling his abusive behavior *abusive!*) Show him your list of his documented outbursts and tell him how each incident affected you. Be specific: you were made to feel nervous, afraid, jumpy, distracted. It is possible that he's in denial or unaware that his behavior is exceedingly offensive and/or negatively impacting your job performance. Offer a graceful way to mend fences without making him lose face, perhaps by labeling the incident a "miscommunication" or "misunderstanding."

- *Thank your boss for meeting with you,* and tell him you look forward to continuing to work together on a professional basis.

- *Watch and wait.* Give your boss the benefit of the doubt. Project a positive attitude that expects and encourages change.
- *If your boss continues his abusive behavior, go to the appropriate personnel to report the harassment.* When you meet with this individual, clearly state that you wish to talk confidentially about a harassment situation. Bring your documentation and outline the offenses and good-faith steps you have taken to remedy the situation. You have now set the process in gear. From here forward, the situation is out of your hands and should follow your company's policy for dealing with harassment.

## The Abusive Boss Owns the Company

*For the assistant whose abusive boss also has the ultimate power of owning the company:* follow same advice above. However, if you fail in your sincere efforts to transform your functionally impaired boss, take my father's advice whenever my sister and I complained about a boyfriend: "Put your track shoes on, kid." Find yourself another job with a boss who respects you for the professional you are.

*And for the abusive boss:* stop being the Boss from Hell because your assistant may one day write an exposé on you and you will find yourself up there on the wide screen. As Jerry Seinfeld used to say, "That can't be good!"

## Two Administrators Hit Their Abusive Bosses Head-On

Here's what an anonymous respondent to my column from Augusta, Michigan, did. She said she calmly walked into her boss's office after one of his screaming "spells" and told him, "I am a professional and deserve to be treated accordingly. I would never speak or act in such an unprofessional way to you, and I expect the same courtesy from you. Stop abusing me, or I'll quit!"

It worked, but only for a short time. Soon enough, his verbal barrage started back up. So, true to her word, this woman started packing her belongings. Alarmed, her boss calmed down and pleaded with her to stay (although he did not apologize). She stayed and he worked on changing his behavior. She reports that while her boss still has an occasional "spell," it is short-lived because she immediately responds with something like, "We cannot work together in this kind of an environment. We cannot afford any emotional outbursts; we just have too much work to do today. It's your choice—do we work or not work?" This, of course, causes him to stop immediately. She obviously likes her job, so she chooses to resolve each individual flare-up as it arises. She explained she was "withholding my name for fear of another screaming spell should he read this." (Some bosses never do grow up.)

Another anonymous respondent writes about having been warned that her new boss had a reputation for going into tantrums every now and then, and was told of his propensity to "carry on disgracefully." The first time it happened on her watch, she stood calmly and observed his "carryings on." Then, she asked quietly, "Are you through?" She did it so masterfully that he was totally disarmed and actually felt quite foolish—and he has never "performed such antics since." (Do you think she might have kids of her own?)

## The Abusive Coworker

The abusive coworker problem is equally as damaging to an employee's psyche and a company's bottom line. Here's a beauty I received:

> Dear Nan:
>
> There is a bully in my department who criticizes me for no reason, goes out of her way to embarrass or discredit me in front of other employees, and seizes every opportunity to make my life miserable. She has even told outright lies about me. She rebuffs all my efforts to become friends, and I feel like a fourth-grader on the school playground. She either (1) is just plain jealous of me, (2) wants my job (for which she is unqualified), or (3) just wants me gone for some reason. I hesitate to mention it to my boss because he'd probably tell me to grow up and ignore her, and I wouldn't blame him. I love my position, my boss, and my responsibilities, but I don't even want to go to work anymore. What can I do?
>
> —Tim in Stillwater, OK

- *Take it seriously.* "In situations where a coworker is attempting to discredit, embarrass, and/or spread lies about you, then it's no longer an issue of 'hypersensitivity.' ... Your job, your reputation, and your career are now on the line," says Tami Dickinson, CPS, executive assistant at Sodexho Laundry Services in Marietta, Georgia.

- *Document every incident.* Include dates and circumstances and keep this tracking journal long enough to make your point. And as Diane Johnson-Hung, an administrative assistant for WEA Trust in Madison, Wisconsin, suggests, "Make sure your documentation is written with facts—what was said, what was done, how you came to hear about the lies, etc., and how you felt afterward."

- *Change your own behavior.* Sometimes the best route to altering someone else's behavior is to change your own. A bully cannot torment someone if you don't allow it.

- *Don't bully back!* The worst reaction is to try to bully the bully. Don't play a game the bully knows how to win. She can handle toughness and know how to make you fearful; that's her forté. Conversely, the bully cannot understand or handle gentleness, so sometimes you can totally disarm her with a calm response.

- *Confront the bully directly.* As soon as the bullying occurs, break off contact by using phrases like, "I'm leaving now," "I don't have to listen to this," or, even better, "I'm documenting your behavior"—and then do it! Later, pick a good (not a stressful) time to convey your objections to her actions. You can use the words *job affecting*, and describe how her bullying behavior (don't mince words) is having a negative effect not only on you, but also on everyone else who has observed it. The bully thinks her behavior is getting good results, and you are pointing out to her that, in fact, the reverse is occurring: she is rapidly losing her peers' respect. Stand your ground, or you will lose more of it.

- *Involve your boss and/or the human resource (HR) department.* Gina Staley, an admin assistant at Airbus in Wichita, Kansas, writes she would go to her boss because, "He should be aware of what Ms Bully is doing; she is spreading lies about you, and you need to protect your reputation." Your company deserves a chance to try to solve the problem with you. Remember, you are doing your management a favor by possibly heading off an expensive lawsuit.

More harassment lulus:

> Dear Nan:
>
> You'll never believe what happened to me today. After months of no takers, I finally got a job interview. And guess what? The HR manager hit on me—he even asked me for a date! I didn't act offended, even though I was, because I wanted to get the second interview. I got it—and, consequently, the job! But now my question is: shall I report his actions or just drop the issue? I don't want to be considered a troublemaker, but on the other hand, I don't think he acted professionally. Am I obligated to do anything?
>
> —Mary Ann in Pacific Palisades, CA

It appears there are still a few ethically impaired managers on the loose! This kind of behavior in a job interview is inappropriate, not to mention illegal. Mary Ann's dilemma is: what does she do now? She could exit the interview. (Why would you want to be associated with a company whose HR manager acts so unprofessionally?) You could get to the second interview and report the behavior to that person. However, you have no established credibility (you are not even an employee) and might be dismissed as a potential troublemaker. Not fair, but reality.

And you thought this was a simple dilemma.

I personally believe that as a professional you have an ethical responsibility to assume accountability for such a situation and take action accordingly. Yes, you have no *obligation* to do anything whatsoever. However, is this professional response? And once again, why would you allow some misbehaving turkey to thwart your chances at a possible dream job? (You already *know* how that annoys me!)

This company has an employee in a position of authority who is not only acting irresponsibly but leaving the company wide open for a potentially costly harassment lawsuit as well. I am fairly sure that any reputable organization would want to know they have a loose cannon like this in their employ (much less in the HR department!).

Let's say that you accept the job and are at some time (when the chickens come home to roost) called into the president's office and told confidentially they are investigating the "reported" misbehavior of the HR manager. You are then asked if anything unprofessional occurred during your initial interview. When you reveal your incident, you may be asked why you did not report it at the time. Your professionalism would reflect better if you had taken such action accordingly.

Mary Ann acted professionally in her interview and has nothing to apologize for or be embarrassed about. However, now that she has the job, this would be my advice to her:

- *Document your initial conversation with the HR manager and any ensuing conversations (if inappropriate) with him.* Store that document in your personal file; then, watch and wait an appropriate amount of time (you can determine this). You need to (1) establish your own credibility as a responsible employee and (2) determine the appropriate individual to approach.
- *Request a confidential meeting with the individual you've identified (e.g., HR director, vice president, president/CEO).* Report your concerns and support them with proper documentation and a statement that you have kept (and will continue to keep) the situation confidential. This meeting can be a great time to establish your role as a professional and the liability you feel toward protecting the company's welfare and individuals involved.

Here's another dilemma from the "what are they thinking" department:

Dear Nan:

I am an account manager in an advertising firm. Two other managers (my peers) are playing out a drama that I don't appreciate. Paul is continually "coming on" to Judy, who does not appear to be bothered by this at all. In fact, she seems to enjoy the attention. Though Judy claims to have a boyfriend and says she is not interested in a romantic relationship with Paul, she also does nothing to stop his flirting, off-color jokes, and touching. Can this be considered sexual harassment if both parties appear to be consenting? Personally, I think their behavior is disruptive to our productivity (and other people are complaining). Am I getting my "britches in a bunch" over nothing? Or do I have any responsibility here?

—Walter in advertising, Red Lodge, MT

Walter, the fact that you're wondering if you have a problem means that, indeed, you *do* have a problem!

The line between harmless flirtation and sexual harassment often is thin, especially when the parties involved appear to be enjoying the interaction. Because their behavior is "job affecting," and because Paul's "off-color jokes and touching" constitute harassment to the courts, you (or your boss) should speak up.

One other point: perception is not always reality. Though Judy *appears* to be enjoying Paul's attentions, this may not be the case at all. She may really be seething underneath, find it offensive, and soon slam Paul *and* the company with a sexual harassment suit. But in order for her complaint to have merit, she will have to express her objection and request that he stop.

The bottom line is: Paul is an employee of your company, so his actions make your company vulnerable to a lawsuit. Even if Judy never objects to Paul's behavior, another employee might, since their activities put you—and other colleagues—in what you have already identified as an "offensive environment." Ultimately, the courts would decide, but everybody would pay a price in time, money, and lost productivity to sort out the mess.

While most sexual harassment complaints are from women accusing men, the reverse does happen. I recall an HR director of a certified public accounting (CPA) firm who once told me about a receptionist named Cyndy, whom she had recently hired. Cyndy had been advised of the company's harassment policy, but had not yet attended any of its training—and it showed! One of the firm's major clients called his CPA one day to specifically complain that he did not appreciate Cyndy's behavior each time he visited the office. Apparently, she flirted with him "outrageously—continually—and once even asked me for a date!"

The client went on to say he was even considering changing accounting firms because he was so uncomfortable visiting theirs. Naturally, the CPA reported this incident to the HR director, who had to take immediate action. The HR director held a crash-course with Cyndy on harassment in the workplace, emphasizing the seriousness of her behavior. Unfortunately, Cyndy didn't "get it"—evidenced by the fact that she ended the session by asking, "Well, how do you expect me to meet men if I can't flirt with them?" Needless to say, Cyndy's employment with that firm was short-lived.

In another female-as-harasser suit, a St. Paul, Minnesota, councilwoman was sued by her male assistant for her "inappropriate sexual behavior." The assistant was awarded damages in court. And remember Mark Foley, the U.S. Congressman forced to resign because of his lascivious e-mails with young male interns?

There's no double standard. If we want the rest of the workplace to behave, we must behave ourselves, as well. I've had male employees tell me they are most uncomfortable when they are standing in the middle of several women who are sharing an off-color joke. If we, as women, don't want to be placed in uncomfortable positions, we have to be careful we don't do the same to our male counterparts.

## Tips in Action

When an inappropriate remark or behavior is directed toward you, you *must* respond if you want it to stop. In fact, the first question that many supervisors will ask when you issue a complaint about a harassing behavior will be: "Have you told the harasser you were offended?" This is important. There are people who know exactly what they are doing when they're acting offensively. However, there are also clueless individuals who have no idea they have crossed a line. Once you tell them so, the latter group will probably cease and desist. Regardless, everyone deserves a chance to clean up their behavior, and they won't be able to do so if you do not tell them you object.

But remember to always take the high road. Because you are offended, it may be tempting to "sling it back" to them with an equally smart remark. *Don't.* This only brings you down to their level (where you cannot afford to be).

**Do and don't examples:**
- John says to Mary, "I'd like to take you out for a hot evening!" *Don't* say: "In your dreams." *Do* say: "No. I don't want to go out with you. Please don't ask me again."
- Your manager stares at your blouse every time he talks to you. *Don't:* Stay silent, but later complain to *his* boss. *Do* say: "I'd appreciate it if you would look me in the eyes whenever we talk."
- Elizabeth says to her assistant, Harry: "Honey, would you get me the Larson file?" *Don't* say (with sarcasm): "Sure, Sweetie!" *Do* say: "Please call me by my name. I don't like to be referred to as Honey."
- Ralph is a touchy-feely kind of guy. As he approaches you, *don't* shout, "Keep away!" *Do* give him a nonverbal response like putting

your hands up to keep him from coming closer. If he presses on, take his hands off your waist, your arm, and say, "Please don't do that ever again," and simply turn and quickly walk away.

## Employers Step Up—*Most* of the Time

Most employers have established training programs to deal with workplace harassment. They hope that by educating their employees, they are less likely to engage in conduct that might offend coworkers. Ideally, unacceptable behavior is quickly identified and corrected so that everyone can get back to work. However, legitimate complaints are still ignored, and unjust accusations are still made.

I argue for common sense on everyone's part. An off-color joke may not be offensive to one person, but the same joke may send another individual into fits. It's no wonder employees are often clueless about what they can and cannot say. Let's all pay attention to each other, be aware when our behavior bumps up against someone's boundary, and do our best to work with each other with respect. Start with an unambiguous policy about abuse, bullying, and harassment; communicate that policy with an across-the-board training program; and respond to rumblings of trouble promptly.

## Can You Use a Company Hotline?

IBM deserves kudos for its "Speak Up" program that gives employees a way to alert the HR department anonymously about intimidation in the workplace. IBM director of global employee relations Harold Newman has advised other companies to follow suit before legislatures do it for them. Newman explains that executives should ask themselves about the price of inaction before they dismiss workplace bullying and abuse as too vague a problem to manage. He encourages all organizations to ask: "What's it going to cost in terms of shareholder value, productivity, or brand image?" Chances are, the price is quite steep.

## Raising the Bar

The U.S. Supreme Court heard two landmark cases that raised employers' level of accountability for workplace harassment.

**Now, as a result of these cases:**

- *You can win a harassment complaint lawsuit even if it is proven management was not aware of the harassment.* This was established in the city of Boca Raton, Florida, lawsuit leveled by Beth Ann Faragher, an individual employed as a lifeguard for the city while attending college (1985–1990). Faragher claimed that she, along with other female employees, was sexually harassed every summer, even though she did not report the offenses (probably for all the same peer pressure reasons that kids don't "tattle" on each other). The "Supremes" ruled that employers are responsible for the sexual misconduct of supervisors, even if they knew nothing about the behavior. This decision established stricter guidelines for the prevention of harassment on the job and put the onus on companies to (1) hire responsible personnel, (2) provide harassment training for all employees, and (3) vigilantly maintain a harassment-free environment.

- *Same-gender sexual harassment in the workplace is actionable under Title VII of the Civil Rights Act of 1964.* This ruling came as a result of the *Oncaler vs. Sundowner Offshore Services, Inc.* lawsuit, whereby Oncaler was working on an oil platform in the Gulf of Mexico as a "roustabout" on an eight-man crew. Oncaler stated that on several occasions, he "was forcibly subjected to sex-related humiliating actions against him by crew members, was physically assaulted in a sexual manner, and threatened with rape." His complaints to proper personnel were ignored, and he ultimately filed a lawsuit against the oil rig company. However, he lost the court case because the state of Louisiana ruled that "same-gender sexual harassment is not actionable under Title VII." Oncaler appealed to the U.S. Supreme Court, who reversed this decision. As a result, same-gender harassment claims are covered today (and no state can rule this way again).

## Are We Going Too Far?

Some people dismiss harassment issues as an overreaction, a power grab, a feminist bias, a full-employment plan for attorneys, a drift toward a "nanny state," hypersensitivity—the list is long. Well, I've got one simple rule: the only opinion that really matters at the end of the day is that of the person being harassed. We cannot judge the merit of someone else's dilemma until we've walked a mile in their boots!

Perceptions differ because people differ. From an outsider's perspective, one may perceive reported harassing behavior to be silly or trivial at first blush. But, believe me, it is truly hurtful and job affecting for the person on the receiving end.

### Here are some examples:
- A waiter is required to wear an ill-fitting and embarrassing outfit.
- An assistant comes to work every morning to find her boss has broken all her pencil points. This requires her to take several minutes to resharpen them under his leering gaze.
- Your boss often says, "Don't even try to talk to her. She's got a whopping case of PMS." Or "It would be a waste of time to give him that promotion because his wife has a great job." Or "Don't ask her to negotiate. She's not hard-nosed enough!"
- A group member is excluded from social invitations offered to everyone else.

The preceding situations may make us wonder if all our concern about harassment isn't a bit overblown. But, believe me, these people feel real pain, stress, and hurt inside. Their productivity often suffers, and they consider themselves true victims. Their "gut feeling" perspectives tell them these incidents are harassment—and who are we to say otherwise? They have already affirmatively answered the question: "*Is this job affecting?*"

Like it or not, if you see it, you're accountable for it.

*The opposite of abuse is cooperation. And cooperation is the conviction that nobody can get there unless everybody gets there.*
                                                                    —Nan DeMars

# Part IV

# You *Can* Keep Your Integrity and Your Job

# 18

# Raises, Not Roses!

## Today's Professional Assistant Has New Respect!

*Nan, this search for my new executive assistant is probably the most important search I will ever conduct.*
—George S. Richards, chairman, president, and
CEO, Sempris, LLC, Minneapolis, MN

George is spot-on today. It was not always like this, however. This was a 1947 newspaper ad for a secretary: *"Wanted— Girl Friday. Must be young, attractive, and preferably unmarried. Pleasant telephone voice, perky personality. Ability to type 60 wpm, take shorthand, spell accurately and run boss's errands. Proven to be loyal and trustworthy. Long hours required."*

Few professional roles have evolved more completely than the "secretarial" one. It's a transformation that has included title, image, responsibilities, recognition, status, salary, and (finally) respect! Considering the fact that the wheels of commerce would come to a screeching halt without administrative professionals, it is a wonder that it took so long!

# The Expanded Role

When Bill Gates delivered the first personal computers, some predicted that secretaries would resist technology. Surprise! They not only embraced it; they became immediate technological wizards. Their expanded responsibilities prompted two important workplace trends to grow in prevalence today: "professionalization" of the clerical staff, and "clericalization" of the professional staff (almost a reversal of roles). Executives are now keyboarding, filing, and the like on their computers, thereby freeing their assistants to handle increased administrative responsibilities.

Another major factor that has contributed to assistants' expanding role is the ongoing layoffs and downsizing of organizations that are struggling with today's economy. Companies are tightening their belts and choosing to not replace key managers; instead, they're handing these new responsibilities over to their assistants. And these assistants are showing that they're more than up to the task.

Augmented responsibilities can include supervising employees and/or departments, planning, budgeting, orchestrating office moves, setting up new information systems, and spearheading special projects. Susan Shamali, CPS/CAP, and 2010 international president of the International Association of Administrative Professionals (IAAP), is a great example of this. As an office services coordinator at PricewaterhouseCoopers LLP, in Grand Rapids, Michigan, Susan recently told me:

> Life has become a bit more challenging since tax return processing duties have been added to my job. I may be the first admin [she's not!] to actually have three separate desks! Each has its own job-related responsibilities. I especially like the records management desk, as it's in the locked files room where I can hide out and actually get something done!

Companies have raised educational qualifications for these employees as well. Today's top-level assistants must often have a college degree, or at least a two-year postsecondary degree. More and more organizations are requiring professional certifications (and paying for them). Examples of these licenses are: the CPS (Certified Professional Secretary) and the CAP (Certified Administrative Professional)—both sponsored by IAAP; the PP (Professional Paralegal) and PLS (Professional Legal Secretary), sponsored by the National Association of Legal Secretaries (NALS); and the CLA (Certified Legal Assistant), which is sponsored by the National Association of Legal Assistants (NALA). In addition to these pedigrees, today's assistants increase their marketability by having a second (or third) language as well. (Spanish and Chinese are most in demand in the United States.)

## Job Description or Job Conscription?

However, we still have a ways to go in terms of clarifying job responsibilities. Case in point: handling personal tasks for a supervisor, an aspect of the job that's always been a sticky wicket. Results from my ongoing Office Ethics Surveys continually reflect that about 50 percent of respondents claim to "occasionally" run personal errands for their bosses and/or have observed others doing so. *However*, very few have reported these responsibilities as having been "specified" in their job descriptions. This suggests a dire need for continued clarification on what is and what is not expected from today's office professional.

A client named Janice called me on her way home from the job interview on which I had sent her (for the search end of my business). The position was to replace a retiring assistant to the CEO of a major public relations firm.

> Nan, the retiring assistant gave me a tour of her executive's office, including his (quite swanky) private bathroom. Upon leaving the bathroom, however, she pointed to the toilet water and said, "That's the color blue he likes in his toilet water!" I reacted with laughter, but the assistant insisted, "No, I'm serious. Part of your job will be to keep the toilet water in his toilet that color blue!" I'm really sorry, Nan, but I would like to withdraw from this interview process; I don't want a job where I have to worry about the color of my boss's toilet water!

This story always hits a nerve with me when I repeat it, because I was personally involved. I will forever regret that Janice withdrew from this high-paying opportunity due to this aspect of the job, but of course, it was her choice. I sent in another candidate with whom the same "bathroom conversation" occurred, and she ended up with the job (and a nice career). Like Janice, she cringed at the "color blue" responsibility as well. However, a week or so into the job, she talked with the maintenance crew, who agreed to monitor this area accordingly. Problem solved. Though there was a time when an admin would automatically comply with such a request, being proactive is now considered a virtue!

## Your "Little White Line"

In fairness to Janice, the silliness of the toilet water was her "little white line"—one that she knew she could not cross and remain happy. Everyone has this boundary of personal ethics that surrounds their activities. It is your personal list of do's and don'ts, and being wise enough to know where that line is will help you avoid all kinds of trouble. When someone steps over your ethical line, you have a right—even an obligation—to push back and insist on maintaining your standards. As Ralph Waldo Emerson once said: "We all boil at different degrees!"

I've heard countless other tales of managers' personal requests that bother assistants. I have the strong opinion that bosses generally will keep asking you to do more and more until they hear "No more!" from you, thereby signaling that they have reached your little white line. And though they'll likely respect your limits once you've identified them, no one will know where your boundaries are until you tell them. You may not be able to list everything that is on your "do" or "don't" list off the top of your head. You may not even discover what they are until pressed to do something you find objectionable, at which time you must speak up clearly and immediately.

Now, you can imagine there are other assistants who regularly check the color of the toilet water in their boss's private bathrooms. They don't mind; it's simply not an issue for them. However, they might find another task or request objectionable. We each have our personal limits and preferences regarding what we will or will not do. What's too intolerable for one of us will not be a problem for someone else, and vice versa.

## Personal Assistants

There are jobs—many that are quite high paying—where an assistant handles just the personal aspects of his or her boss's life. These assistants often travel with their bosses to various homes around the world, hire and fire their household staffs, handle all their personal finances, and even order their wardrobes. Many work for high-profile celebrities, politicians, and philanthropists, and are well rewarded with perks and salary.

The difference, however, is that these assistants have a clear-cut job description that outlines the various aspects of the job. Their expectations are clearly defined and agreed upon at the relationship's outset. I have heard many fun stories from these high-flying assistants who must sign confidentiality agreements (of course). Though they can be extremely demanding, these positions are *never* dull!

## The Trials of the "Office Wife"

Let's face it: there *are* assistants who still fall into the trap of being the proverbial "office wife." You know to whom I am referring—the one who does an excessive amount of personal chores for the boss, such as fetching dry cleaning, purchasing personal gifts and toiletries, picking up the kids, planning vacations, selecting home furnishings, collecting prescriptions, making personal reservations, wrapping gifts, paying bills, feeding pets, and generally anything else the boss delegates (whew!).

Life would certainly be simpler for all of us if we all had access to this kind of help. Considering the ever-increasing stress associated with reconciling the demands of work and family today, it's easy to understand why your boss may be tempted to lean on you for a little bit of extra help from time to time. But watch out for excessive, undocumented personal service requests. The "office wife" trap is a by-product of a lack of communication with the boss about specific duties. The penalties for failing to clearly define the little white line between professional duties and personal favors can range from bruised self-esteem to being held liable for your boss's misdeeds—even to getting fired.

Keep in mind as well that handling personal responsibilities for one's boss is often included in job descriptions for top-level assistants.

It is considered a legitimate attempt on the company's part to optimize this executive's time, and as the assistant, you should be doing your part to lighten his or her burden. Life can be tough at the top, so any practical assistance that saves the executive's time is usually a good value. But even in these situations, you must be sure to do it on the company's time and dime, not your own. You are helping this person achieve his goals, run his life more smoothly and, in general, greasing the wheel he has to steer.

Consequently, *all* of the personal responsibilities in this regard are certainly acceptable—*if* they are agreed upon at the time of hiring and *if* they are documented in your job description!

This is almost always the case with job descriptions for the boardroom-level assistant. However, this degree of clarity is unusual for other administrative professionals at different levels of responsibility. When assistants understand the expectations for help with personal tasks from the get-go, there are no surprises and few problems. Most of these responsibilities are described in vague terms, however, and capped by the catch-all phrase "and all other duties as assigned."

This pattern begs the question: how much is *too* much? The "office wife" role becomes an ethical dilemma when your boss uses you too much for the wrong kinds of personal tasks. It's an amazingly easy dilemma to drift into. Let's say that the company is willing to pay you to be available for that crisis rush to the dry cleaners, and has plainly stated that in your job description. Well, what about the routine trip to the dry cleaner? Now that you know the way, so to speak, do the crisis trips become convenience trips? And what about those other errands and tasks?

There is at least *some* benefit to your boss when you do these things (saving her time lowers her stress, etc.), so your boss might argue that you are only fulfilling the job description's requirements. But you know better. Are you *really* doing what you think the company wants you to do? If your boss expects you to perform personal tasks on company time that would be judged excessive by the company, you have a problem.

Keep in mind that you, your time, and your talents are a valuable company resource. If your boss uses your time for personal purposes and you participate, you are coconspirators in pilfering from the company. If your boss expects you to carry out these chores are on your personal time, and you agree to do them even though you don't want to, you are compromising your own principles by continuing to do them.

# How Much Personal Service Is Too Much?

**Here are some guidelines and ways to recognize that you're doing too many of your boss's personal chores:**

- *Requests are too frequent.* Daily or even weekly requests to run personal errands are generally regarded as inappropriate. But if the requests are infrequent and easy to complete, there might not be much to gain by raising a strong objection. Keep your priorities in order, and don't upset an otherwise fine job over a trivial matter.

- *Compliance costs the company too much.* A boss who ties up an assistant's time with personal tasks is literally stealing a valuable resource from the company, and going along with it makes you an accomplice. Considering the cumulative effect of some of the abusive practices that have evolved in some boss-assistant relationships, this is *not* stated too strongly. If you have to work extra hours to make up for time spent on the boss's personal errands, you and the company are indirectly paying extra time and money to support the boss's bad habit of having you take care of her.

- *Compliance costs you too much.* Let's say your boss wants you to perform his personal errands on your time, without financial compensation or compensatory time off. This is a clear abuse of your services as an employee. Allowing yourself to be taken advantage of like this (1) cheats you of your personal time and (2) diminishes your professional relationship with your boss. In the end, your boss won't respect you, and you won't respect yourself.

- *Your boss is secretive about requests.* Does your boss want you to hide the fact that you are typing his son's school paper from other employees? If so, find a way to decline. This is a sure warning sign that you are doing too much labor of a personal nature. By asking you to keep quiet, your boss is signaling that he knows this is a misuse of your time and talents, and now you do, too.

# Getting Off the Slippery Slope

**You can stop the requests for personal service if you:**

- *Decide how you really feel about the requests.* Are you a passive-aggressive people pleaser, eager to comply, but torturing yourself later for your inability or unwillingness to stand up to your boss and say "no!"? Or are you really and truly okay with the nature and frequency of these requests? (After all, some people enjoy the variety of getting out of the office every now and then to run errands for their boss.)

- *If you decide to make an issue of personal service requests, get prepared.* Document a few weeks of abuses and keep this "memo to yourself" in your personal files. Write down what you were asked to do and how much time it took. At the very least, this is proof of your concern for the problem. And such a file can protect your job and your professional credibility if your boss is ever discharged or disciplined.

- *Examine your job description.* A fair question for an admin to ask in a job interview is: "What kinds of personal service responsibilities are required in this job, if any?" While this is a good way to get everyone's expectations laid out before you accept the position, it's not foolproof. Requests for personal chores have a way of creeping into a boss-assistant relationship. To deal with a situation that is gradually getting excessive, rewrite your job description and include the personal tasks in which you are involved before your next performance review. Your discussion can then be your opportunity to tell your boss that although you prefer not to do these tasks, they seem to be arising more frequently.

- *Discuss your concerns with your boss.* Give your boss a chance to reform. Perhaps he has chosen to forget (or simply doesn't realize) how many times you are being inconvenienced, or perhaps there are temporary circumstances that will soon render the problem moot. Both of you need to be specific to make the expectations clear. You have to say things like, "I don't mind stopping by at the library on my way home, but I dread having to go shopping for your wife." One assistant told me she told her boss she would be happy to handle all the personal services outlined in the job description (and there were many) with one exception: she refused to pick up his dry cleaning. She told him she hated to pick up her own dry cleaning and she didn't want to add his to the list. Apparently, dry cleaning was on the other side of her little white line. Her boss's response? "Fine"—and he deleted it from the list.

- *Learn to say "no" politely, but firmly.* The line between professional duties and personal favors should be clear for all to see after you discuss your respective expectations. Carol Rhodes, CPS, of Carol Rhodes Business Services in Houston, Texas, adds the following important point: "Thereafter, each time you are asked to do something of a personal nature, you can politely refuse, reminding your boss about your job description, your preferences, and your previous discussions. If you are consistent, eventually the boss will stop asking."

- *Finally, focus on the "big picture."* Keep your office's broad goals in mind. A 3M executive once said to me:

> My assistant and I are a team of two and, together, we strive to effectively and efficiently accomplish my job description. To do this, if she has to serve coffee occasionally and run personal errands for me to ease my pressures, it's simply a way that she is helping me perform my job better. Every assistant I have ever had has understood this program and that these responsibilities are simply part of the job. They all help accomplish *our* ultimate goal!

## Communicate, Communicate, Communicate!

This is one area about which you cannot remain silent. It is imperative to open the lines of communication with your managers and discuss the dilemmas that concern you. I hear all kinds of stories from assistants who suddenly find themselves mired down in mundane personal tasks for their bosses—and it remains a point of continuous irritation between them long after the duties are completed. *Example:* A secretary to a major ball club owner told me that she was expected to bring her boss a bag lunch—that she had prepared *herself* for him to eat at his desk—every time he was in town (which was quite often because the team played at "home" a lot). She said that although *she* never "brown bagged" lunch and preferred instead to go out at noon, he insisted on her homemade lunches. She told me that after eight years of doing this, it was finally beginning to bother her! She went into his office one day, sat down, and said: "Could we please have a tuna fish sandwich discussion?" After she explained why she did not wish to continue this practice, his simple reply was: "Good, I was beginning to get tired of your sandwiches, anyhow." Now, who says that we can't mediate the great gaps in communication between us?

Open communication will always serve you well with your boss—and even your potential boss. In addition to asking about the kinds of personal tasks you're expected to perform on the job during the interview, request as well to see the job description. The two rarely match. However, this gives you a chance to begin talking about the discrepancies between them without jeopardizing your chances to get the job offer. You can be 100 percent certain that other personal service duties will seem to somehow "creep in" when expectations are allowed to drift. So go into the job with your eyes wide open. Be wary of situations where the boss seems particularly needy. And don't set yourself up for a nasty confrontation later on because one small aspect of the job (like picking up dry cleaning) turns out to be a surprise. The lack of good communication up front could spoil an otherwise wonderful position and career.

## Respect Is Always the Trump Card

My husband says I will forever wax forth on what he calls the "introduction factor." This occurs when everyone in the company is being introduced with last names, followed by: "This is my assistant, Elizabeth!" If this ever happens to you, step up to the plate, extend your hand, and say, "Hello, I'm Elizabeth Swanson"—and keep doing that until the clueless introducer catches on. It is an egregious but common etiquette breach that managers and executives are introduced with first and last names and the admin is downgraded to "Susie the assistant." Do not *ever* let this happen to you. And if you see it happening to others, step in and ask the individual for his or her last name. Everyone deserves a professional introduction.

This can be a self-inflicted faux pas as well. I wince when I hear someone answer his business phone with first name only. It is just as easy to say "Marvin Anderson speaking" as "Marvin speaking." Unless your company has a policy of not revealing last names (and some do for security reasons), do not degrade your position or your profession by not properly identifying yourself.

A *Sally Forth* newspaper cartoon once had the boss reviewing a list of his assistant's requests in honor of Administrative Professionals Week. He ticked them off: "A raise, an updated printer, a professional seminar, (and even) a day off!" The final note on the list was "Respect." "*Respect*," he ranted. "She's never had *this* on her list before!"

I always tell executives in my seminars that their assistants do not object to serving coffee to them. (In global organizations where international visitors are a common occurrence, it is considered rude if refreshments are not offered.) This kind of hospitality is simply considered being gracious, and I think graciousness on the part of any assistant is always in order. The key word, however, is *respect*. It is how one is *asked* and how one is *treated* that matter most.

A classic example of how an assistant should *not* be treated was exemplified by the book and movie *The Devil Wears Prada* (discussed in an earlier chapter) about the abusive relationship between an assistant and her boss, a major fashion magazine editor. Among other outrageous behaviors toward her assistant (and there were many), the editor would come into the office each morning and fling her huge fur coat and 30-pound Gucci bag on her assistant's desk (and sometimes the assistant herself) with a clunk! Whether it's a Gucci bag or an empty coffee cup, this kind of attitude falls into the "how one is *treated*" category of disrespect and can result in nothing but resentment.

Former Massachusetts governor Jane Swift found this out the hard way. She once had members of her staff babysit her infant daughter on the job when she was lieutenant governor. Her fed-up aides, who felt that this responsibility "devalued" their jobs, went straight to the *Boston Herald* and blew the whistle on their boss. Add this to the fact that what may be acceptable in the corporate world is often unacceptable in the public sector. In addition to the public embarrassment, Swift drew a $1,250 fine from the State House Ethics Committee.

I heard about the most outrageous (and hilarious) request in the personal services category in one of my workshops. An assistant stood up and said, "Nan, I once had a boss who was seeing two different psychiatrists a week." (I recall thinking to myself, "If he had that many problems, I'm glad he was also seeking a lot of help.") Then, she added, "One afternoon, he called me from his car and said, 'Nicky, I'm really running late today and can't make my doctor's appointment. Can you go instead?'" My entire class erupted in laughter. I asked Nicky, "What did you *do?*" She replied: "I went!" After the room settled down, I asked her, "But, what did you *talk* about?" And, she replied delightedly, "*Him!* It was a wonderful hour!"

Who said admin jobs aren't fun?

Yes, the administrative professional job description has evolved drastically from the old days' coffee-and-copier role to one of increased responsibilities, challenges, opportunities, and respect. Developments in office technology enhance this role daily. We must never forget, however, that what makes these positions valuable is that their administrative responsibilities are also of a personal, interactive nature and, therefore, *not* easily automated. These personal skills are what will always make this profession unique and valued.

I have management today to thank for now fully recognizing this profession for what it is: a profession, and one worthy of dignity and respect and increased salaries and perks. But I proudly believe that it is the administrators and assistants of today who are the true architects of this professional recognition. You *know*—and continue to *champion*—your value.

> *Nan, I look upon the hiring of this new executive administrative assistant as filling one of the most important leadership roles in the company. This person will not only reflect an extension of me as a leader, but also will serve as my communicator both inside and outside the company.*
>
> —Greg Flack, CEO, president, and COO, Schwan Food Company, Bloomington, MN

# 19

## The Ethics of Job Hunting

*How to* Look *for a Job While* on *the Job!*

*Life is easier when you learn to plow around the stumps!*
—Anonymous

Dear Nan:

Ethically speaking, how do I look for a job while still *on* a job? I'm aware of increasing layoffs at my firm and am nervous I'll be on the next hit list. I'm uncomfortable about lying to take time off for an interview and even more nervous about addressing the situation with a potential employer (after all, I have to identify my current employer). I certainly don't want my boss to get wind that I am looking; I might be shown the door prematurely. How can I surreptitiously (and ethically) conduct this job search?

—Monie in Decatur, IL

My response: "One looks for a new job while on the current job like one makes love to a porcupine—*very carefully!*"

This dilemma is a sign of our times: job security is at the top of everyone's anxiety list, and you may be semiactively looking for a new job for six months or longer, so this is not a trivial occurrence. Employees who are concerned about being laid off certainly don't want to give their employer even the smallest excuse to accelerate the process. No matter what your current job's shortcomings, you're probably glad to have it and reluctant to let it go before you have the next job in hand. Today's astute headhunters (myself included) are wisely advising their candidates: "Don't quit your day job!"

There's even a word for this new attitude: *presenteeism*, as in the opposite of *absenteeism*. Employees are so skittish about job security that they are extra-conscious of being present on the job, working longer hours, and increasing their responsibilities to not only protect but justify their positions. "Face time" is important again; forget about requests for telecommuting and pushing for flex time.

Nevertheless, every professional needs to steadily move forward in his or her career. "It is not disloyal to anyone to better yourself," writes Peggy Burdick of St. Jude Children's Research Hospital in Memphis, Tennessee. Helen Suarez of Pfizer Inc., in New York City, concurs. "Your career is your responsibility," she explains, "and it should be second nature for you to keep your grapevine tuned for advancement opportunities."

Take heart: you *can* improve your professional future ethically and without jeopardizing your present. When exploring a new job opportunity, keep in mind my three Cs:

## Be Careful

*Keep your personal business private.* This is one situation where you cannot be too careful. While networking has traditionally been the number one route to finding a new job, schmoozing nowadays can be riskier than ever. Be selective about the people with whom you share your plans. Keep in mind that even your best friend—who would never intentionally hurt you or your career—may inadvertently let it slip that you are in the job market. Rumors run rampant when employees are worried about job security.

*Do not use your current employer's time, equipment, or connections without permission.* Be fair. In addition to being the ethical thing to do (after all, you are an employee), it is also prudent. If you are discovered doing otherwise, you will be cast—and remembered—in a negative way. How many resumes have we all found on the company's copy machine, and what did we think of the people careless enough to leave them there? Unless your boss is aware that you are looking for another job and has agreed to help you (use of the copy/fax machines, computer and phone time, postage, even acting as a reference), do not take advantage of her. It's not fair—and dicey besides. Remember: your company has the right to monitor employee e-mails, voice mail, Blackberrys—everything that is part of their equipment. And you will have compromised yourself during your exit interview if your soon-to-be-former employer believes you conducted your job search from your current office's premises.

*Request that prospective employers only contact you at home.* "Be up front with potential interviewers and tell them you would prefer they call you on your personal cell phone and send any inquiries to your home e-mail address," advises Laura Steinbach of Premara Blue Cross in Mountlake Terrace, Washington. "They will respect you, and you'll ease your conscience knowing that your job search was honest and above-board." This means you should provide only your home and cell phone numbers and send out resumes solely from your home computer. You can still respond promptly by periodically checking your personal voice mail and e-mail messages.

*Put a professional image out there.* Prospective employers do not want to hear your latest jingle or Elvis impersonation on your cell or home phone. I once had a client who wanted to change an interview time with one of my candidates. Since he couldn't reach me, he called the candidate's home phone and, ultimately, canceled the interview solely after hearing her "unprofessional voice message" (his words) on her machine. In this same vein, make sure your Facebook, LinkedIn, and similar social media pages are up to date and professional. As we've already discussed, most prospective employers are "Googling" serious candidates to find their personal social media sites. An unprofessional presentation on your part will kill your chance for an interview. While this might not seem fair and isn't something you can prove, it's the reality today! So, first, get your new job. Then you can go back to an informal voice mail message.

*Be discreet in returning phone calls from the office.* Lunch hours and breaks are appropriate times to return phone calls, but keep them to a minimum, and always be sure you are in a private area that is beyond earshot of others. "Remember, you are being paid to work, not job hunt," says Stacia Y. Stokes, All Saints Healthcare in Racine, Wisconsin. Keep in mind that anyone who has scheduled a meeting could burst into a conference room at any time. The last thing you want is to be interrupted midinterview with another employer!

*Be careful not to lie to your employer about taking time off to interview.* This is a biggie. Ms. Ethics, of course, would *never* want you to lie about your reason for taking time off. Just as it is unethical to be paid for time you are taking to seek a new position, it is also unethical to lie to your employer about your reasons for taking time off. "Tell your supervisor you need to take some personal time off (PTO)," suggests Joyce Brown, a CPS in Maui, Hawaii. "PTO is just that: personal. For that reason, it does not require an explanation. Just be sure to give your employer 24 hours' notice as a courtesy."

"If explanations are required for taking PTO, I'd find the next opportunity and grab it with both hands," adds Katherine M. Astleford, CPS/CAP, of CELRP-EC-D in Pittsburgh, Pennsylvania. "If your time off becomes excessive, though, you may want to consider another alternative. Taking vacation time might solve the problem. Requesting a leave of absence would require an explanation, so it should be used only as a last resort."

"Be creative," offers Diane Buzard CPS/CAP, Carillon Investments Inc., Cincinnati, Ohio. "Look at holiday schedules. Perhaps your office is closed on Presidents' Day, for example, but the prospective employer's is not. Or consider tying an interview in with another requested time off. If you are already taking some time off for a medical appointment or school conference, schedule your interview for that same day—and just add an extra hour or two."

Juggle the interview schedules however you must, but keep yourself in good standing with your current employer. Lying about time off can be perceived as the proverbial "dog ate my homework" excuse—and may come back to bite you.

"My boss once interviewed a man for a high-level computer position," says Stacy Walker, CPS/CAP, at McKee Foods Corporation, Chattanooga, Tennessee. "During the first five minutes of the interview, the man made it known that he had taken a sick day from work be there. How revealing! This was definitely an individual whose poor work ethic could not to be trusted. (And, no, he wasn't hired.)"

Employers and search firms are well aware of already-employed candidates' scheduling problems and should be amenable to conducting interviews during a long lunch hour, after work, and even on weekends. Cherrill Mears of Community Transit in Everett, Washington, writes that while searching for a job, she "made every effort to schedule interviews at a time that least inconvenienced my current employer. I would also volunteer to work late or come in early before the personal appointment so that work in my current job was affected as little as possible."

"Potential employers are (typically) more than willing to interview either early in the morning (before 8 AM) or once the normal workday is over (after 5 PM)," adds Lynn Smith of VanSlyck & Associates Inc. in Phoenix, Arizona. "I believe a potential employee would be respected for suggesting it." Carol A. Marroquin, Hankamer School of Business, Baylor University, Waco, Texas, concurs. "If the prospective employer doesn't understand your ethical stance (in not wanting to cheat your employer of your time on the job), then they probably are not the employer you want to work for, anyhow. In other words, if they are not willing to respect ethical behavior, then how will they treat you?"

# Be Confidential

Stress to your search firm that they must keep everything confidential. Working with an agency like this can benefit you tremendously. By representing you, they can save you considerable time and worry. (*Caution:* Work only with a firm that is client paid and does not require you to pay any fee whatsoever.)

"I worked through an agency in my job search while on the job 15 years ago, and the entire process was much easier for me," says L. Montanaro, CPS, from New Haven, Connecticut. Be sure to work only with a reputable search firm that respects the confidentiality of your circumstance. This is key: you don't want your resume to be "shotgunned" to all potential clients of the search firm. While reputable agencies would never do such a thing, there are charlatans who may.

Emphasize to any potential employers as well the classified nature of your job search. If you're applying for a position on your own, always mark your application form and other correspondence as "confidential," and reiterate this fact during every interview. Most human resource professionals appreciate and respect candidates' confidentiality in a job search, but it is always best to have this conversation with them anyway.

It is equally vital to guard your reference information. Give potential employers and your search firm only the references that are safe to contact. Then, be sure those referenced individuals have a heads-up regarding the confidentiality of your search. Prospective employers will understand why you cannot use your current employer as a reference.

Expect a phone interview before a face-to-face interview. This is common now, and it's a good thing for several reasons. You may decide after speaking with someone about the position that it's not one you wish to pursue, and/or the potential employer may determine that you are not a good fit. Either way, you both save a lot of time and effort. Arrange to have the interview with complete privacy and on personal time in order to be able to focus completely. "Phone interviews will allow you to use your cell phone during the lunch hour (for example) and sit somewhere you'll know you have complete privacy," Eileen Holz at Kraft Foods in Glenview, Illinois, offers. Just make sure you don't take *too* long a break!

## Be Considerate

Let your current employer know immediately when you've accepted a new position. It is simple courtesy to allow your employer to be the first to know—not the last. Give proper notice; two weeks is the usual lead time prior to departure, unless your company has a policy of removing employees as soon as they give notice.

Exit your current company gracefully. The "farewell e-mail" to all coworkers is your prime opportunity to exit with class. Some simply state their good-byes and well wishes (this is best), while others attach their résumés in hopes of soliciting new job leads (a bit tacky?). Unless you simply *must* get that chip off your shoulder, skip the drama of an angry "up yours" message. Blasting your boss and/or the company with a "now I can finally tell you what I really think of you" message burns bridges (no kidding!) unnecessarily and diminishes your professional stature. You never know; you may be working with some of these people again someday!

It's also smart to update your job description and desk manual for your successor, and to leave an orderly work space and office surroundings. "Offer to train your successor and/or offer telephone support for them after they start," recommends Patricia Tate, CPS/CAP, secretary at Leeds Presbyterian Church, in Gardendale, Alabama. Your successor will appreciate your thoughtfulness—and your employer will remember your professionalism. Work hard to maintain good relationships with your previous employer and colleagues. Wouldn't you rather have everyone talking about you in a glowing manner after you leave, anyway?

Project a positive and constructive manner. You are not betraying the company or your boss; you are just departing for a career opportunity you can't refuse. If you're granted an exit interview, keep your remarks positive and your criticism constructive. Concentrate on your good experiences and all you have learned. Remember, you are leaving for an advancement opportunity. If you remain upbeat, positive, and helpful from the time you give notice, your boss and your peers will be happy for you.

You write your own history. Your current job, bosses, subordinates, and peers are all a part of this history from the day you walk out the door. You will need good references, so leave on good terms. "Depart in such a way that if you wanted to go back, you could," adds Tate.

Finally, get over any guilt you have about your potential departure. Be proud of the job you have done for your boss and your company, and approach your new job opportunity as another stepping-stone in an ever-evolving professional career.

Sharon Forston at Aerospace Chem-tronics Inc. in El Cajon, California, shares some wise words: "We all have choices . . . that we must make from time to time. These personal choices should promote our own happiness and fulfillment in our careers wherever we work. So shed that uncomfortable feeling and get on with what you need to do." Well said.

## Do I Have to Lie about Being Fired?

Dear Nan:

My most recent job turned out to be a disaster, and, as a result, I got myself fired. I'm okay with what happened because I stood up to my boss and refused to participate in his deception scheme. He owned an employment agency and his slimy practice was to have his sales associates make cold calls into companies and give a false name and bogus company without revealing they

*(continued)*

*(continued)*

were an employment agency. In other words, he was harvesting potential candidates for a certain position under false pretenses. I was always uncomfortable with my company's unethical modus operandi, but I was the assistant to my boss and I was never asked to participate myself. Then, wham—one day my boss asked me to help out in the sales arena, adding these "ruse" responsibilities to my job description. I refused to do so and, bam, just like that, I was terminated.

Well, I'm not feeling so high and mighty anymore. Self-righteousness doesn't pay the babysitter. My ethical dilemma is this: Do I have to lie when I'm asked why I left my previous employer? I can't leave the experience off my resume because it would leave a two-year gap. I've been telling the truth thus far, but get no second interviews or offers. I am well qualified for the jobs I'm seeking, and I've never been unable to find work before. It's almost like I'm being punished for doing the right thing!

—Lisa in Rohnert Park, CA

It is always ironic—and disappointing—when the world does not immediately reward us for doing the right thing. We naturally want to get some credit for making the tough choices. However, I'm proud of Lisa for leaving what was obviously an unethical operation. Had she not done so, that job would have probably ended badly sooner or later, anyway. It may sound funny, but in this case, I commend Lisa for getting herself canned!

**Here are a few thoughts that may help in her next interview:**

- *Say only what is absolutely necessary if asked why you left your last job.* The less you say, the better. You may have been communicating more than the truth with your explanation, and going beyond a few carefully worded statements may be too much. Be matter-of-fact. Don't imply that you're harboring any ill will, since the interviewer assumes you will be talking about this job in the same way someday.

- *Stress the positive.* Help interviewers come to conclusion that the reasons you left your last position are unimportant. Emphasize why you are excited about the possibility of working for their company (do some research here so that you have concrete, detailed examples). Explain why you feel your experience and expertise can benefit them. If they ask you directly, "Why did you leave your last job?," you can certainly respond, "It wasn't the right fit," which is true. Period. That may suffice. (Even employees who are fired for total incompetence can honestly say this. After all, it wasn't the right fit!)

- *If asked directly, "Were you fired?," then you do have to tell the truth.* In this case, I would respond: "I was terminated for refusing to comply with requests by my boss to commit some unethical acts." Practice giving that answer until you can do so naturally and without emotion. If pressed further, declare that "to say more would be unprofessional and violate confidentiality."

Then consider the fact that—without even realizing it—you haven't seemed a bit too eager in previous interviews to "tell the tale" of the former boss that upset you so much. You naturally want the interviewer to understand your situation, but think about it from her perspective: There is no way she can objectively evaluate the rightness or wrongness of your being fired, so she could reasonably conclude (1) you're preoccupied with your mistreatment; (2) you are prone to tell your troubles to others and you'll spill confidential information to anyone in the process; (3) you're a chronic troublemaker—or at least a problem employee; or (4) all of the above. If *you* had these concerns, would *you* offer yourself a job?

Having been burned, it probably goes without saying you'll be a little more selective before taking your next job. This is a *good* thing. It will compel you to keep your eyes wide open to the obvious differences between your own values and those of your prospective employer. In hindsight (always 20/20), you probably are telling yourself you should have acknowledged that ethical gap earlier and started (surreptitiously, of course) to seek a new position.

You sound like a valuable contributor, and you deserve to work for a company that meets more of your needs than just a paycheck. Trust your intuition; does your prospective employer feel like a company you can stand up for and behind in the future, or is a clash of right and wrong inevitable? Now that you're older and wiser, you can apply some of that wisdom to make your next job your best career move ever. And *that* will be your (much-deserved) reward for doing the right thing!

## It's Never Easy

Job seeking, keeping, and even job leaving can trigger ethical dilemmas. But thank heaven we all learn and grow from our experiences—good or bad. And we all overcome challenges to become better people. Think of it this way: if we didn't have those challenges, we would never have had the opportunity to progress. Take heart: you *can* handle it all and keep your ethics intact.

> *This became a credo of mine . . . attempt the impossible in order to improve your work.*
>
> —Bette Davis, actress

# 20

## Start Talking!

### *Everyone Chooses the Ethics of Their Office—Not Just Upper Management and Obvious Victims*

*One's philosophy is not expressed in words; it is expressed in the choices one makes ... and the choices we make are ultimately our responsibility.*
—Eleanor Roosevelt, U.S. First Lady (1933–1945)

True story: For 20 years, Gerard trusted his boss. One day, on his boss's say-so, Gerard notarized the signature on the title of the car belonging to the boss's wife. "She signed it at home," his boss said. "She just wasn't able to come in today to do it herself." Gerard did as he was asked and went back to work, unaware that this was the beginning of the boss's nasty divorce. When the boss's wife found out what had happened, she was (understandably) quite upset. She claimed she never intended to sell the car and slapped a lawsuit on Gerard. Not only did

Gerard receive a considerable fine, but he also lost his notary public privileges—and now carries a felony on his record.

Gerard neglected to follow the first point of his Ethical Priority Compass: protect yourself. He knew, as all notary publics should, to never notarize a signature that you did not personally witness. He had a choice, and he made the wrong one. Though his heart was in the right place (he wanted to please his boss), he momentarily relaxed the ethical habit that had served him so well. Ironically, because now he was no longer a notary, he also lost his job! Our worst wounds are self-inflicted, aren't they?

---

Dear Nan:

I am witnessing a meltdown of my office's ethical standards. It's like everyone (about 25 people work here) has caught the same virus: the selfish, self-centered "me-me-me" bug. They all seem to be behaving in a slipshod manner, fudging (*lying* is a better word), cutting corners, and generally disrespecting each other just to slide through the day and hit the road. The company is making money in spite of ourselves—we have a much-needed product and little competition—so even management seems to not care about the way everyone operates. I love my job as top admin, and I can't give it up without losing seniority and my shot at stock options.

What can I do to turn this situation around? Can just one person make a difference—and where do I start? I can't afford to call it quits, and trying to ride it out is becoming more difficult every day. Is there something constructive that I can do? My attempt to set a good example has not had much of an effect. What else can I do to turn this cesspool into a swimming pool?
—Audrey in Kansas City, MO

---

Audrey has to be feeling pretty alone and disconnected from her coworkers. Who are these people, she wonders, and how did her office culture degrade from "good ethics" to "no ethics"? Can one person make any real difference?

My answer is *yes!*

But you have to talk about it.

# Talk before You Walk

When I asked my readers for their insights regarding Gerard's dilemma and Audrey's dilemma, virtually all suggested more discussion with their bosses *before* actions were taken that could not be undone. "Action should start with a frank conversation with your supervisor about anything you are concerned about," according to Myrna Thompson at Pacific Bell.

**Gerard and Audrey should ask:**
- "Are you aware that _____?" This gets you on the same page. Skip the drama, and make no accusations.
- "Are you aware that this is an ethical dilemma?"
- "Are you aware that situations like this can affect my job performance and possibly the performance of others?"
- "What can we do about this?" The *we* makes it clear that this is something you must all work on together.
- "What can I do (specifically) to help?" You're showing that you don't just want to complain about this situation—you want to do something to change it!

In a perfect world, Gerard's boss will retract his request and Audrey's boss will recognize her as an ally.

"If [Audrey's] company does not respond to these dilemmas, they will lose good employees and customers," says Norma Kasinger, who replied to one of my columns. "There are revolving doors in both the human resource and marketing departments at companies that have an unethical culture."

But what can Audrey do if her boss is part—or most—of the problem (as I suspect might be the case)? Since an office's culture is a reflection and extension of the boss, he sets the ethical standards; ethical "meltdowns" don't just happen. Fortunately, the boss is not the only one who can influence the ethical culture.

What can Audrey do? Let's assume that she discusses her "turmoil" observations with her boss, who quickly dismisses her concern. Now Audrey has a new opportunity to be a part of the solution, and here's what I'd direct her to do: Tell your boss that you want to discuss the dilemmas with your coworkers in an effort to resolve them. Make sure you get his go-ahead to do so (it's good to have permission to stir things up), but don't back down if he tries to stop you (that's a different dilemma). Your scurrilous coworkers are about to encounter the Audrey Factor!

The first conversations about ethics are always the most difficult, but they become easier as the culture of the Ethical Office takes root.

Why just *talk*, you might wonder. Why not take some sort of action? Because talking is a logical first step that lets everyone get a fair chance to tell his or her side of the story (opening the door to conversations that can be real eye-openers). And your alternatives—complaints, lawsuits, and/or finding a new job—will certainly cost the company *and* Audrey more. The most important first step is to start the discussion about ethics at whatever level of comfort you can.

## Informal Ethics Discussions Can Prevent Ethical Dilemmas

Many of the "real rules" of the office are informal, so an informal discussion is a good place to begin. By discussing hypothetical dilemmas ("what should we—or would you—do if such-and-such happened?"), you can, together and in a safe environment, agree on some simple, baseline conduct expectations with your boss, coworkers, vendors, and customers. This will allow you to agonize less often over decisions like, "I wonder if it's okay to say this or do that," and the rascals of the workplace will think twice before asking you to do something questionable.

Don't worry about prescribing acceptable ethical behavior to everyone in advance of every possible problem. People are smart enough to make the connections; they'll reason that, "Since we talked about this topic as a group, I know that if I do this thing, it will really raise people's eyebrows. I think I'd better not do it."

## Informal Ethics Discussions Can Resolve Ethical Dilemmas

When an ethical dilemma does arise, try to pull the person affected aside immediately or shortly thereafter. Ask questions like "What's going on?" or "Are you certain this is the right thing to do?" or similar inquiry. Many people quickly correct themselves, especially when they have had informal discussions beforehand.

Formal ethics discussions are beyond the domain of this book. Your human resources department, company lawyers, and similar decision makers should determine what will be said to whom, and in what manner. By the time official conversations like this take place, the informal discussions have probably failed, and it's probably beyond your control. Formal procedures regarding ethics are always costly for the company to resolve (due to attorney fees, settlement costs, etc.). This is why casual exchanges are preferable; they are faster, less complicated, and less expensive responses.

## Beginning the Ethics Discussion

Ethics discussions are conversations, not inquisitions. Can you and your boss (or coworkers, customers, vendors, etc.) talk about existing or hypothetical dilemmas *today?* If not, is there some news item you can introduce to begin the discussion, such as "What would we/you do if this happened here?"

I have found that "conversation starters" work well with my seminar attendees. My intention is not to script your discussions, but simply to give you a jumping-off point. You can get the ball rolling with just one or two questions, then hang on for the ride while the conversation takes on your office's more pressing topics. Start the discussion with a question that seems interesting to you and your group. If the dialogue lags or becomes awkward, then move on to the next question. This also works well if you want to conduct a general ethics "check-in, check-up" with your boss and/or coworkers.

**Here are some good conversation starters:**
- Is any behavior or action taking place that you would be *embarrassed to see reported in the media?* Why?
- Do you think anyone in the office is doing something *illegal?*
- Do you think anyone in the office is doing something *unethical?*
- Do you *trust your boss?*
- Does your *boss trust you?*
- Do you *trust your coworkers?*
- Have there been any *incidents* in the recent past that made you *ashamed* of your company?
- Is there anything going on in your office that you would feel *uncomfortable about explaining to your kids?* A reporter? Your parents?

- Is everyone—customers, coworkers, vendors—*being treated fairly?*
- Is there any perception of a conflict of *interest?*
- Are there any obvious or subtle *behaviors that seem unfair*, or appear to *undermine the effectiveness* of the work done in your office?
- Has your ability to make an impartial and objective decision been *compromised* or forced to be biased?

Some people have trouble talking directly about the ethics of their conduct, so be prepared to be patient. The person with whom you're talking (perhaps yourself, too) may have to "talk around" the edge of the central questions, tell lots of anecdotes, persist in discussing other tangents, and so on before they get to the point of making a decision or commitment to remedy the dilemma.

One more thing to do: *review your job description before initiating any ethical discussions.* Does your position explicitly or implicitly refer to the ethical dilemma in any way?

## The "What Do We Do Now" Conversations

The worst has happened—you've caught someone in a compromised position, and you have an ethical dilemma you need to talk through with them.

**Here's how to do it:**
- *Before you begin, put yourself in the frame of mind that says everyone deserves the benefit of the doubt.* Also, assume the other person is acting in good faith and telling the truth (at least most of it). Resolve to convey a tone that will not be taken as accusatory, judgmental, or otherwise negative. Stay professional—you are simply seeking facts as the first step to correct a problem.
- *Ask: "Please, may I take a few minutes to clarify a few points with you?"* This is a good way to open a discussion because it is safe. You are being respectful of the other person by courteously asking permission to take time to talk about this.
- *Ask: "Am I to understand that . . . ?"* Then, lay out your understanding of the situation. This gives you the chance to report the facts and circumstances as you know them and the other person an opportunity to correct any misunderstandings under which you have been laboring. It also starts the discussion by having you

both focus on the same facts. Many discussions end right here because misunderstandings are removed.

- *Ask: "Are you aware that this dilemma/situation/problem is serious enough to be affecting our job performance?"* This explains why you are making this your business, and removes the "it's no big deal" and "it's none of your business" excuses. This corporate-speak flags a problem as important enough to resolve for financial and legal liability reasons. Be prepared to describe your feelings of stress, embarrassment, awkward communication, fear, shame, breakdown of trust, ad the like.

- *Ask: "Are you feeling as uncomfortable (there's that safe word again) about this situation as I am?"* Ask this question, and then be quiet to listen.

- *Ask: "What can we do about this?"* Seek consensus around no-fault resolutions. Get a commitment to change if possible, and let everyone walk away with their dignity intact. Remember, the challenge is to resolve the dilemma between expected and actual behavior; it's not just to make everyone "feel better."

What if you encounter resistance and/or denial?

Do not underestimate some people's capacity to cling to irrational and indefensible positions. Some people would rather eat worms while walking across hot coals than admit that they did something wrong.

### Coax them toward acknowledgment of the dilemma with follow-up questions like these:

- "Who is being affected by this questionable behavior?" (Are they nameless, faceless? Customers? People with whom we want a long-term relationship?)
- "What are the harms and benefits to those affected?" (What are their needs, wants, values, expectations?)
- "What would they say if we were completely transparent?" (Does this situation pass the "smell" test, or does it stink?)
- "What are the alternatives?" (There will be suggestions to listen to.)
- "What is your acceptable solution?"
- "How will we know we have resolved this dilemma to our mutual satisfaction?"

# What If the Discussion Does *Not* Resolve the Dilemma?

If informal discussions fail to resolve the dilemma, step back to rethink the situation. Have you learned anything that suggests you can live with these circumstances, therefore neutralizing it as a dilemma that drains you? Can you live with it for now? Or do you remain committed to resolving it?

If you decide upon the latter, then you have to up the ante. The stakes are going to get higher, which means that the consequences are going to get more expensive. Be sure you are prepared to pay the price. Do you really want to fight this battle? Are you ready to press forward, no matter what the friction? Can you deal with the fact that you might even lose your job? Some principles are worth it, but some aren't. Remember your core personal issues and values.

# How to Up the Ante

*Step 1: Write yourself a summary of the situation*, and share it with your personal attorney (not the company's). You'll need this numerous times as you begin "shopping" the dilemma to others who may be interested in helping.

**Clearly articulate:**

- What is the problem?
- What caused the problem? (And are you absolutely sure?)
- Who is affected?
- Who will be harmed?
- Who will benefit (by solving it)?
- Are someone's rights involved?
- Who can help?
- What are the alternatives?
- What action needs to be taken?
- How can this problem be avoided in the future?
- Why can't I and/or the company live with this situation?

*Step 2: Collect evidence* to support your position.

*Step 3: Talk to another supervisor*, preferably someone at or about your boss's level, or someone else with more (or different) authority.

You are soliciting his or her opinion about the best way to proceed.

Talking to someone else has a high probability of wounding your relationship with your boss. Going around him will cause him to worry that you have embarrassed him before others in the company by saying something like, "I'm talking to you because my immediate supervisor won't or can't do anything. He therefore must be weak, unethical, afraid to speak up, or all of the above."

You can try to avoid this by presenting the third-party option to your manager first. You may be able to package this as a win-win option by saying something like: "I realize this puts you in an awkward position, and your hands may be tied, even though I know you wish it were different. May I suggest an alternative? Why don't I take this situation to the human resource department and get their input? That takes it off your desk and makes the HR staff person—not you—look like the ethics policeman. This way, you do not have to upset any other working relationship because of this situation. How does that sound?" This may be an acceptable approach, if it prompts your manager to recognize your commitment to resolving the problem. And the prospect of your talking to others about your concerns may be just the impetus your boss needs to take action. After all, he may worry about being perceived as someone who can't maintain the peace in his own department. And even if this does not occur, at least you've done your best to keep him involved in the process.

You *must* remain absolutely professional in your presentation from this point on. Stick to the facts; focus on the dilemma and the potential consequences to the company—not conflicting personalities, turf wars, and the like. Again, document, document, document the date, time, and substance of every conversation.

*Step 4: Talk to a division head, ombudsman, human resource representative, or other formal "listening post" within the company.* By this time, the company's formal damage control and public relations machinery should begin to work with you to resolve the problem. This is also when you must decide if you believe the company's approach is going to be effective. If you determine that it is not, you have to drop the matter or be prepared for an adversarial relationship.

*Step 5: Formalize legal representation for yourself.* You are stepping into shark-infested waters, and the stakes are escalating rapidly.

Be prepared to hire your own shark to look out for your interests. You may not want to formally engage an attorney—that may be an overreaction that will just compound the problem—but you should have had at least preliminary discussions with an attorney to help you assess your situation by now.

*Step 6: Still no results? Tell your story to the media, relevant government agencies, and citizen groups (the court of public opinion), and/or sue in a court of law.* If you do not find a satisfactory remedy within the company, you have to decide (with advice from your attorney) if you want an adversarial relationship with your employer. You may attempt to remain anonymous in some venues, but not many. Few people or organizations are willing to stick their neck out for someone who is not prepared to share the heat. You'll probably be wondering by this point why you ever grabbed this tiger's tail.

*Step 7: Finally, you always have the option to quit and walk away from the entire situation.* This may be necessary if your mental health begins to suffer. Remember, you have to continue to take care of yourself (it's the first part of your Ethical Compass). You already know I don't like this option, but there are practical reasons people may choose to resign instead of continuing to fight the good fight. The reality may be that you don't want to rock the boat, brand yourself with the stigma of "troublemaker," interrupt your career for a "fight," or worry about getting a reference for your next job. Pretty grim, huh?

Fighting for an ethical stance is often difficult. I have heard the "war stories" of too many employees as they went down their own personal trails of tears. Many of these experiences sound unbearable to me, yet they did it. Tough, ethical decisions have a way of changing you forever—for the better.

# Your Challenge

We already know that management's one-way pronouncements about ethics are the predictable, we'll-always-take-the-high-road stuff. Your job is to push back with questions and challenges based on your experiences in the practical world. Then, somewhere in the middle of that spirited discussion, you, your boss, and coworkers will come up with resolutions to your ethical dilemmas that all of you can accept.

An ethical office environment is in a perpetual cycle of construction and repair as our personal and corporate values and principles stay constant (even though they may not be exactly the same as our coworkers). You cannot change everything all at once, but you can certainly talk about it in a way that starts the process of change.

In fact, who better than you to provide your organization with the unique perspective, feedback, and insight that will spark and sustain ethical conduct? I've seen firsthand that one person's voice—at the right time, asking the right questions—has the potential to transform an office's culture.

Yes, Audrey, you *can* make that difference!

*I wondered why somebody didn't do something. Then, I realized I was somebody!*

—U.S. Vice President Hubert H. Humphrey

# 21

## Doing the Right Thing Never Looked So Right!

### At the End of the Day, You Go Home with Yourself!

---

*It takes 20 years to build a reputation and five minutes to ruin it.*
*If you think about that, you'll do things differently.*
—Warren Buffett

I will never forget Meghan. Fifteen years ago, she walked up to me at the beginning of one of my ethics workshops and said, "Ms. DeMars, I'm so glad I'm here today. I'm a secretary at a utility company, and my boss, who is really a good guy, frequently asks me to do things I think are wrong for the company."

She went on to tell me she was worried that her promotion—maybe even her job—was on the line. She added that the stress from her dilemma was affecting her productivity at work as well as her home life. Then, tears started to well up, and she asked me this powerful question, "Nan, is it possible for me to keep my job *and* my integrity?"

I never saw her after that seminar, but there isn't a day that goes by that I don't think of Meghan. I hope she knows that, yes, it is now more possible than ever to keep her job and her integrity.

## The Ethical Office Is Here

Both management and employees "get it" today: Ethical cultures have successfully gone "live" in workplaces everywhere. Why? Because the Ethical Office is a significant competitive advantage. Management and employees realize that the double or triple bottom line (as ethics are sometimes referred to) relates directly to healthy profits.

**The Ethical Office has three chief characteristics (I call these my "Three Cs"):**

- *A corporate conscience*, which is a shared understanding about the standards for acceptable and unacceptable behavior. This is accomplished by establishing an agreed-upon and documented code of ethics, code of conduct, and/or a mission statement that articulates the company's values and standards of behavior. These should not be the window-dressing variety to be just framed and hung on the wall. The corporate conscience emanates from, and is modeled by, senior management. As a dynamic, living part of the organization's culture, these statements of principles and values inspire employees—at *all* levels of responsibility—to strive to "do the right thing" when making decisions.

- *A commitment to hold yourself and each other personally responsible and accountable for the company's standards.* People working in an Ethical Office believe they have a right and an obligation to their colleagues, both management and coworkers, to uphold their organization's principles. The commitment to principles and values is matched by a commitment to bring out the best in each other. Organizations don't fail because they are too rigorous about doing the right thing or forget how to think and act ethically; they fail because they lose their commitments, and that happens when senior management fails to be the ethical standard bearer.

- *An ongoing discussion of honest communication about ethical issues.* This communication style creates trust, fairness, and an expectation that employees will live up to the company's principles and values as articulated in the code of conduct. In this kind of corporate culture, discussions about "what's the right thing to do" are routine. Challenging someone if they step over the line is a common occurrence, and it's done in a way that is nonjudgmental that simply seeks a better way. Communication about ethics is promoted through expanded employee handbooks (employees need a blueprint on what is acceptable and unacceptable); ethics departments and ethics directors; naming a point person for employees to approach for help; enhanced ethics training; and ethics hotlines. The bottom line: Management is signaling that "it's okay to talk about ethics."

## Good News: It's Working!

Ralph's company recently hosted one of my ethics workshops where he learned about my Ethical Priority Compass. A few months later, Ralph called me and shared the following success story:

> Nan, six of us support the principals of a CPA firm, and each of us has to handle the many travel requests and arrangements of our multiple bosses. Our company has specific guidelines on airline fares (lowest rates) and hotels (reasonably priced). However, I had been continually frustrated with handling these arrangements, as two of my bosses always preferred to travel on a certain airline to gain personal mileage points, and the third boss preferred a five-star hotel (not in the guidelines). In short, all three of my bosses were pushing the outer limits of company policy.

Following my seminar, Ralph said he began discussing his frustrations about these expense accounts with his peers. The other admins said they also had dilemmas and similarly felt uncomfortable bending the rules.

Then, they began talking about my Ethical Priority Compass and their new awareness of their personal exposure and concluded they needed to protect themselves. They soon devised this plan: Each would develop a monthly spreadsheet to be submitted to their supervisors that included their bosses' requests, the date each was made, the date of travel, and a listing of all arrangements—including the costs. Late requests sometimes resulted in higher costs, so if there was a delay in receiving the request, they included the explanation. They went one step further and listed the cost of the lowest airfare available and approved lodging and, if their boss chose to travel otherwise, they listed his/her explanation.

The admins' "transparency" plan worked perfectly. Ralph said that all the bosses pushing the limits immediately changed their lavish ways. The firm's executive administrator applauded these assistants and used them as an example to encourage all employees to remain accountable. The company also saved an immediate and substantial amount of money. More important, Ralph and his fellow admins could sleep more peacefully at night.

There are several lessons here: First, proactive administrative professionals *do have influence*. Second, senior executives are hypersensitive these days to the appearance of unseemly behavior; they know others will view them harshly, as they are supposed to be setting examples. Third, expense accounts are an easy-to-understand trigger that gets conversations about ethical behavior started.

Former Hewlett-Packard CEO Mark Hurd resigned over expense account improprieties that were meant to conceal a close relationship with an HP contractor. The company's investigation concluded that while there was no sexual harassment violation, Hurd had violated HP's "Standards of Business Conduct." The company and Hurd both acknowledged in a joint statement that his poor judgment had "seriously undermined his credibility and damaged his effectiveness in leading HP." In this case, tugging on the fudged expense reports unraveled some surprises. This makes one of my favorite points: nothing is ethically trivial.

When commenting for the *Wall Street Journal* on assistants' handling of their managers' expense accounts, I noted that client companies nowadays want to make sure administrative employees understand that they can't knowingly overlook their bosses' violations. As we discussed earlier, it is no longer acceptable for assistants to take the position, "It's not my job to police my boss."

Today, when high-profile cases with any taint of questionable ethics occur, boards of directors correctly ask for a review of their policies. Assistants are frequently on the front lines of these reviews and, again, they can be held personally accountable.

Ralph's group followed the Ethical Compass as their guide: they protected themselves (they were vulnerable because they processed the reports); protected their company (preventing an embarrassing and perhaps costly incident); and protected their bosses (from a foolish

mistake for chump change, and perhaps even the loss of their jobs).
Everyone won!

## Who Are the Bad Guys?

It's easy to predict the results of managing without secure ethical foot-
ings. Persistent ethical dilemmas cripple service, morale, recruitment,
and innovation. Left unresolved, these dilemmas cause an invisible, in-
sidious drain on the company's productivity and profitability. Consider
the problems that lies, duplicity, theft, illicit behavior, and harassment
cause. Is this the kind of corporate culture that attracts customers?
Retains super employees? Builds profits?

Anyone can slip and need a hand getting back onto the ethical
path. The goal of the Ethical Office is not perfection; it is simply to
do the best we can, as often as we can. And when we can't or don't
or didn't do the right thing, we fix it by *talking about it right away*.
Imagine all the temptations your people have within the company, and
then think about those bad guys out there hoping to take advantage of
you or your coworkers: From hackers and identity thieves to conniv-
ing vendors to disgruntled and ex-employees to information brokers
to scam artists—you can't survive in the jungle without your Ethical
Priority Compass.

## Bobby Jones, Role Model

You already know I'm a golfer. I grew up on the course caddying for
my dad, learned the sport from him, met my husband on the course,
and really haven't been off the links much since I was a kid.

My father's favorite golfer was Bobby Jones, the most accomplished golfer in U.S. history (even ahead of Nicklaus, Palmer, and
Woods). He told me this true story about Bobby—a story that linked
the term *gentleman's game* forever to the game of golf.

Jones lost the 1925 U.S. Open in a grueling 36-hole playoff,
after calling a one-stroke penalty *on himself* over the protests of rules
officials. In one of the final holes, he was addressing his ball, which lay
slightly in the rough, and he noticed the ball move as his iron grazed
the grass (an automatic penalty). When he informed the officials, they
all told him they had not seen the ball move. His caddy had not seen
the ball move. His opponent had not seen it move, nor had anyone
in the gallery seen the ball move. But Jones *insisted* he saw the ball
move, and he charged himself with the one-stroke penalty. This one

stroke cost him the win (and considerable winnings) of the number one tournament in the United States that year. Now *that's* integrity.

## You Are Who You Are

One of the reasons I've always loved the game of golf is that you play against yourself. If you cheat, you cheat yourself. Your golf game reflects who you are. Bobby Jones knew this. And I believe every one of you knows this as well. You may call me a Pollyanna, but I share President Abraham Lincoln's belief in the "better angels of our nature." *We all want to do the right thing—and it's easier when we work in a supportive culture.*

Haven't we all been tempted to just button it and "adjust" to an ethical dilemma instead of confronting and resolving it? We know, however, that these "adjustments" get easier and easier when we start making them routinely. When we don't fight to hold the moral high ground, we quit on ourselves.

## What's the Price of My Personal Integrity?

Dear Nan:

I am an assistant to three realtors. I accidentally saw some highly confidential, personal paperwork that one of my agents had on her desk concerning a sale. She wasn't supposed to have these papers; heaven knows how she came by them. By acting on this information, she took advantage of a situation and made substantially more money than she would have otherwise been entitled. I feigned ignorance and asked her about what I saw. She became defensive and then rushed off to an appointment. The next morning, at a meeting with the other agents, she pushed through a big raise in my salary. I deserved the raise anyway, but this was quite a bit more than I expected. After the meeting, she told me I could keep my job if I "forgot" everything that had occurred the prior day.

Keeping this secret feels like carrying a loaded gun that could go off at any moment. If I say anything to the wrong person, my

*(continued)*

> *(continued)*
>
> boss could lose her license, her job, and maybe even go to jail. If I keep her secret, life will probably go on as normal. Part of me wants to clear my conscience, but then I would feel bad for ruining this woman's career. Another part of me wants to forgive and forget her lapse of judgment. She has never done this sort of thing before, and she told me she will never do it again. Should one mistake send her career down the drain? And, should I be the one to pull the plug?
>
> —Phyllis in Hoboken, NJ

What's your price to do the deed, keep quiet, and look the other way, Phyllis? You have already been compromised. You may still see yourself as an innocent bystander, but you aren't. And you have only a fraction of the control you think you have over the final outcome of this situation.

Here are the facts: A crime has apparently been committed, you know about it, and you have benefited by keeping silent. From the outside, you look like an accomplice. You need to "put on your track shoes, kid" (my father's words again) and run—don't walk—to a senior manager in the firm, who can make sense out of what has happened.

This is the kind of situation that invariably unravels and makes everyone involved look guilty. People don't need much to jump to conclusions. Just the hint of unethical behavior is enough to derail a person's career.

Phyllis has to protect herself first and foremost because she knows about the situation, has been offered what might be construed to be a bribe for her silence, and may now be considered an (albeit unwitting) accomplice to her boss's illegal behavior. She needs to get out ahead of this situation before it gets away from her. By reversing her passive role and becoming a proactive advocate for doing the right thing, she may be able to at least avoid personal legal problems. It is doubtful whether she can keep this job, and it is almost certain that she is facing the demise of her relationship with this boss.

Phyllis also needs to protect her company. Its clients, financial welfare, and reputation are at risk. Would any senior manager *not* want to know about this kind of misbehavior?

Finally, Phyllis is too close to the situation to make any credible judgments about what should or should not be done relative to her boss. That's the senior manager's job. If the company decides to believe that this is her boss's first and last transgression, then forgives and forgets, that's the company's business.

Kathy O'Donnell, CPS, administrative assistant at Ingersoll-Rand Company in Bethlehem, Pennsylvania, writes that "Phyllis sounds like a classic enabler when she says '. . . but then I would feel bad for ruining this woman's career.' Her boss did that all by herself by choosing to act unethically in the first place." Yes, Phyllis has to speak up and, in her words, "pull the plug," by explaining exactly what happened—including her less-than-flattering role in it.

International Association of Administrative Professionals (IAAP) Florida division officer Janice Socher, CPS, says:

> No pay increase is worth the price you are paying now, or worse, the price you will have to pay if and when the situation is discovered. I know because I sold out one time also. I still regret the decision I made and can't shake the feeling that I chose money over principle. If I could turn back the clock, I would simply say "no" and avoid putting myself in a position to be manipulated. Like me, Phyllis must move forward and learn and grow from this experience.

## Summary: There Are Many Keys to the Ethical Office

This book is about how to build an Ethical Office—*your* Ethical Office. If I had but one wish, I would inspire every person in every workplace to begin thinking and talking about their day-to-day ethics. Creating the ethical office does not require a lot of money, but it does take time.

### Besides my Three Cs (above), employees need to:
- Feel *safe* to express ethical concerns.
- Have a designated person or department to approach with their concerns.
- Feel free to ask *any* kind of question.

- Know their concerns will be taken seriously and kept confidential.
- Feel confident there will be no repercussions from opening the ethical discussion.

People who work together must learn to talk to each other in a different way that allows a discussion of tough questions to occur. If we could all begin communicating about the ethical dilemmas that worry and frustrate us, people would begin making different choices—and we could transform the workplace!

## The Benefits

The case for the Ethical Office is a *moral and economic imperative*. Office ethics remain the hinge upon which countless other productivity-building programs swing. It's just that simple: *If you improve office ethics, you improve productivity, and when you improve productivity, you improve profitability.*

When people who work together share a common understanding of office ethics, they work smarter, with more enthusiasm, and get more of the important tasks done. Lies, second-guessing, deceptions, fabrications, harassments, favoritism, lack of trust, lack of confidence, and cover-your-behind activities are the aspects of office interaction that drag people down and drain them of their potential contributions. Imagine an office team that could collaborate without all of the "ethical static" confusing the communication.

Building an Ethical Office comes down to managing the practical aspects of everyday tasks and relationships, and no one is better positioned than administrative professionals.

## The Ethical Office at a Glance

Here is a recap of my top suggestions for those taking on this challenge:

**Nan DeMars's 23 GOLDEN KEYS to Opening the Door of the Ethical Office**

1. *Try to see things as they are, not as you wish them to be.* In the midst of a mess, you may be more comfortable pretending to be "confused" or to deny the facts. But the way out of the mess is to challenge

yourself with the tough questions, starting with this one: What is *really* going on here?

2. *Admit it when ethical dilemmas bother you.* When a person accepts the fact that there is a problem and there are going to be consequences, things get very, very clear—very fast! Matters remain muddy as long a person thinks he or she can be lucky enough or clever enough to avoid the issues. You have to live with your own actions (or inactions), and remember: even choosing to do nothing about a situation requires making a decision!

3. *Lead by setting an example of good ethical conduct and good ethical problem-solving skills.* A good example can have a powerful effect on the work environment. It's vital to share your sense of what's right versus wrong, and you owe it to yourself and your company to reconcile the differences between you and others as they arise.

4. *Never give the impression that you "do not care" about the improper actions taking place.* You *do* care or you wouldn't be reading this book.

5. *Get used to the idea that ethics are not a luxury you can afford only during good times.* Ethics are forever, good days and bad. Ethics may actually help you survive tough economic times—people will remember how steadfast you are, just because you are the exception. "Going along to get along"—compromising—just to keep your job is a short-term strategy with long-term consequences to your reputation. When layoffs begin, don't be surprised if you are first to lose your job. Those who maintained their integrity through difficult times will be the last to go.

6. *Commit to being involved in ethical discussions.* Office ethics are about what gets done and how. As a person at the hub of operations, you are entitled to have a voice. In fact, today's new accountability *requires* you to speak up.

7. *Anticipate ethical conflicts.* Develop a sixth sense for ethical dilemmas by looking behind the curtain of what you are intended to see and believe. Again, ask yourself what is *really* going on.

8. *Communicate well.* Tell the truth. Be open. Be concise. Provide your boss and coworkers with the complete facts as you see them. Ask for feedback, and give it to others, about specific conduct and dilemmas. You can do a lot by shifting negative self-talk (e.g., "I can't do anything about it") to positive self-talk (e.g., "How about if we try it this way, instead?"). Making simple statements about the company's principles and values ("We don't do that here," or

"That's not the General Mills way of doing things") can inspire employees to change their behavior and make their next decision the right one.

9. *Do not judge, shame, or blame others.* This only puts distance between you and your coworkers. Accept the reality that people are not always as ethical as they think they are. We tend to judge ourselves by our best actions and best intentions, and judge others by their worst.

10. *Define ethical expectations early in your relationships.* Even the job interview isn't too soon to establish your ethical boundaries. An executive at 3M Companies once told me, "If I was interviewing a new assistant and learned she would do exactly as she was told, no more or no less, I wouldn't change her for the world. I wouldn't *hire* her, either."

11. *Support your boss's efforts to uphold high standards for ethical conduct, communicate about ethics, and solve ethical dilemmas.* Communicate your respect and trust in her ethical judgment, and let her know you have high expectations for her as well. If your boss is careful about communicating honestly, you know it's important to her that you do likewise. Does she know you support her efforts? She might not, so tell her!

12. *Expect the best in people, and you will usually get it.* People tend to live up—or down—to others' expectations as they perceive them. They really *do* want to do the right thing, so help them!

13. *Be patient with each other.* Don't expect perfection in yourself or your boss. When performance ebbs and flows (and it will), review the good and bad news as soon as you can. Be candid and look for ways to set and meet more reasonable goals in the future. Your boss will not always have the right answers, nor will you. You have an obligation to speak up and make recommendations. Passive compliance is destructive, so be proactive and assume responsibility.

14. *Be consistent and predictable.* Build a track record of dependability. Fulfill your promises, and exceed expectations. The best surprise is no surprise. One of the finest compliments your boss can make is: "Oh, don't even *think* about asking Luke to do that (unethical deed). He would never even consider it."

15. *Pay attention to details.* This builds mutual trust and candor. By sweating the small stuff, your boss has confidence that you are watching his or her back.

16. *Nurture the communication process with your boss.* Don't let your communication interplay get stagnant. Keep it fresh! You will not keep your job if you ignore this. Never mind your unbelievable qualifications or the generous and forgiving nature of your boss. If you don't have a positive "chemistry" when working together, you will be looking for a new job soon.

17. *Ask questions.* Questions promote communication, transfer information, encourage candor, and furnish feedback. When in doubt about what is going on, or if you wonder how you should handle something, *ask*.

18. *Be organized and stay focused, but stay flexible as well.* No one knows better than you that one phone call can change the order of the schedule for the day (maybe even the week). Your boss counts on you to stay on track and keep him on track as well. But he also counts on you to switch gears at a moment's notice.

19. *Dodge the ethical traps of overthinking and cynicism, both of which lead to inaction and ineffectiveness.* Take people's good intentions at face value, and give them the benefit of the doubt—at least until proven otherwise.

20. *Speak up whenever you feel any unethical behaviors may be slipping in, when you sense your collective ethics are getting sloppy, or when you think convenience is becoming more important than character.* You must be very clear in your response to this: Don't participate in the unethical behavior. Express your objections and concerns right away. Be a problem solver by suggesting alternatives. Help others understand how unethical conduct in the office detracts from the company and everyone who works there.

21. *Practice tolerance.* You may not have the final or only word on what is right or wrong. You may not even have all the information or thought about it from the other person's perspective. Though self-righteousness may make you feel superior, it accomplishes nothing. Explore ethical dilemmas with a spirit of honest inquiry and seek the best outcome. Others' views of others are important.

22. *Be a mentor for those who follow you.* You will forever be remembered for the example you lead, the guidance you provide, and the support you give to those around you in your constant vigilance to maintain the Ethical Office. You can leave a legacy of being the caretaker, the monitor, even the conscience of your workplace. Who would *not* want to be remembered this way?

23. *Finally, protect your key assets.* These include good health (for which you need a daily routine, regular affirmation, and healthy habits); a strong self-esteem (learn or accomplish something); a desire to improve a situation (follow your moral code); good communication skills, and your reputation as a person of integrity. So watch yourself diligently. If you start losing or gaining weight, for example,—or whatever you do when you are under stress—sit down and objectively evaluate your situation. Ethical dilemmas can be a slippery slope; we often don't realize we are sliding down one until we have skidded to the bottom. Do you remember the story about the little frog who accidentally fell backwards into a pail of scalding water, hopped right out, and saved his life? His sister, however, wasn't so lucky. She was placed into a pail of lukewarm water and, each day, the heat was increased a little bit more . . . until she was cooked. You don't deserve to be cooked!

# Yes, You Can!

We live in a world these days whereby we are occasionally seduced by a culture of shortcuts, cost cutting, fictions, and misbehavior that erode the Ethical Office. The culture of the unethical office is promoted by unethical employees. But it cannot be sustained if ethical employees step up to the plate and halt the mischief.

*Time* magazine reported that Enron whistle-blower Sherron Watkins was sitting on her bedroom floor unpacking her boxes after her company closed its doors. She found a sticky notepad that CEO Kenneth Lay had distributed to every Enron employee a few years before. It had this quote from Dr. Martin Luther King, Jr.: "Our lives begin to end the day we become silent about things that matter." Sherron said, out loud to herself, "Wow—think about all those who remained silent."

I know you are no stranger to ethical challenges. We learn more every day about the ethical failings of company leaders and policies. The response requiring the least effort would be to become cynical about trying to make the workplace more ethical. We're tempted to ask what a single person can possibly do—especially if that one person is *you*. We're tempted to dismiss company leaders' exhortations to do and be "better" because we suspect it's only a matter of time before he is caught with his hand in the proverbial cookie jar. Wondering "why bother?" is an understandable response.

But I urge you to persevere—to not let the cynics win. Your coworkers long to believe that they work for an ethical and honorable enterprise, and will eagerly support you if your example overcomes their cynicism. While the hounds of the media bay for sensational exposés and corporate failings, we must continue to work in the quiet, where people still care about doing the right thing.

Throughout this book, I've asked you to rethink the way that you handle the ethical dilemmas you encounter. I want you to start talking about ethics among your coworkers, and discuss how these matters affect your profession's decisions. I want you to commit to doing a little office "remodeling" to make it more fair, more honest, and less stressful—in short, more ethical. Perhaps you want to stop a specific wrongful practice, correct an injustice, cut down on the petty bickering and infighting, or just give your boss a wake-up call that the rules of conduct are a bit too loosey-goosey for the good of the business.

Your leaders will not be able to build a more ethical workplace alone. They need your help. If they are to be strong, ethical leaders, you must be equally strong, ethical followers. You have a responsibility to speak up, make yourselves heard, and let your bosses know that you support their efforts to build a more ethical business. To do so, you must concentrate on the process by which those results are achieved—who does what and how do they do it. If your leaders do not lead you toward increasingly more ethical practices, you have to initiate those actions yourself. You may look like followers on the organizational chart, but you can each lead by example!

And you *will!* Building a more ethical office is not a quick or easy assignment to give yourself. You will encounter resistance because change makes people uncomfortable. But your organization's productivity, profitability, and, ultimately, its well-being depend on your consistent efforts to do the right thing for the right reasons.

You have an important role to play in this process, even though you may feel your contributions and efforts are so small as to be inconsequential. That's just not true. The small decisions we make are small steps leading in the right direction—toward more ethical workplaces.

More than 20 years ago during the Iran-Contra hearings, America listened to secretary Fawn Hall tell how she smuggled classified documents out of Colonel Oliver North's office under her clothes—just because he was the boss and she was the loyal assistant, and in spite of what federal law dictates. Activity like this would be the exception today. I truly believe that by 2030, the Ethical Office will be the standard. The arc of history favors more ethical behavior, not less. Take heart, persevere, and stay optimistic. You *can* make a real difference.

Now is the time for us to be our best professional selves and to be sure we are on the side of the angels. Don't wait for someone else to inspire, cajole, or even shame you into establishing an Ethical Office. Begin today, and reap the rewards so many have found in doing the right thing.

You *can* make a real difference. And in some situations, you are the *only* one who can do so.

## Back to Bobby Jones

Jones was praised throughout his career for observing this rule of golf, which cost him great personal expense. But he forever refused to acknowledge or accept *any* praise for observing the rule. In fact, his response was always: *"You might as well praise a man for not robbing a bank!"* What he did was the *right* thing to do.

What's so hard about that?

> *If you have integrity, nothing else matters. And, if you don't have integrity, nothing else matters!*
> —Harvey Mackay, best-selling author

# Acknowledgments

First and foremost, I wish to thank all the admins and their managers, at all levels of responsibility, who have contributed to this book. I have met you through seminars, interviews, and events, and we have shared thousands of hours of conversations. You know who you are. My insights and writing have been immeasurably enriched by your generosity. Thank you for freely and honestly pouring your hearts out with your stories of the ethical dilemmas you have faced in the workplace—some with happy endings and some with not-so-happy endings. It is because of *you* that the Ethical Office is becoming a reality today.

In addition, I have the following individuals to thank:

*Brad Lee Thompson*, my associate and editor extraordinaire. There was hardly a sentence I wrote that you did not improve with your wizardry. Thank you, Brad, for contributing your superb talent, for sharing my passion for creating the ethical workplace, and, perhaps most of all, for our treasured friendship over the years.

*Gordon Warnock*, senior agent at Andrea Hurst Literary Agency. How did I become so fortunate to have you represent me? From the get-go, you understood and embraced my passion and became a tireless advocate for my work. Gordon, your enthusiasm and efforts have raised the potential for the improvement of workplace ethics in the future.

*All of the great people at John Wiley & Sons, Inc.*—you have all been terrific. In particular, I wish to thank *Lauren Murphy*, associate editor, who so carefully spearheaded the entire project and left no detail unattended. Thank you, Lauren, for making this such an enjoyable process. *Christine Moore*, thank you for your expert, finely tuned editing, and also for understanding and championing all the personal stories of employees. And *Susan Moran*, senior production editor, thank you for your expertise in wrapping it all up and making it a joy to read. What a team!

On a personal note, I wish to thank my sister-in-law, *Rochelle Hummel,* for all her grammatical expertise and loving critique. And a special thank you to my Best Friend Forever, *Kathy Junghans,* for always supporting my work and walking through this entire project by my side. You forever know when I need you.

Finally, I must thank my other "BFF," my husband, *Lou De-Mars.* Lou, you could have written this book yourself. During our 39 years together, you have patiently listened to my stories when I return from a seminar, been my sounding board at any hour of the day (or night), put up with my rantings and ravings about injustices I may see in the work world, never trivialized them, and always, always—when appropriate—added your invaluable insight and input to helping me find solutions. Thank you for believing in the Ethical Workplace—and in me.

# About the Author

Nan DeMars is an internationally recognized thought leader and practitioner in the area of workplace ethics. Her energizing, interactive workshops, seminars, and speaking engagements have helped employees at all levels of responsibility realize greater productivity and higher levels of job satisfaction by creating more ethical office cultures. For more than 30 years, she has demonstrated in all types of industries that good ethics result in good business outcomes. She is author of the popular book, *You Want Me to Do WHAT?: When, Where, and How to Draw the Line at Work*.

Nan is president of Executary Services, a consulting firm providing workplace ethics seminars and keynote presentations, as well as placement services for executive assistants.

She is a past international president of the International Association of Administrative Professionals. She is the Office Ethics columnist for *OfficePro* magazine and writes often for the *Star Tribune* in Minneapolis and other publications. Nan is a frequent guest on both U.S. and Canadian TV and radio and is often featured in national and international periodicals as an expert on workplace ethics.

Additional information on Nan's background and training can be found on her Web site: www.office-ethics.com.

Nan lives in Minneapolis with her husband, Lou, and their cats, Ginger and Fred.

# Index